Victory Girls, Khaki-Wackies, and Patriotutes

Victory Girls, Khaki-Wackies, and Patriotutes

The Regulation of Female Sexuality during World War II

Marilyn E. Hegarty

NEW YORK UNIVERSITY PRESS
New York and London

NEW YORK UNIVERSITY PRESS
New York and London
www.nyupress.org

Library of Congress Cataloging-in-Publication Data
Hegarty, Marilyn E.
Victory girls, khaki-wackies, and patriotutes : the regulation of
female sexuality during World War II / Marilyn E. Hegarty.
p. cm.
Includes bibliographical references and index.
ISBN-13: 978-0-8147-3704-0 (cloth : alk. paper)
ISBN-10: 0-8147-3704-8 (cloth : alk. paper)
1. Women—Sexual behavior—United States—History. 2. World
War, 1939–1945—Women—United States. 3. Soldiers—Sexual
behavior—United States. 4. Sexual ethics for women—United
States—History. I. Title.
HQ18.U5H42 2007
306.7082'097309044—dc22   2007027210

New York University Press books are printed on acid-free paper,
and their binding materials are chosen for strength and durability.

Manufactured in the United States of America
10 9 8 7 6 5 4 3 2 1

To Zani with love

Contents

Acknowledgments

I am grateful to several individuals and institutions who supported me during the years that I researched and wrote this book. From the beginning, Dr. Leila J. Rupp and Dr. Susan M. Hartmann have been staunch supporters; I am deeply grateful to both of them. To the anonymous readers of the manuscript, I thank you for your time and effort; your critiques and comments greatly improved this book.

My data gathering for this book was made possible by funds from several sources at The Ohio State University: the Ruth Higgins Award of the Department of History; the Alumni Research Award of the Graduate School; and the Elizabeth D. Gee Fund for Research on Women Award of the Department of Women's Studies. I would like to thank the *Journal of Women's History* for allowing me to reprint my article "Prostitute or Patriot: The Representation of American Women's Sexuality in Popular Literature during WWII" (vol. 10, no. 2, Summer 1998), which appears here as chapter 5.

In the course of my research, many individuals made this enormous task a bit easier. I am particularly grateful to David Klassen at the Social Welfare History Archives Center of the University of Minnesota; Bill Creech, at the National Archives in Washington, D.C., who introduced me to the records of the Social Protection Division; Barry Yerby, at the National Archives Center in College Park, Maryland, who went above and beyond anything a researcher could expect as he assisted me with the records of the Navy's Bureau of Medicine and Surgery; Bertha Ihnat at The Ohio State University; and the people at the Rockefeller Archives, who were quite helpful during my time there. My research took me to several other sites; to all those who provided assistance, I offer my thanks.

As I transformed this project from a dissertation to a book, several colleagues and friends were very helpful. I thank especially Birgitte Soland, Donna Guy, David Staley, Jessica Pliley, James Lenaghan, and

Rob Faber. It was my good fortune to find freelance editor Judy Duguid, who polished the manuscript, and Deborah Gershenowitz, Senior Editor at NYU Press, whose enthusiasm for the book and the final stages of its publication are gratifying. To all of you, and to many others in Columbus and at NYU Press, thanks for caring and for lending your talents.

Several special people in my life provided needed encouragement throughout the process. To my sister, Ginger, I say thank you; I am fortunate to have you for a sister. To my daughters, who always believed their mother was "smart," I offer my heartfelt thanks. My work has benefited from Leila Rupp's keen insight, her excellent suggestions, and her belief in my scholarly ability. In addition to the academic, scholarly, and professional support Leila provided during the past years, she kept me going whenever my spirits sagged; I will be forever grateful.

And last, but assuredly not least, I want to say much more than thank you to Suzanne Damarin, without whom none of this would have been possible. Thank you for sharing the good times and the hard times. Thank you for sharing your incredible knowledge; our conversations have enriched my work and my thinking. Thank you for supporting me in so many ways over the years, for believing in me when I found it difficult to believe in myself. And finally, thank you for loving me.

Abbreviations List

ASHA	American Social Hygiene Association
ASHA Papers	American Social Hygiene Association Papers, Social Welfare History Archives Center, University of Minnesota, Minneapolis
BSH Papers	Bureau of Social Hygiene Papers, Rockefeller Archives Center, North Tarrytown, New York
CCC	Civilian Conservation Corps
CTCA	Commission on Training Camp Activities
FSA	Federal Security Agency
NA	National Archives, Washington, DC
RG 215	Record Group 215, Records of the Office of Community War Services, Social Protection Division
RG 18	Record Group 18, Records of the Army Air Force
RG 52	Record Group 52, Records of the Navy Bureau of Medicine and Surgery
RG 287	Record Group 287, Uniform Crime Reports for the United States and Its Possessions, Federal Bureau of Investigation, U.S. Department of Justice
NAPCSP	National Advisory Police Committee on Social Protection
NSA	National Sheriffs Association
NWACSP	National Women's Advisory Committee on Social Protection
OCWS	Office of Community War Services
ODHWS	Office of Defense, Health and Welfare Services
OWI	Office of War Information
SPD	Social Protection Division
USO	United Service Organization
USPHS	U.S. Public Health Service

Introduction

In 1995, as the United States celebrated the fiftieth anniversary of the end of World War II, and in 2004, as it celebrated the sixtieth anniversary of D-Day, the country remembered and honored the heroism, hardship, and sacrifice that characterized the war years. For the most part the retelling focused on men and military matters. The story of World War II has not, however, been entirely gender blind. The historical record has been enriched by the work of numerous scholars who have delineated women's contributions to the war effort.[1]

While the contributions of women in the armed services and in defense work have been studied and analyzed, we have less knowledge of the ways that civilian women experienced the militarization of their everyday lives. Over time, women, across the globe, have provided numerous support services for the state and more particularly for the armed forces of their respective countries.[2]

This book offers a different account of women in the United States during World War II that makes visible part of a troubling chapter in the history of American women in wartime. It is not a comfortable story to tell. From exploration of the ways that the apparatus of the state manipulated female sexuality across lines of race, class, and ethnicity, a darker story emerges of a process by which some women became "patriotutes." This term, a blend of *patriot* and *prostitute* coined by the U.S. Public Health Service (USPHS) physician Otis Anderson to describe women who entertained the troops in order to maintain morale, stigmatized numerous young women who had responded to their nation's call to support the war effort.[3]

Archival records contain a complex story of thousands of women who supported the war effort not only by providing labor power but also by providing morale-maintaining services to the military, such as attending dances at military bases and servicemen's clubs. Inevitably, the latter sexualized services raised public and private fears regarding the present and future impact of the wartime disruption of the gender system.[4] At a time when the state had initiated a campaign to protect the nation from prostitutes carrying venereal diseases, female sexuality seemed particularly dangerous. While Rosie the Riveter became a national icon, many other women who served their country received no commendations but were branded, in a sense, with a scarlet letter.

This account of the militarization of women plays out against a backdrop of a complex and often contradictory morals campaign launched by the apparatus of the state during the Second World War. The story revolves around official policies and practices, as various government and social agencies attempted to control venereal disease, particularly in the armed services, through the repression of female prostitution.[5] On the surface, then, this seems like an account of an official program to repress prostitution and to protect national health from venereal disease. Underneath the public discourse, however, the story is far more complex. On one level, federal agencies found female sexuality disturbing, even dangerous; on another level, official wartime discourse included plans to use female sexuality in support of the war effort. Stereotypical images of wartime women and men, full of assumptions about male and female sexuality, were commonplace in official discussions. The wartime state's interpretation of sexuality produced a monolithic discourse regarding both male and female sexuality. It valorized a militarized type of masculine sexuality, reinforcing a persistent notion that "manly" soldiers would regularly seek out women for sex. The same process operated to cast female sexuality as threatening not only to the war effort but also to the larger society and therefore justified the repression of potentially dangerous and diseased female sexuality. Such discourses often served to minimize complex and critical issues of race, class, and ethnicity, which in reality were significant factors in the repression campaign. I do not attempt to resolve the numerous contradictions inherent in the policies and practices of the wartime state but rather aim to illuminate the complex relationship between women and the wartime state and to show the ways that complexities, contradictions, and ambiguities influenced American women's (and men's) lives during the Second World War.

While this account focuses on women in the United States, their experiences are part of a larger international story. Important scholarship has uncovered numerous wartime sexual support systems that served military forces in other countries' systems, such as the enslavement of women as comfort station prostitutes that the Japanese high command deemed "necessary to the war effort."[6] Other scholarship considers the experiences of wartime women in Germany, where, for instance, prostitutes (and lesbians) were sent to concentration camps and exterminated or forced to work in bordellos at the camps. England, France, Portugal, and many other nations involved in the war had their own militarized policies for prostitutes and for women more generally.[7]

Moreover, military reliance on women's service, especially sexual service, has a long history: the 1860s British Contagious Diseases Acts required compulsory examination of prostitutes and suspected prostitutes in selected military areas to limit the spread of venereal diseases.[8] Focusing on "poor outcast women," plainclothes police could identify a woman as a "common prostitute" and force her to submit to venereal disease tests. If she tested positive, she was remanded to a lock hospital. In Italy in the 1860s, the Cavour Act regulating prostitution required prostitutes to register with police, undergo twice-weekly vaginal examinations, and be hospitalized if they were venereally diseased; the act remained in effect until 1958.[9] During the First World War both the United States and Great Britain established policies to control female sexuality in order to reduce venereal disease. In the United States, the Commission on Training Camp Activities (CTCA) was charged with controlling venereal diseases in the military. Great Britain's "war within a war" operated on different levels depending on geographical location.[10]

Whatever their circumstances, women during wartime could not escape the militarization of their respective societies and the means by which the state "maneuvered" to both mobilize and control female sexuality, although their experiences varied greatly, depending on factors such as race, class, and ethnicity. The complexities of women's relationship to the wartime state also became more evident when women's public presence increased as the United States mobilized for war.

The joining of women's patriotism and their sexuality in the term *patriotute* is not surprising given the various forces that operate on women's lives. The close connection between the concept of citizenship and military service (the citizen-soldier) complicated, from the start, perceptions of women's wartime contributions. Linda Kerber explains the relationship between citizenship and (historically male) military service by pointing out that "the word 'citizen' carried military overtones and permeated the concept of citizenship since its origins."[11] Leisa D. Meyer concurs that "the military is a critical bastion of state power and service within it is a determinant of the rights of citizens."[12] Over time women and men have had different relationships to the state; the question of citizenship also depends on factors including, but not limited to, race, class, ethnicity, religion, and sexuality.

During World War II, many citizens who fulfilled their wartime obligations were not, however, recognized as entitled to all the rights of citizenship. For example, when the American Red Cross initiated a national campaign to encourage everyone to give blood as a sign of "a new kind of democratic citizenship," race discrimination denied full citizenship to African Americans. The Red Cross segregated and marked black blood and "reinstantiated Jim Crow."[13] For second-generation Japanese American citizens (Nisei), state officials in charge of internment created "a kind of conditional citizenship," reflecting an assumed lack of loyalty to the United States. Male Japanese citizens could try to reclaim their citizenship by shedding blood for the United States in the armed forces.[14] African American women saw military service, despite segregation, as a step toward gaining full citizenship rights.[15] Women, during times of war, have participated in many ways to meet the obligations of citizenship, but seldom has their wartime service been defined or respected as such.[16]

Existing scholarship has documented the stories of the millions of women who agreed to do their part to support the war effort in factories, shipyards, and defense plants.[17] While these deviations from normative gender roles challenged the sex/gender system, a gendered process of redefinition that contained female labor power in a discourse or language of domesticity and femininity mitigated the threat. As a 1940s newsreel exclaimed: "Instead of cutting the lines of a dress, this woman cuts the pattern of aircraft parts."[18] Media images and messages informed the public that under every working woman's clothes remained a feminine body attired in silk and lace.

Sexualized services, however, were less easily redefined in acceptable terms. The sexual innuendo that often framed female sexualized mobilization is strikingly illustrated in a perfume advertisement featuring a seductively clad woman accompanied by the caption "Spell 'IT' to the Marines."[19] Even the Women's Army Corps came under attack as rumors spread that they were prostitutes or lesbians.[20] Many other women have left records that tell of the sexual harassment they endured during this period.[21] Articles such as "Public's Health: Program to Prevent Young Girls and Women from Involvement in Prostitution and Promiscuity" typified a parallel discourse that evolved in response to perceived dangers that surrounded female sexuality.[22] This type of article, and there were many of them,[23] suggested in unsubtle ways that by peeling away the layers, the overalls, the feminine attire, one would find a body with the potential to spread disorder. The discourses that circulated around wartime women engendered suspicions that problematized wartime women's responses to the war effort. Such varied but gendered discourses operated to keep women positioned at or beyond the borders of patriotic citizenship.

The state called upon women to serve their country while simultaneously denying them credit as they met the needs of wartime. While the national interest demanded total mobilization for war, deeply embedded attitudes toward female sexuality served to complicate the issue of women's place in wartime society. One senior official, Charles Reynolds, illustrated how intensely emotional these attitudes were when he equated prostitution with treason.[24] The category of "prostitute" quickly became unstable, stretching to include so-called promiscuous and potentially promiscuous women. This instability is well illustrated by the gendered term *patriotute,* which combined both positive and negative connotations and produced a symbol of a potentially subversive female individual.

This study examines, in part, wartime constructions of female and male sexualities. Female sexuality was represented by both the sexually dangerous (female) individual and the sexually alluring (female) morale builder, who became conflated with each other. Masculinity/manliness and war/soldiering have a longtime connection. Following R. W. Connell, I suggest that we consider servicemen as located at various sites of "institutionalized masculinity."[25] During wartime the iconic soldier was manly, heroic, the protector. While the public image of the servicemen may have been "masculine in a particular way," not all servicemen qualified for iconic status. The hierarchical structure of the military made distinctions based on race and class. Race-based attitudes circulated throughout the wartime campaign against venereal disease. Government officials tended to focus on an allegedly high rate of venereal disease among blacks. As Alan Brandt points out, "[H]igh rates of infection were attributed to the premise that blacks were promiscuous."[26]

The state had jurisdiction over a complex structure that reached into diverse social spaces and established a plethora of wartime policies. By examining official records, this study traces the emergence and evolution of wartime policies, particularly toward women in the United States. In considering such "techniques of power" as they operate through various state institutions, one can gain some understanding of the complex ways that the state exerts and maintains control over individuals and groups. Within this power structure are also strategies of dissent and resistance.[27] We will see, as the story progresses, that wartime women spoke back to power in a variety of ways, even though the space within which to resist was constrained. During the period of mobilization and continuing throughout the war, numerous ambiguities and paradoxes, both in government and in social policies and practices, not only created tremendous pressures in the everyday lives of individual women and men but also made concerted resistance difficult.

General Reynolds, with his charges of treason, along with other officials who had concerns that wartime women could subvert the war effort, proceeded to wage an all-out war on prostitutes and so-called promiscuous women, who came to personify venereal disease. In the years before Pearl Harbor, the army and navy, the Federal Security Agency (FSA), state health departments, and the American Social Hygiene Association (ASHA) formulated the Eight Point Agreement (see Appendix 1) regarding venereal disease control through, in part, the repression of prostitution and contact reporting. These eight points mark the official start of wartime sociopolitical efforts to control female sexuality. In 1941, the May Act (see Appendix 2) made prostitution within specified areas around military bases a federal crime.[28] The federal government then created the Social Protection Division (SPD) to serve as a watchdog over women's morals. American women became a suspect category, subject to surveillance for the duration of the war. In the following years, as many more women became visible in areas previously closed or forbidden to them, sociosexual tensions heightened.

By focusing on the complex series of government and social interventions regarding female sexuality in the World War II period, one can trace the evolution of a discourse concerning a female potential for immoderate sexuality that resulted in an imposition of the labels *prostitute* or *promiscuous* on numerous wartime women. Lauren Berlant notes that often "extravagant sex is a figure for general social disorder" and can "create panic."[29] In imagining any woman, particularly any young woman, as "hypersexualized," the state strengthened its rationale for policing female sexuality.[30] As the United States prepared for war, the apparatus of the state, in an attempt to deal with the recurrent wartime problem of venereal disease, launched a campaign to suppress prostitution and to curtail the activities of so-called promiscuous women. Prostitutes have historically been depicted as carriers of venereal diseases, and the World War II campaign to preserve national (male) health enmeshed numerous women, some who were prostitutes as well as many who were not, in a web of criminality, deviance, and disease.[31] As the country moved closer to war, female sexuality was in a sense nationalized, and a discourse of obligatory sensual patriotism circulated around American women. Magazines and newspapers featured stories, articles, and advertisements that encouraged women to do their part.

The media operated as a crucial locus of support for both mobilization and control of female sexuality. The policies of government propaganda agencies, such as the Office of War Information (OWI), its Magazine Bureau, and the War Advertising Council, indicate the close working relationship between government and media.[32] Popular magazines, for example, urged wartime women to support the war effort in a variety of ways. The United Service Organization (USO) recruited respectable young white women for recreational activities and encouraged them to be friendly and open with servicemen. But at the same time many women had to be wary about appearing to be too intimate. As women became visible in new ways to the gaze of the public, their behavior came under close scrutiny. The state's claim that women's bodies were necessary to the war effort in both factory and dance hall clashed with more traditional ideals about women's proper roles and confounded women's wartime service. Consequently, state and social authorities, while mobilizing women to depart from their assigned spaces and provide diverse wartime services, also spoke of their concerns that women in public would become sexualized and masculinized. Such contradictions provoked fear and confusion in the public mind. Paradoxically, many women who responded to wartime mobilization did not appear as patriotic citizens; instead, the female body came to represent a threat to the national welfare. Rooted in the past, a notion of the female body as essentially disordered began to circulate, exacerbating social anxieties related to impending war.

During World War II, women's bodies were nationalized and their sexuality militarized: women's laboring and sexual bodies were, in a sense, drafted for the duration.[33] The draft called men to serve their country, and women likewise received their orders: to be patriotic and support the war effort, in part by maintaining servicemen's morale.

"Men who KNOW Say *no!*" Poster, 1944. Social Welfare History Archives, University of Minnesota.

As numerous women volunteered to entertain—to provide pleasurable companionship for—the troops, the already unclear boundaries between acceptable and transgressive female sexuality grew even more nebulous. It became difficult to separate acceptable morale-maintaining sexuality from dangerous promiscuous sexuality at a time when female sexuality was simultaneously needed and feared. All too often, the distinction between the "good girl" and the "bad girl" collapsed. Women's contributions to the war effort, subject to rumors of promiscuity and colored by sexual innuendo, became tainted with charges of sinful and transgressive sex. Growing perceptions that the new wartime woman would spread contagion and disrupt the social order through her promiscuous sexuality led to policies for more stringent control of women. Prostitutes, promiscuous women, and their inevitable consequence—venereal disease—became the enemies on the homefront.

Chapter 1, "The Long Arm of the State," takes us directly into the heart of the campaign to control venereal disease by repressing prostitution. It presents an overview of the institutions and agencies of the state apparatus that participated in the campaign. We see how quickly the campaign to repress prostitution expanded to include so-called promiscuous and potentially promiscuous women. The intention in this chapter is to illuminate the sweep of the state's interventions in the realm of female sexuality. I subsequently look back in time to identify some salient factors that laid the foundation for attitudes and policies toward women in the war years.

Chapter 2, "Prelude to War," deals with the months and years immediately before Pearl Harbor. To illuminate many of the issues and events that provided an infrastructure for the officials involved in the World War II repression campaign, this chapter examines venereal disease policies during World War I and in the interwar years. In the early twentieth century, charity girls, flappers, and the "New Women" had challenged gender norms and provoked concerns regarding female sexuality. Progressive reform focused, in part, on prostitution and produced several prostitution studies that served as sources of information for state officials in the late 1930s and 1940s. During World War I a link between prostitution and venereal disease in the military led to the establishment of the CTCA. In this early period, state intervention in everyday life was quite visible, more so than in the past. As the United States mobilized for war once again, state officials gathered to discuss expected problems regarding female sexuality. They looked back in time and reviewed past records and reports as sources to draw from in shaping the emerging campaign to repress prostitution and prevent venereal disease in the current crisis. The persistence of attitudes toward, and interpretations of, female and male sexuality are evident from a comparison of the earlier records and reports with the emerging dialogue during the Second World War.

Chapter 3, " 'Reservoirs of Infection': Science, Medicine, and Contagious Bodies," illuminates the tensions between two concepts of venereal disease: contagious disease and moral failing. This chapter excavates the roots of a persistent negative discourse focusing on female sexuality through an analysis of historically specific representations of women in sociocultural and medico-scientific sources. Over time, such representations produced a powerful discourse of dangerously deviant female bodies that ultimately contributed to the wartime measures to control and contain female sexuality during the Second World War. Not only women (nonwhite and white) but also black men were affected by sociopolitical discourses that marked them as sites of venereal infection while simultaneously rendering them invisible in terms of contribution to the war effort.

Chapter 4, " 'A Buffer of Whores': Military and Social Ambivalence about Sexuality and Gender," discusses how programs to regulate prostitution were juxtaposed with military reluctance to repress prostitution. In the larger society, responses to repression were also complicated by support for regulated prostitution. This chapter considers the effects of militarized sexuality on servicemen and on women, as well as military prophylaxis policies that supported the notion that men, especially servicemen, need sex. I suggest that the constant attention paid to sex, including safe sex, in the military also served as an incitement to sex, as a way to prove one's manliness.

Chapter 5, "Spell 'IT' to the Marines: The Contradictory Messages of Popular Culture," explores two strands of sexual discourse in print media of the 1940s. The first strand, found in a wide range of periodicals, from mass-circulation popular magazines such as *Look, Life, Newsweek, and Reader's Digest* to professional journals such as *Probation, Federal Probation,* and the *American Journal of Public Health,* focuses on the condemnation of prostitutes and promiscuous women as vectors of venereal disease. The second strand, found in three types of periodicals—homemakers' magazines (such as *Woman's Home Companion, Ladies' Home Journal,* and *Good Housekeeping*) targeting middle-class women, romance magazines (such as *True Confessions*) targeting working-class women, and magazines targeting African Americans (*The Crisis, Negro Digest*)—consists of more general portrayals of female sexuality and tends to militarize sexuality as a female wartime obligation.

Chapter 6, "Behind the Lines: The War against Women," examines specific wartime measures intended to control female sexuality and discusses several ways that the female body was marked as deviant. It includes a section on the professional women who participated in the campaign and troubles the notion of protection. The consequences for women charged with criminal and/or moral transgression emerge from case studies and statistical reports. This chapter also presents several instances of overt resistance to the policies and practices of the repression campaign.

In my conclusion I argue that the 1950s emphasis on family and domesticity is, in part, a response to wartime disruption of the sex/gender system. Wartime women should not, however, be seen as passive or as mere victims of the state apparatus. In spite of the persistence of sex/

gender ideologies, women experienced change; and through their wartime services, these women invariably challenged, though at great expense, the sex/gender system. Complex forces operated to mobilize and control women's sexuality during World War II; an analysis of the process helps us understand the consequences of the war for women in the United States, both for the duration and in the postwar years.

1

The Long Arm of the State

Six months after the attack on Pearl Harbor, in June 1942, nine hundred girls and women were arrested on morals charges in Oklahoma City, Oklahoma. These arrests came about as a result of the efforts of local, state, and federal government, assisted by various social agencies, which were launching a campaign to control the spread of venereal disease during wartime through the suppression of prostitution. In cities and towns across the country, thousands of women were arrested on morals charges during the next four years. Many of the women involved were neither prostitutes nor venereally diseased. Nonetheless, officials of the state referred to them as "patriotutes."[1]

While it is not unusual for the power of the state to increase during wartime, it is not always evident how deeply the state penetrates individual lives.[2] Historian Cynthia Enloe has pointed out that both military and civilian authorities attempt to "maneuver different groups of women and the idea of what constitutes 'femininity' so that each can serve military objectives."[3] The wartime state needed women to assume a variety of supporting roles, including that of building and maintaining morale, but they simultaneously feared the results of encouraging women to act in masculine and sexualized spaces such as factories, public dance halls, bars, and military service.

While historians John D'Emilio and Estelle B. Freedman have noted that the "meaning and place of sexuality in American life have changed over the last three and a half centuries,"[4] we can nonetheless identify the persistence of particular concerns regarding female sexuality. Fear of female sexuality, often perceived as dangerous, can be found throughout history, especially in times of change.[5] As a result of preconceived notions about and attitudes toward female sexuality, increasing numbers of women were arrested on morals charges, incarcerated, and forced to undergo venereal disease testing. As the country prepared for war and more women moved into public spaces and engaged in nontraditional activities, government officials became concerned that women might engage in disorderly (sexual) behavior. Persistent notions of female sexuality "as a source of social disruption"[6] led to increased surveillance of women whose activities challenged sex/gender norms. Fears that uncontrolled female sexuality would endanger male health and thereby diminish the nation's strength gave birth to the term *patriotute*. This term was used primarily to describe women who, in responding to the nation's call to service, crossed an all-too-ambiguous line between the good and the bad woman.

Government, military, and medical authorities as well as social reform authorities began to develop plans to protect the wartime state and male health that attempted to control dangerous female sexuality by focusing on a link between prostitution and venereal disease. Disorderly female bodies, in the official discourse, posed a threat not only to homefront defense plans but also to social stability in general. Seeking to ameliorate the chaos of wartime and "to protect the armies of field and factory,"[7] the government of the United States took action by initiating a campaign to repress prostitution in order to defuse the danger posed by disorderly women. In 1939 representatives of state health departments, the army, the navy, the FSA, and the American Social Hygiene Association (ASHA) met and formulated the Eight Point Agreement, setting out "measures for the control of Venereal Diseases in areas where armed forces or national defense employees are concentrated."[8] The agreement covered services that should be developed by state and local health and police authorities in cooperation with the Medical Corps of the U.S. Army, the Bureau of Medicine and Surgery of the U.S. Navy, the USPHS, and interested voluntary organizations. Point six of the agreement called for "all assistance possible to the cooperating agencies to bring about a reduction in exposures to venereal diseases through the repression of prostitution, both organized and clandestine."[9] (See Appendix 1 for full text of the Eight Point Agreement.) In May 1940, the Eight Point Agreement received the endorsement of the Conference of State and Territorial Health Officers, the International Association of Chiefs of Police, the National Sheriffs Association (NSA), the American Bar Association, the American Medical Association, and other professional and civic organizations. Ness called the Eight Point Agreement a "declaration" of the federal government's policy on the repression of prostitution. The agreement also covered matters such as early diagnosis and adequate treatment, quarantine of infected persons, education, and development and stimulation of support for the preceding measures.[10] In addition, it called for the "gathering of information" from servicemen regarding sexual contacts (with any women, not just with prostitutes), as well as the reporting of this information to the appropriate authorities. This agreement marks the official start of wartime sociopolitical efforts to control female sexuality. The passage of the May Act in July 1941 added another weapon to the government's arsenal. Prostitution became a federal offense in areas around defense plants and military bases. (See Appendix 2 for the full text of the May Act.)

During this period of policy debate, the army and navy, USPHS, FSA, and Department of Justice met and recommended to Paul V. McNutt, the FSA administrator (and also director of the Office of Defense Health and Welfare Services [ODHWS]), that a section be set up within the ODHWS to "implement" point six of the Eight Point Agreement. As a result, in early 1941, the SPD was established within the FSA. Later in the year McNutt, acting in his capacity as FSA administrator, "delegated the administration of his responsibilities to the SPD."[11] Eliot Ness, formerly of the Federal Bureau of Investigation and more recently the sanitary commissioner of Cleveland, became the director. (During the first few months of the agency's operation, Bascomb Johnson served as interim director.) Since the prostitute was already conflated with "other women differing from them only in nomenclature,"[12] it is apparent that the campaign to eradicate venereal disease served a purpose that exceeded disease control.

Official plans to control female sexuality became complicated, however, by simultaneous governmental efforts to mobilize women to support the war effort in a variety of ways. Wartime women were not only asked to labor in the factory and the shipyard but also called upon to provide services that would sustain military morale. Morale building and morale maintenance emerged as significant concerns of the state apparatus; the military must be fit to fight both physically and psychologically. Government officials assumed that women would provide such services to the military, and they did. There was, however, a hidden cost for many women, who often (inadvertently) crossed an ambiguous and fluid line dividing acceptable and unacceptable behaviors; the patriotute became a symbol for such women. The subject of male sexuality was both present and absent in these discussions. Since many authorities took as a given the male need for sex, their concern was not to prevent men from sexual liaisons but rather to ensure that they would be protected from venereal disease and fit to fight.

Mobilization and the State

The magnitude of health-related defense problems became evident as early as 1939. The USPHS engaged in sanitary reconnaissance work in army maneuver areas, expanding its endeavors to ensure a safe environment and to protect and maintain national health as mobilization and industrial expansion progressed. USPHS concerns covered contagious diseases, water supply, waste removal, nutrition, and related problems that would or could occur as a result of overcrowding and material shortages.[13] The surgeon general, Thomas Parran, noted in his 1941 annual report the possibility of total war. He stated that it was critical to move beyond seeking health primarily for its value to the individual. "Now," he said, "we must obtain it for the nation's security."[14] Assistant Surgeon General Vonderlehr also addressed national health, speaking of "the necessity for comprehensive defense of the nation."[15] Maintaining high military morale, according to the authorities, had become even more important given the logistical problems emerging in areas such as transportation, housing, sanitation, health, and recreation as the nation mobilized for war. In short order, population density increased in manufacturing cities; some small towns and cities expanded into overcrowded "boomtowns." Population distribution also began to change significantly as many people moved around the country; military forces traveled to maneuver areas, and workers and families headed to defense production areas. The large numbers of men summoned to report to their draft boards in 1940 ultimately added to the movement throughout the country.

In these situations, control of communicable diseases, including venereal disease, was of paramount importance.[16] At the time, venereal disease was extremely difficult to treat or cure. Not only were venereal diseases considered shameful, but they required lengthy, painful, and costly treatment. Total cure could not be ensured, and treatment was inaccessible to large segments of society. Penicillin, which could cure venereal diseases quickly, did not become available until 1944, and then only in limited quantities. According to government officials such as Surgeon

General Parran, Paul V. McNutt of the FSA, and officers of the army and navy, as well as officials of the ASHA, if prostitutes and promiscuous women infected servicemen with venereal diseases, the resulting loss of manpower could sabotage defense efforts. Officials were, however, well aware of the magnitude of venereal disease in at least one segment of the male population when, in 1940, the Selective Service adopted the practice of routine blood testing for all draft registrants summoned to report for induction. While statistics indicated that sixty thousand of the first million draftees (6 percent) were rejected due to venereal disease, these numbers failed to remove the spotlight from females (including women in the military) as sexually promiscuous and as vectors of disease. Moreover, the rejected men were, for the most part, sent back to their communities untreated. In mid-1941, according to the USPHS surgeon general's report with regard to deferred individuals, "in twenty-two states, the District of Columbia, and Hawaii, where this information was available for tabulation only thirty-one percent of the cases were brought under treatment or shown to be already under treatment."[17] But as the disease discourse continued to focus on transgressive female sexuality, including but not limited to prostitution, the scope and message of disease prevention narrowed significantly. The double standard, which took on new life in this period, served to shield numerous servicemen from charges of promiscuity while instructing them in how to protect themselves from sexually transmitted diseases. In general, white men's bodies would remain unmarked by disease, while women, especially nonwhite and working-class women, as well as black men, were marked as actually or potentially diseased.[18]

The venereal disease campaign of the Second World War era involved not only the branches of the federal government but also state and local governments. Law enforcement groups such as the FBI, local police departments, sheriffs' organizations, and women prison superintendents all participated in the organized effort to protect the nation's health and wartime efficiency through the vigorous repression of prostitution and the eradication of the alleged threat posed by promiscuous women and girls. The army, navy, USPHS, FSA, and ASHA joined the fight, as did women's groups and concerned public citizens. As the repression campaign progressed, the activities of the SPD ensured that solutions to the problem of venereal disease remained focused on women. For example, in newspaper accounts regarding the closing of red-light districts and brothels, the authorities referred to vice districts as "swamps that bred malaria-carrying mosquitos."[19] And in Rapid City, South Dakota, girls who were "continually on the streets and whose behavior for any reason seems questionable were approached by the VD nurse or the police-woman and asked to come to the clinic for examination."[20] The campaign to control venereal disease and to protect the health of the nation by protecting the men of the armed forces from dangerous or diseased women served not only as a gendered system of domination and control but also as a rationale for official surveillance of women's activities. As mobilization for war progressed, women's increasing economic, social, and geographic mobility challenged systems of control, even if unintentionally. When government agents increased the level of interventions into women's lives, more, albeit limited, overt resistance would emerge.

By late 1940 it was clear, at least to certain officials, that there was little chance of avoiding American involvement in the war. Talk of more widespread mobilization became part of the public discourse of preparedness, and government officials continued to discuss the topic of mobilizing and controlling female sexuality behind closed doors. Historian Cynthia Enloe points out that women can provide support services for the military if the military is certain that the state apparatus exerts sufficient control over women. The control, however, needs to be "invisible."[21] While most women were probably not aware of the state's consuming interest in their sexuality, they did recognize the problems and the opportunities offered by wartime service. Women continued to enter areas in the public realm formerly closed to them, as they responded to the needs of national defense. Women migrated to take defense work, joined the women's armed services, moved near military bases to be near husbands, and volunteered to meet the need for morale-maintaining entertainment for servicemen. But as numerous women, often traveling alone, waited at train stations and bus terminals, the authorities saw camp followers—that is, prostitutes. Meeting their wartime obligations, women entered public and disorderly spaces, including dance halls and servicemen's clubs, as well as male spaces, such as factories and the military. Many women who provided support services for the war effort engaged in activities that still seemed somewhat inappropriate when judged by prewar gender norms. They were, after all, socializing and dancing with men who were strangers, behavior not expected of a "respectable" woman. The USO was able to avoid accusations of impropriety by employing a rhetoric of respectability, by recruiting only middle-class white women, and by "functioning as a normative force that emphasized women's domesticity and sought to contain female sexual activity to marriage."[22] But many other women who engaged in similar activities fell under a cloud of suspicion, becoming liable to charges of prostitution and promiscuity and therefore subject to intense surveillance and possible arrest.

I do not mean to suggest that prostitution did not exist at this time but rather to argue that *prostitution* and *promiscuity* became elastic terms, commonly used to interpret numerous women's diverse wartime activities that were sometimes, but not always, sexual. M. Jacqui Alexander asks why the state "marks sexual inscriptions" on particular bodies. She argues that one way that the "state deploys power" is by "drawing symbolic boundaries around sexual difference." The criminalization of different or deviant sexuality "functions as a technology of control [and] becomes an important site for the production and reproduction of state power." She also notes the ways that particular bodies are sexualized within the polity and argues that "the focus on state power is not to imply rationality or even internal coherence. In fact, what is evident in the legislation and other contextual gestures surrounding it are paradoxical and contradictory ways in which the state exerts its will to power."[23] The figure of the patriotute embodies such a paradox. For the authorities she symbolized threatening female sexuality, the patriot and the prostitute, the good and bad female, inseparable.[24]

As government officials took the lead in conceiving and implementing extensive social hygiene policies, the publicly stated strategy in the war against venereal disease remained the repression of prostitution.[25] But in short order, the category of disease-bearing females expanded to include so-called promiscuous and potentially promiscuous women. While the draft and industrial conversion to war production sparked discussions and debates, little official disagreement or debate arose regarding the seemingly contradictory plans to both mobilize and repress female sexuality. For wartime officials, allegedly venereally diseased women posed a clear and present danger to national health and therefore to national defense.[26] As the government authorities broadly applied the terms *prostitute, promiscuous,* and *potentially promiscuous* to numerous wartime women, the state erected a framework within which female sexuality would be not only mobilized and controlled but also pathologized and demonized during the war years.

Federal Agencies: The Social Protection Division

In early 1941 the SPD of the Office of Community War Services (OCWS), a division within the FSA, was formed to coordinate the war against venereal disease. The SPD launched its campaign by focusing on "the repression of prostitution," point six of the Eight Point Agreement. The passage of the May Act (July 1941), making prostitution in and around military areas a federal crime, gave the division a powerful tool to control prostitutes and so-called promiscuous women.[27] The SPD soon came under the leadership of Eliot Ness, who served as director from 1941 to 1944. Eliot Ness and the SPD, already hard at work in 1941, became more publicly visible in short order. The ODHWS issued the following statement to public officials regarding the function of social protection:

> The broad objectives of the Social Protection Section are the safeguarding of the armed forces and the civilian population from the hazards of prostitution, sex delinquency, and venereal diseases. To accomplish these objectives the Section will gather and evaluate information with respect to prostitution and related conditions in cities and counties adjacent to military establishments, the statutory and administrative measures designed to combat such conditions, the extent to which these measures are enforced, and the results achieved. It will implement community activities directed toward the protection of women from sexual exploitation and the social rehabilitation of prostitutes and other sexually delinquent women.[28]

This statement of purpose summarizes the SPD's intent: to protect the armed forces and civilians from "bad" girls and women who will infect men. From the start the campaign did not confine its policies to prostitution but extended its reach to other women perceived as sexually delinquent.

In addition to the major federal agencies, numerous committees, some preexisting the establishment of the SPD, participated in the campaign to eliminate prostitution. The Interdepartmental Committee, for example, which brought together twenty federal agencies (e.g., the FSA, SPD, army, navy, USPHS, FBI, and Children's Bureau) had been established by the Council of National Defense in January 1940 to assist the

FSA's director in dealing with health and other defense-related problems.[29] The Interdepartmental Committee met regularly to discuss emergent problems and to monitor progress in the war on prostitution.

Public Relations, Statistics, and Legal Issues

On occasion, state officials recognized that certain aspects of the repression campaign could produce difficulties for and provoke challenges against many of their policies and practices. When, for example, an Advisory Committee on Social Protection met to discuss "problems and programs," FSA head Paul V. McNutt opened the meeting by saying, "You have the most delicate task there is in this whole defense program, and there are opportunities for getting into no end of trouble."[30] Over time, state officials developed concerns about legal aspects of the campaign and were challenged regarding statistics employed to support repression. In referring to the "tremendous job" facing the committee, McNutt reminded them that repression of prostitution "is of vital importance to the whole defense program." Charles P. Taft, from the Division of Health and Welfare in the SPD, spoke next on the question of public relations. He stated: "It isn't that we are fearful of publicity if we are doing the right thing." McNutt and Taft sought the opinions of those summoned to the advisory committee because they thought their status as outsiders (i.e., not directly serving in the SPD) would create an impression that the campaign to repress prostitution as well as the broader effort to control female sexuality had widespread support. In fact, as discussed later in this chapter, it was opposed by individual citizens and businessmen as well as by many military officials. Realizing that they were vulnerable to a variety of legal challenges, McNutt and Taft also had other concerns that went beyond public relations. As the repression campaign progressed, statistical anomalies and federal intervention in local affairs created spaces for serious challenges to the campaign.

Legal concerns included, but were not limited to, "widespread use of suspicious person charges," search warrants issued for possible rather than probable cause, hearsay evidence, and entrapment.[31] "The Constitution guarantees that there will be no unreasonable searches and seizures and that a warrant must be issued by a judge only upon probable cause."[32] Legalities were also complicated by a lack of uniform practices: for example, some law enforcement agencies regularly arrested prostitutes without warrants and without fear of repercussion, while others would not arrest unless they caught the prostitute in the act.[33] In Hattiesburg, Mississippi, for instance, the mayor was reluctant to support repression. While he did not condone "illegal traffic," he was concerned to remain within the "letter of the law."[34] In many cases the evidence used to justify harassment and arrests was based on hearsay and contaminated (not legally useful) by the interpretations of the investigators. If federal authorities failed to maintain confidentiality, the investigators feared libel suits.[35] Such diverse policies added to the confusions and ambiguities that characterized the war against venereal disease and prostitution. Despite these legal concerns, challenges to wartime policies were minimal. The text of legal briefs provides some insight into the lack of visible support for women's civil liberties by traditional supporters of civil rights. For example, with regard to quarantine and other administrative regulations that deprived citizens of liberty, one legal brief made two important points in support of the government's right of a compelling interest in female sexuality: "All liberty is subject to reasonable regulation in the interest of the general welfare," and "the so-termed May Act . . . offers specific example of the authority of Congress to treat with the suppression of venereal disease [through the repression of prostitution] as incident to the exercise of granted powers found in the Federal constitution—to declare war and support armies."[36]

Another potential problem for state officials pertained to reports containing statistics. Much of this statistical information served as a rationale to continue the campaign to repress prostitution and to support requests for additional funding for social protection programs. Government officials, operating with a set of preconceived ideas, claimed that female prostitution and promiscuity were rampant and that prostitutes and promiscuous women were disease carriers who threatened the health of the armed services. Not only prostitutes but also promiscuous teenagers were at one point blamed for 90 percent of the venereal disease cases among servicemen.[37] It is important to note, however, that numbers are not necessarily neutral but can encode the underlying values of the enumerator.[38] Different agencies, numerous subgroups, and individual officials participated in amassing statistics on a variety of topics; often their reported results conflicted with one another or produced a partial story. For example, when the venereal disease rate in the army showed a marked jump, the increase was, in fact, due to a new

policy that allowed the induction of fifty-five thousand men with venereal disease.[39] This information did not, however, alter the notion that
women spread venereal disease.[40]

Challenges to official statistics came from varied sites. A newspaper
article noted that "the reported prevalence of VD may have been exag-
gerated; incidence is one thing, prevalence is another."[41] In May 1940
Dr. Walter Clarke (ASHA) complained to Dr. Parran (USPHS) that an
editorial in *New York Medical Week* had accused the ASHA of inflating
the VD rate, calling its statement that one out of every twenty people in
the United States had syphilis a "gross and deliberate exaggeration" for
the purpose of "scaring" the public into "taking certain steps against
venereal disease" and backing up ASHA's claim for more financial support. Clarke suggested that it would be a good idea for the ASHA
and USPHS to "promptly get together" and agree upon the numbers.[42]
Throughout the campaign, such questionable statistics would be employed and challenged.

Despite pointed questions regarding ASHA statistics from Dr. Sheldon Glueck during the SPD conference of June 14, 1941, few answers
were forthcoming.[43] The conference participants moved on to a number of topics, including quarantine for infected women, procedures for
contact reporting, and policies regarding venereally diseased men rejected for military service. Vonderlehr suggested that "properly handled,
through the investigation of each of these selectees and volunteers with
VD we will find quite a number of contacts"; if the contacts named
were prostitutes, the USPHS invoked the quarantine laws against prostitution.[44] In other words, diseased men declared ineligible for military service returned to their communities, where, in many cases, no
treatment was provided. But any woman named as a contact would
be tracked down and perhaps quarantined. If the women named were
prostitutes, the USPHS would post quarantine notices on their houses.
Vonderlehr allowed that he had some "misgivings" regarding the efficacy of quarantine but stated that it was a temporary measure pending
better cooperation from law enforcement officials. Completely ignoring
the significance of diseased men freely circulating throughout society, he
concluded by saying that "there is a grave need throughout the country
for isolation centers for women."[45]

Katharine Lenroot of the Children's Bureau discussed at length investigations carried out by the bureau to "get some information first hand
on the situation surrounding young people in various communities." To

aid in the process, the bureau engaged two experts in social protection: Captain Rhoda J. Millikin of the District of Columbia Police Women's Division and Eleanor L. Hutzel, Fourth Deputy Commissioner, Chief of the Women's Division, Detroit Police Department. Millikin and Hutzel, along with members of the bureau, made "observation visits" to towns and cities experiencing rapidly growing populations and reported back on related problems. Of particular concern were the "undesirable forms of recreation" that emerged in such areas. Reports emphasized "that many young girls are involved in situations, either of grave moral danger, or directly described as situations of prostitution, girls even as young as 13, 14, 15, or 16 years."[46] Statistics regarding the age of females classified as prostitutes or promiscuous also presented difficulties. They often focused on extreme youth—sometimes as young as ten or eleven—and were challenged as erroneous in several instances.[47] Lenroot was concerned that, in many communities, "there is no one responsible for keeping young people from participating in undesirable activities or for giving them the various types of special care which their problems demand."[48] Female officials, many of whom had backgrounds in Progressive reform, seemed more committed to rehabilitative solutions than male officials. By the 1940s, however, protection for such young women often involved arrest or apprehension and detention without charges. This focus on youthful offenders served (as did other aspects of the campaign) as scare tactics, warnings to girls and women to monitor their behavior and to meet their parenting responsibilities.

Charles P. Taft raised the issue of local law enforcement, with its necessary corollary, the "backing of public opinion" and "the protection of women and girls who are involved in this difficult situation."[49] *Protection,* as we have seen and will continue to see, was a term subject to interpretation, as evidenced by the first concrete item introduced, the "question of public relations": that is, convincing the public that it must support the fight to protect male citizen-soldiers from contamination by women and girls. Presenting the war on venereal disease as critical to the war effort and to national health, officials urged all citizens to help defend and protect their country. Since many attendees at the June 1941 SPD meeting were civilians, Taft suggested that their advice and reactions would have greater influence on public opinion. He exhorted them to "give great importance to the method of public education so that it secures the widest possible support."[50] Government officials recruited numerous individuals and groups to take a message into their

"Don't be Her pin-up boy." Poster, 1940. Artist: C. D. Batchelor.
Social Welfare History Archives, University of Minnesota.

communities: that prostitutes and promiscuous women endangered the strength of the nation. The list of those recruited to lobby for repression was a lengthy one, including professional women, clubwomen, physicians, lawyers, police officials, sheriffs, businessmen, and educators. The breadth of the campaign against "disease-spreading" women expanded rapidly. Large numbers of supporters of repression advocated policies that increased suspicion regarding wartime women's activities at the same time that women's visibility in public places had also increased. Discussions during the June 1941 meeting made it clear that mere female presence in a dance hall or even at a bus or train station constituted a potential problem. And despite some minor concern about the violation of civil liberties, by and large the campaign went ahead under full steam.[51]

The National Advisory Police Committee on Social Protection

Eliot Ness acted quickly to pull numerous groups into the SPD's orbit. He called together law enforcement officials from all over the United States to discuss wartime problems. Out of this meeting came the National Advisory Police Committee on Social Protection (NAPCSP), established in June 1942. According to its statement of purpose, "The Committee was formed to assist in the enforcement of the Federal government's Social Protection Program and to develop new and effective techniques of police enforcement pertaining to the repression and prevention of prostitution."[52] The committee, appointed by Paul McNutt (FSA), consisted of twenty-one police officers from fifteen states, plus representatives from the army, navy, USPHS, FBI, and ODHWS, which included the SPD. Shortly after the formation of the NAPCSP, the OWI released a press statement: "The National Advisory Police Committee on Social Protection today called upon police and law enforcement officials throughout the country to stamp out prostitution."[53] In a report to McNutt, the NAPCSP acknowledged its "professional obligation" to stamp out prostitution so that the "Army, Navy, and war industries are not to be decimated by casualties due to venereal diseases."[54] This committee became one of the most active groups in the campaign to repress prostitution and to control so-called female sexual delinquency.[55] This is not to suggest that local and state police were always in agreement; laws and attitudes varied widely in the forty-eight states and U.S. territories.

The NAPCSP had numerous subcommittees, including separate committees on prevention, repression, enforcement, and cooperation. The task of the cooperation group involved convincing the public, some of whom still favored "varying degrees of regulation or toleration" of prostitution, not only that repression and law enforcement were necessary but also that they substantially lowered the venereal disease rate. This subcommittee planned to issue manuals on social protection especially designed for police officers and also began planning "an information service to all local police officers, giving them the latest developments in the police field of social protection."[56] Ness called a meeting to discuss the proposed manuals, using "Indiana's War-Time Program against Venereal Disease" as a model since this program seemed successful. Michael Morrissey, chief of the Indianapolis Police, strongly suggested that the manual be written by a well-respected police official and that it "tell the story" in a manner understandable to "cops": in other words, to appeal to the policeman's viewpoint. The manual was to be kept simple and brief, aimed directly at police officers and presenting a clear picture of the ravages of venereal disease. It would point out useful laws applicable to morals offenses (by women) and would remind policemen that they had a duty to enforce such laws. This strategy appeared necessary since many police departments opposed this key policy change and continued to support segregated districts as the efficient way to handle prostitution. The manual also stated that the common practice of using prostitutes as informants would no longer be acceptable. According to Morrissey, policemen should be told, without further elaboration, that repression must be the wartime policy.[57]

NAPCSP not only put together a manual for policemen but also produced pamphlets such as *Does Prostitution Breed Crime?* This four-page pamphlet included information on the role of the police in the prevention of juvenile delinquency (often used as a code word for "potential" female promiscuity). It called for community support and outlined some prevention strategies, stating that "proper discharge of police obligations and responsibilities requires dealing with the individual violator whose conduct menaces public health and safety, and close observation of places and conditions which may be regarded as breeding places for crime and delinquency."[58] The second page took the form of a response from the superintendent of police of Terre Haute, Indiana, who confirmed that the segregated vice district in Terre Haute's West End constituted just such a place. This "notorious" district, where at one time three hundred to four hundred prostitutes operated within an area of three or four square blocks, had 104 prostitutes working in 1942.[59] The superintendent claimed that "with the closing of the vice district, the effect on crime was noticeable," with robberies, aggravated assaults, and other crimes decreasing by a third in a two-year period. Anyone reading this pamphlet could hardly avoid the message that prostitution was both a criminal act and a practice that supported the commission of other serious crimes. The pamphlet concluded with a statement by the NSA in support of repression as well as the group's statement of plans to continue to combat prostitution in the postwar era.[60] During this period, however, arrests for prostitution included charges against women, far outside vice districts, for so-called morals offenses.

The Committee on Cooperation ultimately succeeded in enlisting the support of the American Bar Association and the Interstate Crime Commission in particular to "teach prosecutors and judges the importance of and need for cooperating with the Federal Government in repressing prostitution."[61] As a result of police activity toward "cooperation," the Council of the Criminal Law Section of the Bar Association "voted to appoint a special Committee on Courts and Social Protection."[62] In cooperation with the ASHA, the council accepted the task of developing a model for a uniform prostitution law to be used throughout the entire nation. For a variety of reasons, including federal, state, and local conflicts, such a law was never passed.[63] In addition, the committee was determined to obtain the cooperation of military police, both army and navy, "in securing evidence for court cases": that is, getting soldiers and sailors to testify and name female contacts.[64] Military police, they assumed, could exert more immediate, on-the-spot pressure on individual servicemen to name contacts. In this manner, servicemen, who moved around so much and who were often reluctant to name names (if they knew them), would come under pressure when they were most vulnerable—when encountering the military police or when making use of prophylaxis facilities.[65]

Discussions at a meeting of the NAPCSP's Committee on Enforcement, held on November 20, 1942, highlight some of the problems that officials faced as they engaged in repression. Representatives of the army, navy, state health departments, and SPD joined the law enforcement officers who made up the committee to discuss ways to handle a variety of situations. In speaking of persons "who own local facilities" such as taverns and taxicab companies patronized by prostitutes, Ness (SPD) held that they "should not be thrown into jail."[66] Rather, the local police should first inform such persons that they or their establishments had been identified as involved in questionable activities that jeopardized their licenses, thus inspiring cooperation. Colonel Turner (army) spoke about the importance of contact reporting, and McCullough (navy) said that anytime local military commanders failed to cooperate, the police should notify Ness. The ensuing discussion revolved around questions such as how long women could be detained pending venereal disease testing, where to hold a woman who was arrested on a morals charge, and what to do about first offenders. Most participants agreed that after women had been arrested, health officers should detain them and require testing for venereal disease. However, the time that such women spent in jail varied, ranging from twenty-four hours to seven days. Several meeting participants objected to this practice, since many of the women detained did not have venereal disease; they suggested a faster release time, with the requirement that women be held liable if they were not "available for examination."[67] Several police officers took harder stances, making statements such as: "I think they should all be held," "We are gambling with lives now," and "If we have to go to extremes it is best to win the war. . . . I suggest not too much consideration."[68] While male "go-betweens" deserved a warning, female suspects received no such consideration. Although some officials seemed to take a softer stance, they did not object to jailing numerous women, many of whom, in fact, were neither prostitutes nor venereally diseased.

NAPCSP's Committee on Enforcement had a full agenda at this meeting; it also debated the topic of taverns, curfews, and "pickups." One committee member wondered if members "weren't advocating prohibition," but the majority favored curfews. Ness then praised Chicago's policies, stating further that "an analysis of the infections shows that many soldiers are being infected by pick-up women in beer parlors." Chicago had attempted to solve that problem by prohibiting lone women from sitting at a bar. A policeman from Virginia went even further, saying "eliminate women [from bars] entirely is the only way." In Indiana women could not sit or stand at a bar, but several women together could get table service. However, if one went to another table, "she is not served and must go back to her own table." Not everyone agreed with these practices; even Ness suggested that these "curtailments raised the question of liberty."[69]

Ness spoke again to the members of the Committee on Enforcement regarding the success of the law enforcement campaign; he said that red-light districts had been closed in three hundred cities. Colonel Turner (army) claimed that the VD rate in the army, in late 1942, was "the lowest in history,"[70] allowing Ness to claim credit for a successful repression program. In fact, the lower venereal disease rate owed much to improved as well as widely available prophylaxis. The official use of statistics to support repression programs became particularly necessary because law enforcement officials and other individuals were not yet fully convinced that repression was the best plan. Nonetheless, as red-light districts closed, making contact with prostitutes became more difficult. Of course, sexual encounters did not cease. Other women and girls, depicted in popular and official media as the girl next door, "who may look clean, but . . . ," became more vulnerable to sexualized encounters. If they were named as contacts (whether or not intercourse occurred) by a venereally diseased serviceman, the statistics confirming widespread sexual promiscuity increased.[71] When such statistics were reported in print media, the notion that numerous nonprofessional girls and women both were promiscuous and had venereal disease gained strength. For example, a claim that "fully 90 percent of the Army's cases in this country are traceable to amateur girls—teenagers and older women—popularly known as khaki-wackies, victory girls, and good-time Charlottes" appeared in the *Nation* in 1945.[72] Pressure on servicemen to name a woman or girl as a contact could well have artificially inflated the statistics regarding promiscuity. Unreliable, incomplete, and erroneous statistics were, as we have seen, the subject of many official discussions.[73] The Committee on Enforcement ended this meeting with some comments on continuing problems with lawyers who got prostitutes out on bail and judges who merely fined prostitutes,[74] practices that the committee wanted to stop. Given that the category of prostitute did not necessarily apply only in a traditional sense, it seems clear that women's civil liberties did not overly concern many authorities.

The NAPCSP's numerous meetings illuminate the scope of the anti-venereal-disease campaign. SPD representatives, who were always in attendance, discussed matters such as a requirement for licensing all places of commercial entertainment, thereby making it easier for the authorities to close down the questionable ones by canceling their licenses. They also discussed getting laws passed to "regulate wages and hours of employment for females." California, for example, proposed measures to close night work to women.[75] The SPD worked vigorously to gain the support of various law enforcement officials, the judiciary, and certain "expert" women. The dialogue at these meetings is, moreover, revealing of the male officials' distrust of and even disdain for women in government positions and especially for those in social work. When Mrs. Burgoon, a social protection regional supervisor, suggested that a female representative of the Department of Public Welfare could be appointed for rehabilitation and prevention work, several male officials commented that there was a great deal of resentment throughout the state against so-called social workers.[76] In general, male authorities perceived social workers as ineffectual and generally resisted or derided women's involvement in the campaign. Chief Morrissey responded negatively to a suggestion that a (female) medical social worker or a trained policewoman might be more advisable. Morrissey claimed that his "experience with policewomen was not encouraging inasmuch as he had inherited all of his women, and they didn't even make good telephone operators."[77] Given such attitudes toward women, even women of the professional class, it is not surprising that less privileged women were fair game for the officials responsible for repression. Nonetheless, the SPD needed women's support to sell the idea of repression. Ness would soon approach women's organizations to elicit their support for the campaign.

The National Women's Advisory Committee on Social Protection

On June 9, 1943, the SPD held a conference to discuss the "woman's role in social protection."[78] Taft (OCWS), McNutt, and Ness spoke to the representatives of numerous women's groups for the express purpose of enlisting them to support the repression of prostitution. McNutt began by informing the attendees that the "success of the Social Protection Program depends upon you and the support that your organizations can give the work we are trying to do."[79] According to McNutt, a recent Gallup poll indicated that more than 60 percent of the men and women polled still believed that "medical examinations (of prostitutes) were an effective means of controlling venereal disease."[80] Even more problematic to the SPD's program, "only 24 percent of the men and 34 percent of the women polled had accepted the kind of program which the Social Protection Division is administering today."[81] The public feared that closing brothels would put their daughters at risk of sexual predation;[82] clearly the SPD needed help in mobilizing public opinion to conform to its view. Turning to women's groups to explain the SPD program, officials spoke of how confident they were that respectable women would "feel it [repression] is right." Supposedly, these women would now listen seriously to the SPD's ideas and agree to help "to obtain the support of public opinion generally and widely throughout the country."[83] Out of this conference emerged the National Women's Advisory Committee on Social Protection (NWACSP). Discussions with the women's groups seem quite one-sided, as the only voices heard in the records are male voices. Ness and other officials lectured rather than listened, seeking to gain uncritical support. Ness and the others were, nonetheless, able to point to the NWACSP as evidence of "good" women's support for repression. Male-dominated organizations such as the ASHA seemed to be taken much more seriously. Ness, with barely a pause, went on to meet with numerous other groups and organizations to urge them to support repression. He spoke to and requested cooperation from hotel and restaurant associations, taxicab companies, individual cabbies, local governments, and groups of concerned citizens.[84]

Confining the Bad Women and Girls: Civilian Conservation Corps Camps and Quarantine

Faced with limited jail space, many law enforcement officials became concerned about the logistics of detaining large numbers of suspect women. As a matter of fact, policemen often raised the question: What do you expect us to do with all these women?[85]

Ness introduced a possibility: either the SPD or the FSA had an opportunity to acquire approximately thirty Civilian Conservation Corps (CCC) camps. These camps could then be used to warehouse women arrested or apprehended on morals charges as law enforcement ran out of jail space.[86] The problem of lack of facilities had already come up in March 1941 at a meeting of one of the many advisory subcommittees on social protection. The conversation had turned to the "problem of young girls" and a lack of quarantine and detention facilities.[87]

Ness spoke extensively about the camps. Formerly owned by the FSA, they had lost funding and had been turned over to the army. Ness, Taft, and Turner met with army officials, who agreed to give thirty camps to the SPD. To be operated by local or state governments, these camps received funding through the Lanham Account, which provided supplementary grants to communities experiencing problems due to increased population.[88] Ness stated: "We are working out a closely controlled program with minimum standards" (for the camps). In reference to minimum standards for detention facilities, he "wondered" if there were such standards and whether it was even necessary for the committee to "give any attention" to the matter.[89] The CCC camps were, in fact, used more or less as they were; they lacked amenities and were often in isolated areas. Stephenson (navy) suggested using the camps as an alternative to jail in order to save women from having a criminal record. He made a distinction between hardened prostitutes and women who were "infected by accident." But Stephenson's ideas did not meet with wide approval.[90] In June 1942, the subject of CCC camps came up again when Vonderlehr (USPHS) discussed a plan to acquire one or two of such camps in each state. Vonderlehr also spoke about funding the camps, saying, "[I]t is proposed to start these camps at the federal level, and later attempt to get the various state governments and state health departments to take them over."[91]

Health departments in several states adopted plans to quarantine women who had or were suspected of having venereal disease. In Georgia, for example, the state board of health "declared a quarantine on venereal diseases . . . and has promulgated rules for its enforcement. . . . [P]rovisions are made for the establishment of isolation or detention hospitals for the detention and treatment of these [venereally diseased] persons."[92] In a number of other cases quarantine laws had been invoked against prostitution. The state of Florida appeared "outstanding" in its use of quarantine, according to Vonderlehr, who said that Florida quarantined for syphilis and gonorrhea by placing a "Keep Out" sign with a communicable diseases warning on houses of prostitution. Such a method, as Vonderlehr noted, "breaks up the house."[93] In addition, numerous women were, in fact, confined in the CCC camps.

Repression at Work

During a public lecture in 1942, Eliot Ness stated that "the repression of prostitution can and will be accomplished in one of two ways, first and most desirable is through full co-operation and support of state and local law enforcement officials. However, should voluntary cooperation in any community prove unsuccessful then the second and less desirable method of enforcement would be employed, that is, the May Act."[94] Proposed by Representative Andrew J. May in January 1941 and passed in July 1941, the May Act made prostitution in military areas and defense-related areas a federal offense.[95] The SPD visited noncooperative areas that failed to adopt or resisted repression programs and warned local officials that the May Act would be enforced if necessary. In January 1942, for example, an SPD field representative made an inspection tour in Columbus, Georgia, and Phenix City, Alabama, both in close proximity to Fort Benning.[96] Columbus had closed its red-light district during the First World War; however, "surreptitious" prostitution still operated. Phenix City was a place with a reputation as a "border town and a law unto itself." As of January 1942, approximately a dozen "establishments were flagrantly operating" and providing prostitutes, gambling, and liquor for the soldiers from Fort Benning.[97] This type of situation is representative of those that galvanized the SPD people.

The report on Columbus and Phenix City featured many of the problems that characterized the SPD investigations: allegations unsupported by statistics, the marking of certain female bodies as excessively sexual, and an emphasis on resistance to repression on the part of police, military, and local officials. Mr. Arthur M. Fink, the associate director of the SPD, informed Director Ness of the conditions in Columbus and Phenix City. The investigator claimed that in Phenix City, under the guise of waitressing, anywhere between fifteen and twenty-five girls were in reality working for the "purpose of making pick-ups." The women and their customers, according to this report, then "repaired to beds in the rear." Fink contended that there were "well authenticated" reports that each girl had been known to service fifty to seventy-five men in a twenty-four-hour period. Moreover, the city officials seemed to accept such practices, giving "evident consent." If further evidence were necessary to support the contention that city officials were in collusion with the purveyors of vice, Fink stated that, due to politics, vice crusades did not generally last long in Phenix City. In Columbus, the ongoing investigation determined that a similar problem existed. The investigator stated that local officials, including the police, were not "especially vigilant" and did not interfere with the operations of numerous hotels, tourist courts, and rooming houses that served as sites of prostitution. The conditions in Phenix City and Columbus were further exacerbated by a failure of officers at Fort Benning to formulate any antiprostitution policies. As Fink noted, "There has been no understanding on the part of local officials, police officers or military officials as to the reasons for wanting a thoroughgoing repression program."[98]

The SPD field representative met extensively with various officials, including the commanding officer of Fort Benning. While a venereal disease control officer had been on site, his efforts had been "stymied because of the failure of the camp to take a stand on venereal disease control, and the subsequent failure of the communities to provide adequate control."[99] Meetings were held with editors of the local newspapers, a common SPD tactic intended to whip up public opinion against prostitution and against those officials who failed to support repression. The representative also met with officials such as the mayor, councilmen, lawyers, judges, health officers, law enforcement officials, private welfare organizations, schools, service clubs, and women's groups. The first step involved bringing local and military officials together to formulate a repression program. The second involved agreeing to enforce repression policies. In Phenix City, the SPD claimed success in mobilizing the mayor and the city commissioners to support repression; the threat of enforcing the May Act most likely influenced the decision. In Phenix City, brothels and the hotels (as well as similar facilities in Columbus) were closed. Lacking a separate vice squad, the chief of police and the sheriff spearheaded the campaign of repression. The SPD also had some success with the Phenix City court system, which responded by imposing heavier monetary fines for prostitution; but as probation officers were not yet integrated into the system of repression, control of prostitutes was limited. The state legislature also approved a "more specific definition for prostitution." This measure provided weapons necessary to deal with the prostitution problem; in cases where the definition seemed inadequate, city officials "interpreted the statutes broadly."[100] The report concluded by noting that once military support was forthcoming in declaring some establishments off limits to servicemen, placing military police in both communities, and providing local courts with information gathered from infected servicemen regarding their experiences and contacts, the military disease rate decreased. Some military and medical officers disagreed, arguing that closing of red-light districts resulted in higher venereal disease rates.[101] In either case, women bore the brunt of the blame for spreading venereal disease.

Columbus experienced some difficulties forming a vice squad but ultimately instituted an "active repression program."[102] A significant factor in a number of such towns and cities remained a lack of law enforcement personnel; in many cases this led to appointing female officers to handle the arrested girls. Columbus officials finally authorized such a move. Generally the appointment of female police officers was a vigorously contested matter. Detention facilities, always a problem as arrests increased, could have been a problem in these cities. However, since numerous women "disappeared once the heat was on,"[103] the lack of jails became moot. Surveillance of dance halls and recreation centers (often tasks relegated to women) increased in both Phenix City, Alabama, and Columbus, Georgia.

Race and Class

The SPD used reports by their field representatives to claim, in their own words, "proof upon the basis of experience that repression experiences can be effective and sustained."[104] Division representatives went on to visit Fort Knox in Kentucky, although by this time the VD rate there had been lowered considerably. Their interest focused on the venereal disease control officer at the fort, who kept extensive statistics on sites of infection and in particular on the "colored" troops. Captain Jones, the VD control officer, indicated that the VD rate for 1942 showed a rate of only 20 per 1,000 for white men but 124 per 1,000 for black men. He contended that "60–70 percent of colored soldiers pay professional prostitutes who ply their trade in the colored district near 7th and Walnut."[105] This gave the SPD a clear target, namely the "colored district," where presumably the rate of venereal disease was high. Jones did not mention that the lack of adequate recreational facilities disproportionately affected black soldiers, especially in the South, where they were denied entry to public facilities. While such reports, in the words of a senior SPD official, "are devised for the use of the army surgeon and are not in any sense the responsibility of the SPD," the SPD met, nonetheless, with various post officials to discuss the venereal disease problem among black servicemen.[106]

The allegedly high rate of venereal disease among African Americans led to a focus on black soldiers. This focus marked black male bodies and strengthened the stereotype of African Americans as, in the words of a physician (unnamed) quoted by James H. Jones, a "syphilis soaked race."[107] Many physicians challenged the accuracy of the statistics, and Raymond F. Clapp (SPD) sent corrected statistics to Katherine Lenroot (Children's Bureau).[108] In addition, an official from the FSA informed Eliot Ness about the erroneous statistics.[109] While reports of flawed statistics proliferated in private memos and meetings, the ASHA held a conference in 1943 to "consider practical measures whereby Negro voluntary organizations can best join in united action at federal, state and local levels aimed at reducing the venereal diseases as a serious handicap to health and efficiency."[110] While the ASHA thought it necessary to educate the black population on the topic of sexually transmitted diseases, African Americans had established venereal disease control programs prior to 1943, though they received little assistance from health services. When health services were offered in Alabama in 1936, black persons responded in large numbers. Unfortunately, the services had little to do with preventing or curing venereal disease; the infamous Tuskegee experiment left black male syphilitics untreated.[111] In 1942, Paul B. Cornley, associate professor of preventive medicine and public health at Howard University, wrote to Dr. Clarke (ASHA) in response to a proposed education project among "Negroes."[112] He reacted favorably to the project, especially educational materials specifically geared toward the black communities. Cornley informed Clarke that the USPHS had already been working along similar lines and suggested that both organizations set up an "advisory committee . . . of six or seven Negro leaders in education and public health work to give guidance to development of these activities." He also suggested that a "full-time Negro field worker, preferably a doctor," be appointed as liaison between the ASHA and the USPHS.[113] African Americans who had long supported health education and treatment pointed out, albeit subtly, that such plans and programs would work better if African Americans were involved. Official attitudes—racist and sexist—complicated and diminished the efficacy of venereal disease programs.

The U.S. Public Health Service

The medical aspect of the campaign to eradicate venereal disease operated primarily through the USPHS. Whenever possible, local public health departments responded positively and quickly to the call to prevent or treat venereal disease. They expanded both clinic space and facilities for examinations, although many areas of the South remained lacking in adequate treatment facilities. In several southern states, public health nurses had the task of locating women named as contacts, who would then be held in local jails and forcibly, if necessary, tested for venereal diseases. Committees of concerned citizens also did their part to keep the public health campaign active. The attempt to involve persons and organizations such as tavern keepers, hotel managers, and taxicab operators was less successful; the SPD continued to exert pressure on such groups. The Travelers Aid Society agreed to assist the Public Health Service by interviewing persons who resided outside the communities where they were apprehended.[114] Welfare agencies were also mobilized to interview women who were apprehended and to provide public health officials with the names of local persons served by the county welfare departments. The cooperation between welfare and public health is indicative of the class bias of the campaign; individuals or families who had received public assistance were situated at or beyond the borders of respectability and were perceived, at best, as potentially promiscuous. Since welfare, at this time, served more white persons than black, white lower-class women made up a large percentage of women taken in for questioning and mandatory venereal disease testing. Social class served in this case as a marker for deviance. However, given the years of the Depression, one must consider that class membership had been disrupted. Thus it is entirely possible that some women, regardless of prior class status, were marked as lower class on the basis of contact with relief agencies. While individuals and agencies spoke with genuine concern about the perils of venereal disease, their everyday policies were influenced by gender, race, and class stereotypes.

The May Act Enforced

On May 21, 1942, the *Washington Post* reported that the May Act had been invoked for the first time on May 20. Secretary of War Stimson had designated twenty-seven counties in East Tennessee in the vicinity of Camp Forrest as the areas where the act would be enforced.[115] One year later, Helen Hironimus, warden of the Federal Reformatory for Women at Alderson, West Virginia, analyzed the information regarding the first hundred violators of the May Act. These women, sentenced to Alderson, did time for periods ranging from three to twelve months. In her report, Hironimus discussed the official interpretation of the type of woman or girl that the authorities had expected to transgress: "A flashily dressed, gay and reckless young woman with a certain amount of sophistication . . . [or] a homesick, bewildered young girl . . . expecting to marry her soldier sweetheart" but unable to locate him. This did not, however, turn out to be the case; rather, as Hironimus stated of the offenders, "the war changed their destinies." Of the hundred women, ninety-four women came from submarginal industrial and agricultural areas and would otherwise have remained in poverty and obscurity. They were, according to Hironimus, "ill-equipped for the rapid whirl of soldiers, easy money, beer taverns, and freedom from drudgery, drabness, and monotony." The other six women had followed their sweethearts or husbands and allegedly "resorted to prostitution when their funds were exhausted."[116]

Of the women arrested and sentenced, sixty-eight were white, twenty African American, and twelve Native American. Seventy-three received sentences from ten to twelve months. Their ages ranged from fifteen to sixty-five; only ten were older than thirty-five. Ninety-two women scored between "dull-normal and imbecile" on the IQ test administered. Some had prior encounters with the law, having been arrested on misdemeanor charges. The authorities could not, however, find actual evidence of involvement in prostitution: in other words, ninety-six women did not have venereal disease. Hironimus claimed that the activities of "a large number of the women . . . who are occasionally sexually promiscuous . . . would have escaped the attention of law-enforcement agents had their companions not been soldiers." She reported that while these women had many medical needs, they had a "relatively low rate of venereal disease." She mentioned only four as having gonorrhea, saying this might be "further evidence of the limited sex experience of some of the girls." This case study cast doubt on the claim that so-called promiscuous women spread venereal disease throughout the armed services. While some of the women sentenced to Alderson admitted to sexual relations with servicemen, occasionally for small sums of money, Hironimus pointed out that typically a young woman in this situation felt "bewildered at finding herself . . . confined for doing something she considered her own personal affair."[117] Clearly these young women did not define themselves either as prostitutes or as mentally deficient promiscuous women. There is no evidence that these women did not complete their jail time despite their low incidence of venereal disease and the lack of evidence of their "involvement in prostitution." Their bodies, white and nonwhite, were, however, marked as low class and of subnormal intelligence and therefore, in a psychiatric diagnosis, as liable to sexual excess. Potential promiscuity became a rationale for incarceration. But Hironimus's study shows how a sexually unsophisticated woman who took advantage of wartime opportunities could easily find herself accused of prostitution for "doing something she considered her own affair." Moreover, the authorities had broad powers to accuse, arrest, try, convict, and imprison numerous women on the basis of arbitrary and flexible definitions of prostitution.

Two months later on July 1, 1942, the authorities invoked the May Act for the second time in twelve counties near Fort Bragg, North Carolina. In one county, 161 persons were arrested; in another, 140 "prostitutes" were arrested and tested for venereal disease, with 53 testing positive.[118] According to official sources, the publicity that surrounded the use of the May Act resulted in a mass exodus of prostitutes, who thereby escaped arrest.[119] During an interdepartmental meeting in September 1942, officials contended that prior to enforcement six hundred prostitutes had been active around Fort Bragg. When the decision was made to continue enforcing the act, local officers and military police decided "that it would be unwise to attempt a cleanup before the 20th because payday (military) was later."[120] Mr. Tamm (FBI) said when the act had been invoked a few days before payday, 448 prostitutes had disappeared from one area. The authorities could find only 52 but also arrested several operators of brothels and houses of assignation and juke joints. In all, according to this account, the arrests numbered 75, with 16 convicted.[121] Tamm said most of those were operators of establishments, but he also pointed out the leniency of the federal judges who tried the cases. He related the case of a cab driver who was termed a "key figure" in one of the prostitution operations. Found guilty, the cab driver was "fined one cent for violation of the May Act."[122] A discussion ensued regarding possible legal difficulties around enforcement. The question of constitutionality arose, as one official pointed out that "the Act constitutes an illegal power of contress": that is, federal interference with states' rights. Another area of concern and possible ground for challenge was the scope of the area: twelve counties in North Carolina and twenty-seven counties in Tennessee. "A hundred miles from the army camp is an unreasonable distance."[123] Legal concerns abounded as the campaign progressed: undercover operations (some by citizens groups), investigations by nongovernmental agencies, arrests without warrants, arrests on mere suspicion, lack of evidence, wide distribution of confidential reports, and the fear of libel actions for unsubstantiated material were troubling but did not deter repression in its broadest sense.[124]

While the FBI continually assured police officials that the agency had no intention of "supplanting" local officials or "substituting" federal officers for those of the states, Mr. Tamm noted that "when the May Act was invoked, Mr. Hoover sent in a squad of approximately 158 agents who worked with officials in the various communities and with the military police."[125] Before the invocation of the act, the FBI conducted a survey in the area around Camp Forrest, Tennessee, and determined that "500 prostitutes were operating in the area." Subsequent reports indicated that "the activities of Special agents of the FBI in these two areas up to January 31, 1944, brought about 784 convictions (of prostitutes and procurers)."[126] But the FBI noted that as soon as they left an area, prostitution returned. They insisted upon "vigorous and continuous law enforcement" as the only way to maintain a successful program.[127] FBI officials made a point of mentioning the inadequacy of "a sob sister or a psychological approach" to "clean out" such areas."[128] In other words, they took the criminal approach to prostitution and promiscuity and denigrated the attempts of social agencies to prevent criminal charges in some cases of alleged female sex delinquency.

The Long Arm of the Law: Federal Security and Social Protection

According to Edward V. Taylor (SPD), by 1944 the SPD had helped "to fuse the activities of law enforcement, health departments and social service agencies in an attempt to meet community needs and to eradicate to the point that it is possible the spread of the [venereal] diseases."[129] The SPD also extended its tentacles outside the continental United States, attempting, for example, to influence sexual policies in Mexico and British policies in the Caribbean. While the SPD most assuredly emerged as a notable force in the war against venereal disease, it seems clear that its war on venereal disease, symbolized by the figure of the patriotute, had the potential to target any woman. It was naive, at best, to think that venereal disease could be diminished in any significant measure by ignoring men. But, of course, men were not really ignored; they were protected by government policies and practices both from diseased "bad" women and from "good" women who maintained the men's morale. (The state apparatus continued to call upon America's patriotic young women while simultaneously casting doubt on their patriotism.) The wartime state's interpretation of sexuality and gender produced a monolithic discourse around a category "woman": she was imbued with sex; she was all sex; she was a dangerous individual capable of destroying male health and thus the nation's strength.

In the next chapter, we look backward in time and consider factors that provided an early framework for the wartime repression campaign. The apparatus of the state was concerned about not only controlling female sexuality but also avoiding repercussions as a result of both soliciting women's services in support of the war effort and simultaneously accusing women of soliciting men for sex. Fear of female sexuality was nothing new. Perceptions of dangerous women have long been part of official discourse and popular culture. As wartime necessities disrupted the gender system, the state was determined to control the extent of these disruptions, to ensure that they were limited to "for the duration." Officials looked to the past for workable strategies. There was a vast body of material to draw on to frame the morals campaign of the 1940s; the state would rely on past policies, practices, and gender ideologies to wage a new war against the patriotutes.

2

Prelude to War

While the military sector realized that, in the event of war, plans for military engagements would necessitate more modern tactics and techniques, both the military and other government officials continued to look to the past for strategies to fight against venereal disease and the so-called reservoirs of disease—prostitutes. Hence, the roots of the sexual discourse that influenced World War II policies were deeply embedded in the socio-scientific lore of the past. Since neither a quick nor an effective cure for venereal diseases existed at the time, the authorities relied on past experiences for ideas to assist in planning prevention strategies for the present and future.[1]

Social protection officials, who would ultimately control the venereal disease program during World War II, relied heavily upon individuals and groups active in earlier moral reform efforts of the Progressive Era as well as upon officials who had been involved in programs to protect servicemen from venereal disease during World War I. Bascomb Johnson, director of the Law Enforcement Division of the 1917 CTCA, agreed to lend his expertise to discussions and planning sessions regarding venereal disease and prostitution during wartime.[2] The CTCA was established by Secretary of War Newton D. Baker after receiving a report from his investigator (Raymond B. Fosdick) regarding the appalling conditions at army camps in the Southwest. Fosdick enumerated problems such as "drunkenness, vice, and debauchery" as well as prostitution and venereal disease.[3] Alan Brandt points out that what began as an attempt to keep the troops free of disease, especially venereal disease, soon expanded to a more ambitious effort to "rid the nation of vice, immorality, and disease."[4]

World War I provided an opening for what has been called "an opportunity to evaluate the effects of a national appeal for [sexual] continence." In an attempt to keep servicemen "fit to fight," the government aimed to prevent exposure to medical and moral hazards by persuad-

ing servicemen that sexual restraint was "a virtue comparable to patriotism."[5] Winick and Kinsie state that "as a result the U.S. became a
vast sociological laboratory for testing social hygiene measures."[6] The
CTCA set up a program of athletics/manly exercise/competitive sport
and urged the military and community to work together to provide
amusement and recreation for men on leave. The World War I program
to control venereal disease and prostitution served as a model in the following years. While engaging in a new effort to repress prostitution and
prevent venereal disease during World War II, the state expanded its in-
terventionary role, reaching even deeper into the everyday life of the
American people.

Government, military, and medical officials interested in forming a
new version of the CTCA sought information on the commission's operating procedures. Officials of the ASHA immediately offered their expertise. Heavily involved in venereal disease prevention for many years, the
ASHA continued to advise the army, navy, and USPHS in a capacity similar to its role during World War I. As a result of numerous meetings and
conferences, the ASHA was asked "to assume the same voluntary role
in quietly obtaining the facts and developing public opinion and civilian
cooperation for the protection of soldiers, sailors, civilians, and workers
in essential industries, that it played during the [First] World War."[7]

Jean B. Pinney, editor of the *Journal of Social Hygiene* during the
1940s, put it this way: "Many of the problems which confronted pio-
neer social hygiene workers of those first years of the national campaign
against venereal diseases, prostitution, delinquency, and public indifference and inaction, are much the same as those faced today in the present national emergency, particularly in regard to today's problems of
prostitution and social protection."[8] Pinney stated that experienced social workers believed that it would make good sense to apply the policies used in the past to current conditions, since their earlier reform efforts had "dealt a deadly blow to a gigantic evil."[9] The World War I
notion that "the sexual impulse could be curbed through instruction,
exercise, and wholesome entertainment" recurred in the World War II
discourse but was challenged by a competing idea that (white) servicemen's sexuality could or should not be interfered with.[10] While continence and chastity remained a theme, it was no longer the only option.
Taking a more pragmatic view, especially of sexuality and servicemen,
military and some government officials favored preventive and prophylactic measures. Other segments of the population (white women and

nonwhite men and women), however, remained vulnerable to state interventions in their sexual lives. Influenced by past attitudes toward, and interpretations of, potential problems in the realm of sexuality, the state became overly invested in controlling female sexuality.

State officials, both women and men, who worked in the interwar years in areas such as prisons, reformatories, the judiciary, and police departments added their suggestions to organizing the repression effort.[11] In addition, fact-finding individuals and groups utilized the large body of Progressive Era studies and analyses regarding prostitution.[12] While the magnitude of the war against prostitution, female promiscuity, and venereal disease during World War II exceeded that of World War I, the presence of advisers such as Johnson and women who began their professional careers in the 1910s and 1920s ensured the continuation of a strain of (white) middle-class social and moral reform in the 1930s and 1940s. The early-twentieth-century studies had concentrated on lower class and nonwhite vice districts. The World War II campaign to repress prostitution and control female sexuality had a much broader scope. State officials focused more generally on female sexuality and looked to more varied social locations. Lower-class bodies in the so-called vice districts were no longer the only bodies liable to surveillance.

On Female Sexuality

By the start of the twentieth century, female sexuality had already become a topic of study and analysis. With an acknowledgment that women, too, were sexual beings came new problems that were not only personal but also social. As Joanne J. Meyerowitz points out, such departures from traditional norms "attracted public notice."[13] Print media of many types featured issues on female sex and sexuality by Freud and the sexologists and on flappers, bohemians, suffragists, and more. Often the women depicted were stereotyped as mannish, neurotic, oversexed, undersexed, or otherwise deviating from the expected norms. Bram Dijkstra argues that at the turn of the century scientists "transformed . . . gender conflicts . . . into a 'scientifically grounded' [Darwinian and eugenicist] exposé of female sexuality as a source of social disruption and degeneration."[14] That many young single women, across class lines, had already engaged in male and female relationships, some of a sexual nature, provided evidence for such claims. At the same time that young women were frequenting public entertainment establishments, a parallel discourse of vice and related crimes and their relationship to public entertainment received public attention. The apparatus of the state took notice.

During this period significant numbers of women, many of them former social workers, entered police work; under the heading of crime prevention or "protection," policewomen's goals were "to reduce the vulnerability of teenage girls and young women to sexual exploitation, which they thought encompassed virtually all instances of premarital sex."[15] In a study of adolescent female sexuality that spans the late nineteenth and early twentieth centuries, Mary E. Odem looks at, in part, the emergence of an "elaborate network of legal codes and institutions designed to control the sexuality of young women and girls."[16] By 1920, many female adolescents and young women were perceived no longer as victims of sexual exploitation needing protection but rather as sexually active and in need of discipline. Many women's everyday lives underwent enormous change in the interwar years, but as women once again assumed new wartime roles, older attitudes toward female sexuality remained embedded in the discourse of prevention and protection.

Repression in the Years before Pearl Harbor

In October 1940, Major General Charles R. Reynolds, MD, spoke to a special session of the American Public Health Association on national defense and venereal disease. He went back to colonial times to emphasize the seriousness of the problem. He claimed that George Washington had "directed the attention of the commanders of the armed forces to the gravity of venereal diseases" as spread by camp followers. Ever since, according to Reynolds, the women who followed the troops had been "the chief cause of disability and consequent loss of efficiency in the military establishment." Ignoring the predominance of sexually transmitted diseases in the civilian male population, Reynolds came quickly to the point. "Throughout military operations," he stated, "it is the prostitute who supplies the venereal infection; it is the prostitute who must be controlled to prevent venereal disease in the military forces." He went a step further, however, referring not only to prostitutes but also to "other women differing from them only in nomenclature."[17] In this analysis, which typically omitted the military's dependence on women, proximity to the military could automatically define a woman as a camp follower —that is, as sexually promiscuous. As we have seen, the state fully agreed.

The representatives of the main groups propelling the World War II campaign against prostitutes, promiscuous women, and venereal disease agreed that social hygiene was a critical area of preparedness activities. "Careful planning—based on stern realization and grim determination —was the foundation of the Federal program of venereal disease control."[18] A significant aspect of this "careful planning" became mobilizing public opinion in support of the repression of prostitution. Operating concurrently with the focus on women as vectors of disease, official meetings discussed topics such as increasing prophylactic materials and facilities for servicemen, removing penalties for servicemen who contracted venereal disease, and possibly drafting and treating venereally diseased men.[19] Men could engage in sexual relations, use prophylaxis, and, if they became infected with a venereal disease, receive medical treatment. But women named as contacts were perceived as always already infected or infectious and therefore a threat to national defense.

In January 1941, Dr. Vonderlehr (USPHS) wrote to various officials and agencies regarding the "vital relationship of venereal disease control to current national defense efforts" and the importance of "broad community participation" in VD control. "All public spirited citizens," he said, should be enlisted to support this campaign. McNutt praised the ASHA's work in support of repression as a "great service to the nation." He then requested continuing assistance from the ASHA in "cultivating and organizing public opinion in support of law enforcement to reduce prostitution and sex delinquency to a minimum."[20] This seemed particularly important in light of public opinion polls that indicated that the public favored regulation. Public opinion posed persistent problems. A Gallup poll taken after repression had begun (1942) indicated that 55 percent of those polled still favored regulation. Sixty-one percent of the men and 49 percent of the women said yes.[21] Regulation meant that prostitutes would be required by law to operate in a segregated district and would be subject to regular medical inspection. If found diseased, they would be confined in a treatment facility; if free of venereal disease, they would be issued health cards to that effect. The subject of longtime controversy, regulation appealed to segments of the public and the military for a variety of reasons. On one level, support for regulation reflected a pragmatic view by military officials con-

cerning male sexuality as well as an acceptance of male sexual prerogatives. On another level, public attitudes were more complex, encom-
passing a number of reasons: businessmen's profit motives, community
fears that servicemen might resort to rape if prostitutes were not available, women's fear of rape, and perhaps doubt regarding the possibility
of men remaining chaste.

Despite public concerns that emerged in support of regulation, Ness
and his agency moved quickly to close down vice districts, eliminating
several hundred in a short space of time. Although the SPD claimed a
good success rate, many officials, including Surgeon General Thomas
Parran, perceived the mechanisms for enforcement as weak.[22] Pro-re-
pression officials from government, military, medical, and social institutions sought legislation that would provide the enforcement mechanisms they found lacking as they attempted to close down red-light
districts and arrest prostitutes. With the passage of the May Act in July
1941, they would achieve their goal.

In the meantime, government, medical, and social agency officials
continued to review and discuss repression policies employed during
World War I. In March 1941, Charles P. Taft, the assistant director of
ODHWS (serving under McNutt), held one of many meetings to discuss
a federal social hygiene plan.[23] Dr. William F. Snow (ASHA), Vonderlehr (USPHS), and Bascomb Johnson attended. Taft once again called
upon Johnson to explain the law enforcement policies used to repress
prostitution during World War I and to give particular attention to a
comparison with the proposed May Act. Johnson recalled, in part, that
the country had been divided into districts, each one having specific legal and protective measures. Plans had been drawn up for detention
houses and reformatories to contain women and girls.[24] Johnson stated
that during the First World War most of the administrators were army
officers and that both men and women served as field officers, with the
men handling law enforcement and the women in charge of women and
girls. He recommended that a civilian be placed in charge of the coming
effort, but he stressed the importance of full cooperation by the army
and navy. He then called attention to the word *cooperation* as problematic, since there was at that time "some difference of opinion" among
naval officers regarding repression. The army and navy officers present
assured Taft that they would support any "workable" plan.[25]

That the World War II effort to formulate a coherent social hygiene
program was complicated by "turf wars" became evident as this meet-

ing proceeded. Katherine Lenroot, of the Children's Bureau, wanted a woman in charge with a staff of women. The representative from the FBI wanted to ensure the primacy of his agency's police power. Various other officials, including Captain Rhoda J. Millikin, the director of the Women's Bureau of the Metropolitan Police Department in the District of Columbia, spoke to their own agendas.[26] Many women involved in the campaign, such as Captain Millikin, Katherine Lenroot, Helen Hironimus (prison system), and Miriam Van Waters (prison system), belonged to a group influenced by Progressive reform. Their definition of protection for women and girls incorporated middle-class biases about the working class. They accepted the notion that working-class women were potentially promiscuous, but they favored reforming the women so that they would fit into appropriate class and gender categories. Upon rare occasions, individual women argued for practices such as more realistic sex education for young people, especially women. For example, Dr. Valerie H. Parker, chair of the Social Hygiene Committee of the National Council of Women of the United States, wrote in an ASHA pamphlet that "direct sex character training" was necessary, rather than "the vague and half understood statements concerning purity." She believed that adequate training could help "avert juvenile tragedies."[27] For the most part, however, professional women, while speaking of protection, seemed to have been in agreement with the government's suggestions for a repression program that concentrated on women. Protection, then, had a punitive element.

One lonely voice disagreed with the seeming consensus, that of Aimee Zillmer of the Wisconsin Board of Health. She spoke strongly against attitudes toward social hygiene on the part of many military officials in the prewar period. "I remember," she said, "at a social hygiene day in St. Louis on February 5, 1941, my utter disgust with army officials who stole the show by practically squeezing out any moral, spiritual or educational considerations of social hygiene."[28] She was referring, in part, to attitudes toward servicemen, who were represented as courageous and brave but unable to "face a fancy lady and resist her." Zillmer went on to cite a navy official who, a few months earlier, had spoken about navy men's "disgust" at the focus on venereal disease but who responded favorably to more positive arguments for "staying clean." Suggesting that negative attitudes would have later repercussions, Zillmer stated, "I think we have done youth a great injustice."[29] Her cautions—that both men and women should receive reasonable sex education and

"A Sailor Doesn't Have to Prove He's a Man." Poster, U.S. Navy, 1942. Courtesy of National Library of Medicine/ National Institutes of Health.

that men, too, should be held responsible for promiscuous behavior— went unheeded. Instead, the war against venereal disease continued to equate women and venereal disease.

The May Act Hearings and the Criminalization of Female Sexuality

In late 1940, Major General Charles P. Reynolds introduced a new concern, "mechanized" prostitution, to officials engaged in venereal disease control. He claimed that since contemporary women had great mobility and used various means of transportation, especially automobiles and trailers, many more women followed the troops. This widely circulated theory gained strength from constant repetition, as in the discourses that repeatedly branded the women who "flocked" to areas of military concentration as promiscuous. While prostitutes certainly did business in military areas, not all women in these areas were prostitutes. Presumptive terminology tainted women who were on the move for non-sexual purposes. A mythology of mobilized prostitution, especially after the institution of rationing, served also to strengthen the idea that numerous women were engaging in unpatriotic subversion of defense measures. Reynolds, in fact, referred to prostitution as "a Fifth Column in our midst to be dealt with accordingly."[30] Many persons, both female and male, were, of course, on the road for a variety of reasons related to mobilization. Nonetheless, women who, in supporting the defense effort, deviated from the travel norms that defined prewar behavior became suspicious individuals. Such attitudes indicate that, even at an early point in the campaign, prostitution and promiscuity were often broadly conceived categories, applied indiscriminately. Official perceptions regarding rampant promiscuity gained strength when the venereal disease rate continued to climb even as prostitution districts were closed down.[31] Support for federal legislation increased.

In January 1941, Representative Andrew J. May of Kentucky presented a bill to Congress that would make prostitution in the vicinity of military bases and defense-related areas a federal crime. The Committee on Military Affairs held hearings on the May Act during March 1941.[32] The committee numbered twenty-seven and heard testimony from representatives of diverse groups, all in favor of legislation to criminalize prostitution. Reports of the hearings indicate that the fight against venereal diseases focused almost entirely on women. The proposed legislation was, in fact, referred to as the "suppression of prostitution bill."[33] Representatives of organizations such as the ASHA, the American Legion, and the Children's Bureau, as well as several military chaplains who favored moral suasion as a strategy to reach men and convince them to resist promiscuity, testified in support of the May Act. The day after the hearings opened, Mayor La Guardia of New York informed the *New York Times* that not only did he endorse the act, but also he had suggested an amendment to make it "even more forceful and effective." La Guardia's proposal that the act include "loiterers" in the vicinity of cantonments, or training stations, not just prostitutes, illustrates how the campaign moved beyond an attack on commercialized prostitution. He also recommended that the government be authorized to seize property used for immoral purposes, including automobiles and trailers.[34]

Dr. Arthur T. McCormack, state health officer of Louisville, Kentucky, was one of the first to speak in support of this legislation. Testifying as a member of the Conference of State and Territorial Health Authorities, McCormack stated that the group was "unanimously in favor" of the proposed legislation. On the basis of his experience during World War I, he pointed out that federal legislation conferred the power of persuasion: "[Y]ou are able to persuade a great many people to do things that you could not do if you did not have the authority that is conferred by this legislation." He suggested that the threat of federal intervention could diminish the need for actual prosecutions. McCormack then raised the question of "reasonable distance," since widespread use of automobiles and other improved means of transportation meant that men on leave could and did travel long distances and that women, too, had greater mobility. McCormack pointed out that the size of the zone around the camp was of "very great importance" and a "very serious practical problem," given the high rate of venereal disease among servicemen.[35] Apparently the area of the zone never became standardized, since a significant portion of Tennessee came under the control of the May Act in 1942.

When the hearings returned to the need for federal legislation, McCormack pointed out that a large percentage of the men stationed at Fort Thomas and Fort Knox, Kentucky, had venereal disease. He claimed that a "great many" prostitutes operated in the immediate neighborhood of both camps but that because of a lack of effective law enforcement measures not much had been done to eliminate the problem. Moreover, McCormack said that without a federal mandate on repression of prostitution a particular type of problem resulted. "Cincinnati," he said, "has enforced its laws very well indeed, and that has resulted in driving most of the prostitutes over to Newport, Kentucky where they are welcome and where they like to have them because it increases business in Newport, and as a result they have succeeded in infecting not only soldiers but a great many of the civilians in Cincinnati, because the men seem to follow the prostitutes there, as they do in other places." The chairman then inquired whether the doctor had any up-to-date information regarding the activities of these women. McCormack replied that "there is one very curious thing that is happening": on the night before payday at Fort Knox between 50 and 150 automobiles carrying women arrived in the general vicinity. He claimed that his investigators referred to these women as "grass grabbers" who "go around in these cars, get under the trees and set up business for the night, and are gone the next morning." The doctor went on (at length) to make the case for the absolute necessity of federal legislation that would "centralize authority" and support uniform prosecution of (female) offenders.[36] Many who testified in favor of passage of the May Act stated their support in terms of the need for federal intervention if local law enforcement did not comply with the directives to clean up red-light districts by vigorous suppression of prostitution. Accusations, like the one made against "grass grabbers," proliferated and lent strength to the call for federal intervention. The machinery for controlling female sexuality was set firmly in place with the passage of the May Act in July 1941. The battle on the homefront, based not only on charges that some American women were already engaging in sexually "deviant" behavior but also on an expectation that many more would do so, began well before entry into the "real" war on December 7, 1941.

Sexuality and Surveillance

Once the May Act became law, the SPD increased its investigations of so-called problem areas. Surveillance had, however, been occurring for some time. In response to a request from McNutt (FSA) for information regarding the activities of the ASHA on "national defense problems," Dr. Clarke (ASHA) reminded McNutt that Dr. Snow had already deposited a complete file of the ASHA's reports of "undercover studies" with the Office of the Surgeon General of the United States.[37] Clarke reiterated the ASHA's general position on educational and environmental measures, which were "intended to foster the most advantageous exercise of sex functions in life." But he also stated that "certain pathological practices such as commercialized prostitution and certain communicable diseases such as syphilis and gonorrhea, spread mainly by sex contacts," had to be "corrected," since army, navy, and defense workers would become disabled as a result of venereal disease. Furthermore, he maintained that "since prostitution constitutes the principal means of spread of these diseases," national defense demanded a solution. The magnitude of the early campaign became visible: "209 undercover investigations of prostitution and allied conditions" had been carried out by the ASHA from September 1, 1939, to January 1, 1941, in twenty-nine states and the District of Columbia.[38] Given that representatives of the association had discovered numerous areas of problematic sexual activity, Clarke reiterated the necessity of "adequate law enforcement against prostitution and juvenile delinquency."[39] He told McNutt that the association was regularly informing state and local officials of "situations" in need of remedial action in order to protect the "health and morale of the armed forces." The FBI acted on such information; the records indicate a significant rise in the number of women arrested on morals charges. FBI statistics for 1941 and 1942 show arrests of women under twenty-one increasing by 64.8 percent for prostitution and by 104.7 percent for "other sex offenses."[40]

The Battle on the Homefront

The state apparatus had a clear target in existing prostitution districts, but officials also planned a preemptive strike on women deemed potentially promiscuous. In general, planning sessions for the implementation of the war on venereal diseases made it clear that women were viewed as both sexually available and sexually suspect. The authorities discussed ways to use women for varied forms of entertainment in order to maintain male morale while simultaneously acting to control and contain so-called dangerous female sexuality. For example, James E. Moore, a physician, while engaged in a discussion about service clubs, called for the availability of "wholesome activities: pool, billiards, cards, etc., and young women for game or dance partners."[41] The USO mobilized carefully chosen young women to serve as hostesses for servicemen and "assumed that white middle-class women were inherently sexually respectable and feminine." "It groomed these 'good girls' to represent the USO. . . . [T]hey conducted work that helped to maintain the role of the virtuous woman in this time of crisis."[42] The Cincinnati USO bused three hundred girls from Cincinnati to Fort Knox every other Sunday. They departed in the morning, lunched at Fort Knox, served as dancing hostesses at a tea dance, and returned home around 11 o'clock in the evening. After a few weeks the same service was provided on the intervening Sundays to Camp Atterbury.[43] Many other young women;

traveling alone or in groups, were not so fortunate; unprotected by the USO's excellent reputation, they might be perceived as "mechanized prostitutes."

In Louisville, Kentucky, a committee of citizens appointed by the director of public welfare and functioning under the Welfare and Recreation Division of the mayor's Military Affairs Committee identified a need for a center for transient servicemen. Accordingly, in March 1941 the committee opened such a center where servicemen could engage in a variety of activities, including meeting girls and dancing. The committee also called for a hospitality program to integrate servicemen into the community through churches and invitations to Sunday dinner.[44] Paradoxically, then, numerous women, in complying with wartime obligations, traveled beyond traditional gender boundaries and became vulnerable to charges of suspicious behavior. For example, when women volunteered to attend dances at military encampments, they traveled in buses and trains, but at the same time magazine articles referred to trainloads of girls arriving in military areas as, at best, potentially promiscuous.[45]

On rare occasions an official figure exhibited concern about the use of women as hostesses or in other capacities in support of servicemen's morale. For example, the assistant dean of women at Ohio State University was initially very reluctant to permit "her girls" to travel to dances at nearby Lockbourne Air Base. Newspaper articles such as "Sweethearts at Ease," by Ovetta Culp Hobby, responded to similar concerns. She thought that wives, in particular, might want to know more about the army innovation of "hostesses." Speaking of the importance of maintaining morale, Hobby discussed hostesses as part of the "giant housekeeping problems of the rapidly expanding army." She wrote about her public relations job in terms of putting out "personalized news," saying that she intended to keep women—wives, sweethearts, mothers—informed about the kind of news that they were interested in. In representing the public relations arm of the War Department, Hobby was charged with reassuring the female public that hostesses were performing an ordinary domestic task and were not "loose" women who would tempt their men to sexual transgressions.[46]

It is not surprising that women would have some misgivings regarding the presence of hostesses and other women mobilized to entertain the troops, since warnings about so-called promiscuous women proliferated. Places of public transportation, for example, featured posters cautioning servicemen about loitering women, depicting lone women as most likely soliciting. Influenced by the prevailing and widespread notion that prostitution flourished around military camps and bases, many women feared for their men's moral virtue. In light of the public campaign against venereal disease–bearing girls and women, women who participated in defense-related recreational activities for servicemen were all too often viewed with suspicion. Amid a discourse of female sexual deviance, the state called upon women to volunteer for morale service. But as we have seen, male morale based on female companionship, which was sexualized in the prevailing discourse, often placed women in dangerous spaces, regardless of their reasons for joining the mobilization effort.

These conflicting attitudes toward women who traveled beyond normative spaces strengthened beliefs held by certain government and civilian officials that unrestricted female sexuality would result in an epidemic of venereal disease. As sexuality, particularly female sexuality, became the topic of numerous publications, reports, and meetings, the discussions and debates regarding the venereal disease problem produced a discourse of anticipatory stigmatization around women's expected sexual activities. In February 1941, Dr. Moore, who was chairman of the National Research Council's Subcommittee on Venereal Diseases and who served as a frequent witness, appeared before a joint army-navy committee to speak about the causal relationship between prostitution and venereal diseases. His testimony reinforced a notion that mobilization and war would loosen social constraints and that immoderate female sexual activity would ensue. This, in turn, would spread venereal disease, imperil the health and efficiency of the armed forces, and sap national strength. Dr. Moore epitomized the contradictions of the war on prostitution and the venereal disease campaign. In March 1941, for example, he spoke strongly in support of the repression of prostitution as an effective measure for "minimizing potentially infectious contacts." And in the course of his lengthy speech, he also provided insight into the mobilization aspect of female sexuality as he advocated providing hostesses at service clubs to maintain morale. Then again, Moore is also on record as considering the viability of regulated prostitution as a means of providing clean sex for servicemen. It should also be noted that Moore was a consultant to the Tuskegee experiment (1932), at which time his belief that venereal disease manifested differently in blacks and whites did much both to rationalize the experiment and to maintain the fiction that blacks were inherently different from whites.[47] Moore was not the only official who inscribed sexual deviance on raced and gendered bodies.

Venereal Disease Control Strategies

Numerous individuals and agencies continued to present their plans to reduce venereal disease in the armed forces. The ASHA continued to plan for venereal disease control by focusing on education, particularly for servicemen. Sex education, a contentious issue, had different meanings for a variety of organizations and individuals. For the ASHA, the outbreak of the war in Europe and the inevitability of American involvement gave a sense "of history repeating itself." ASHA leaders thought that the First World War could have "provided the ultimate teachable moment." However, social and political opposition, as well as the brevity of U.S. participation in the war, limited the association's success. The ASHA expected to be more successful this time, since the federal government seemed ready to play a more active role in the fight against venereal diseases through a well-coordinated program for the repression of prostitution.[48] Over time, the ASHA engaged in efforts to educate young people regarding the horrors of venereal disease, its links with prostitution, and the dangers of promiscuity to the nation, to the family, to the body, and to moral character. During the Second World War, the association continued its efforts to dissuade young men and women from promiscuous sex.

While the ASHA contended that the best way to prevent venereal disease was through education, other participants in the campaign continued to discuss more direct intervention, such as federal regulation of prostitution or federal legislation to suppress prostitution. Some officials challenged the idea of more explicit sex education as a viable strategy, contending that providing prophylactic information would increase immorality rather than decrease disease. And the very idea of providing women with sexual information was anathema to many of those involved in the social hygiene campaign. Paradoxically, while sex education and "pure" womanhood seemed a contradiction in terms to many officials, they continued to view women, in general, as liable to promiscuity. After all, according to a popular VD poster, even the seeming pu-

"She May look Clean . . . But . . ." Poster, ca. 1941–45. Courtesy of National Library of Medicine/National Institutes of Health.

rity of the girl next door was open to doubt.[49] There was a widespread sociopolitical perception that "immoral" women posed the most significant threat to national health, and this perception continued to retard a comprehensive war on venereal disease.

Official teams had another plan; they began to conduct numerous studies in diverse areas throughout the United States. The military, for example, did a survey of commercialized prostitution conditions in so-called problem areas in California in 1940.[50] And in 1941 the ASHA published a report reinforcing the belief that some women would likely cause problems: "[I]n all probability the problems of prostitution would become conspicuous again as the nation prepared for defense and possibly for war."[51] As a result of such suppositions, the ASHA and the Bureau of Social Hygiene conducted 531 studies of prostitution, leading the authorities to state that "dangerous conditions existed" across the United States.[52] Local and state health departments sent investigators into various localities where prostitution, promiscuity, and venereal disease "flourished." Connecticut health officers, for example, visited ninety-six towns and cities between July 1940 and June 1941. Particularly troublesome areas, characterized by female prostitution and promiscuity, such as Hartford and New Haven, received multiple visits, eighty-two and forty-one respectively.[53] The Detroit Police Department also did its part by arresting "a group of women each day and night on morals charges." Some were known prostitutes, and others were so-called first offenders; all were held in jail and examined for venereal disease.[54]

In June 1941, the Second Army (approximately seventy-five thousand men) held field maneuvers in southern Tennessee. The governmental responses illuminated the gendered workings of the VD campaign. The public health system set up VD clinics within existing health departments and opened special clinics in other locales. In each of the ten counties in and around the maneuver area, a deputy sheriff worked full time to "apprehend prostitutes and arrest female vagrants." Vagrants could be women who were not local to the area, but the charge of vagrancy could also be used to arrest "on suspicion of," as in the case of women perceived to be potentially promiscuous. Numerous women were arrested, held in jail, examined for venereal disease, and, if found infected, remanded to quarantine facilities. "Those suspected of being prostitutes and who had negative blood tests on the first examination were held in most instances for a second examination a week later." Women who were arrested on charges of vagrancy but who tested negative for venereal disease received a fine. Inability to pay the fine resulted in a sentence to the workhouse. Ultimately officials determined that only about 14 percent of the male cases of venereal disease originated in the maneuver area; 86 percent of the men had acquired venereal disease elsewhere.[55] Such statistics did not reach the public, leaving the impression that prostitutes and "loitering" women managed to infect significant numbers of servicemen. While the repression campaign may have reduced sexual contact in the maneuver area, it did not stop the soldiers from engaging in sexual relations. It was not intended to. Rather the war against venereal disease was more often fought by randomly accusing American women of immorality. When addressing the public, the SPD used the specific term *promiscuous girls and women*, though in private, by using the term *potentially promiscuous*, it failed to make clear distinctions between and among women.

Official discussions of female sexuality in articles such as "Prostitution as a Source of Infection with the Venereal Diseases in the Armed Forces" led to meetings to discuss the necessity for contact tracing of allegedly diseased women. A representative memo discussed, in part, repression of prostitution, including factors such as eliminating segregated districts and individual brothels and refusing to tolerate "flagrant solicitation," whether it occurred on the streets, in cabarets, in dance halls, in honky-tonks, or by "trailer girls." A discourse of (bad) women on the loose circulated privately and publicly in state documents, professional publications, and the popular press, forging a link between women and the contagion of sexually transmitted diseases.[56] Many officials had no doubt that as large numbers of men became concentrated on military bases and in wartime industrial boomtowns, "hordes of harlots" would soon follow.[57] As venereal diseases, prostitution, and female promiscuity filled the agendas of committee meetings, hearings, and memos by concerned and interested officials, individuals, and agencies, no one in attendance seemed to disagree with the claim that prostitutes were responsible for the spread of venereal diseases. Many also assumed that numerous other wartime women would not only exceed the bounds of their assigned sexual space but also carry venereal diseases.

The resulting publicity regarding investigations tended to overshadow different solutions such as moral suasion and education regarding the perils of venereal disease. The extent of the policies and practices of the state apparatus as they affected women during the period of preparedness and mobilization for the Second World War has been, for the most part, underreported.[58] In the years and months immediately preceding Pearl Harbor, the homefront was not a secure place for women. Government officials called upon women to provide a variety of defense-related support services as the nation prepared for war. But at the same time, government officials and members of social agencies developed plans to prevent and control venereal diseases in the armed services through the repression of prostitution. Numerous women, many of them not prostitutes, became subject to repression. Once any woman stepped outside the traditional boundaries of female space, she entered an ambiguous space where she could be seen as "promiscuous." We turn in the next chapter to the role played by the sciences and medicine in the war on the homefront against venereal disease and women.

3

"Reservoirs of Infection"
Science, Medicine, and Contagious Bodies

The wartime definition of contagious bodies was a product of discourses of medicine and science, including the social sciences. These discourses include not only those circulating during the 1940s but also those of the preceding decades. Ideologies, theories, stereotypes, attitudes, and perceptions of gender, class, ethnicity, and race that surfaced and resurfaced during the war years both reflected and reinforced preexisting assumptions regarding particular bodies as always prone to deviance and disease. Because the disease in question was venereal, the bodies in question were constituted as dangerous, both morally and medically. During World War II a belief that some bodies (female and nonwhite) were dangerous shaped government policies and social attitudes.

Sexually transmitted diseases have a long and complicated history.[1] Controversies over venereal diseases and their interpretations converge at an intersection of political, philosophical, medical, moral, racial, class, and gender dialogues. Thus discourses of venereal disease have often exceeded the boundaries of science and medicine. During the Second World War, syphilis and gonorrhea represented not only communicable diseases but also signs of danger and disorder in the social body, particularly in its female aspect. Complex sociocultural meanings surrounded, and continue to surround, concepts and categories such as disease, sin, deviance, race, women, and prostitutes, to name a few.

In the early twentieth century, when the physician and experimental scientist Paul Erhlich discovered an arsenic-based treatment for syphilis, he referred to it as a "magic bullet." The new drug, Salvarsan, seemed to offer hope that another serious communicable disease could be controlled, perhaps even cured. But in spite of this scientific breakthrough, venereal diseases remained in the realm of the unspeakable, emerging

only occasionally to be considered as medical rather than moral problems. When Thomas Parran, MD, was appointed surgeon general of the
USPHS in 1936, his priorities included lifting the silence and removing
the moral stigma around venereal diseases. Nonetheless, a connection
persisted between venereal disease and sin. In 1940, for example, when
Paul De Kruif discussed Erhlich's discovery, he still referred to the ar-
senical treatment as "a deliverer from the scourge of that pale corkscrew microbe whose attack is the reward of sin, whose bite is the cause
of syphilis, the ill of the loathsome name."[2] And while Parran spoke of
treating venereal diseases just like any other communicable diseases, he
too could not completely escape from the influences of his time, including the belief that race affected the etiology of disease. For example, the
surgeon general wrote that "it is not his [the black man's] fault that the
disease is biologically different in him than in the white, that his blood
vessels are particularly susceptible so that late syphilis brings with it
crippling circulatory diseases, cuts his working usefulness in half, and
makes him an unemployable burden upon the community in the last
years of his shortened life. It is through no fault of hers that the colored
woman remains infectious two and one half times as long as the white
woman."[3] Wittingly or unwittingly, such statements contributed to a
belief that venereally diseased African Americans not only were biologically different from white people but also posed unique dangers to the
larger society. Women, both black and white, and black men became
the primary signifiers of venereal disease, allowing a perception of white
men, especially servicemen, as innocent victims of these diseases and by
extension the most moral members of society. Such discourses, which
marked particular bodies and left others unmarked, continued, over
time, to confound wartime attempts to deal with sexually transmitted
diseases in a medical framework. Historian John Duffy notes that while
"existing medical knowledge defined the limits of health activity . . .
that alone did not determine what would happen."[4] Nonmedical factors
such as politics, economics, religion, and issues of class, race, ethnicity,
and gender all influenced perceptions of and policies regarding venereal
disease and its prevention and control during World War II.

The competing discourses that circulate around the topic of venereal
diseases illuminate the clash between medical and moral perceptions of
sexually transmitted diseases. Alan M. Brandt, in his work on the social
history of venereal disease in the United States, considers "venereal disease in its social constructions." He analyzes the ways in which three

factors, "sex, disease, and medicine," both "engage social fears" and operate to "express these anxieties" around the subject of venereal disease.[5] Historian Elizabeth Fee adds that "social, political, religious, and moral conceptions influence our perceptions of disease, just as do scientific and medical theories."[6] She also points out that "a fundamental cultural ambivalence" is manifested in a continuing debate regarding studies and treatments of sexually transmitted diseases. "Are venereal diseases infectious diseases just like many others," or do they represent "social, moral, or spiritual afflictions?"[7] According to Charles E. Rosenberg, disease is an "elusive entity." He contends that "explaining sickness is too significant—socially and emotionally—for it to be a value-free enterprise."[8] During World War II, servicemen suffered from a curable disease, but women and disease became synonymous.

Constructing Deviant Bodies

The production of the sexually promiscuous and diseased woman of the Second World War becomes somewhat easier to comprehend when considered in light of similar medical, scientific, and sociocultural manifestations in prior times. Rosi Braidotti has traced the presence of traditional and historically continuous categories of the "other," such as "sexual difference (i.e. man/woman), sexual deviance, race, ethnicity, and the non-human." She views otherness through the lens of "monstrous" beings, who, in her words, "help us understand the paradox of difference as a ubiquitous but perennially negative preoccupation."[9] That state and social authorities were preoccupied, in a negative way, with expectations of an imminent explosion of "monstrously" excess female sexuality in the late 1930s and during the war years cannot be denied.

In his book *Evil Sisters*, Bram Dijkstra follows a similar path.[10] He explores the construction of the dangerous female body in bioscience and popular culture, especially in the early decades of the twentieth century. Dijkstra analyzes the figure of the female vampire, who presented a clear and present threat to the virility of the white heterosexual male. Appearing in popular media as the "vamp," such women were both alluring and dangerous. Depicted as sexual predators, vamps were held responsible for destroying manhood. Reading such scholarship in conjunction with the numerous studies of prostitution and promiscuity that proliferated in the Progressive Era, one can identify continuously negative attitudes toward female sexuality, which made possible designations such as the World War II patriotute—another destroyer of manhood. In spite of, or perhaps because of, actual changes in women's material lives during wartime, these deeply embedded attitudes reemerged and adapted to the necessities of war. They continued to exert an influence on perceptions of what constituted appropriate or inappropriate womanhood. In this process, many myths about female sexuality acquired a patina of truth.

Recent scholarship looks closely at the relationships among women, science, and medicine, particularly in terms of the framing or marking of the female body. The editors of *Body/Politics: Women and the Discourses of Science* remind us that "many of the crucial focuses for scientific contestation have involved or invoked the feminine body."[11] And as Jennifer Terry and Jacqueline Urla have indicated, the idea of "embodied deviance" has, "since the nineteenth century, been part and parcel of a larger effort to organize social relations according to categories denoting normality versus aberration, health versus pathology, and national security versus social danger."[12] In the nineteenth century, for example, the criminal anthropologist Cesare Lombroso wrote on certain troubling social elements, among which were delinquents and prostitutes. Lombroso, according to Nancy Harrowitz, grounded his methodology in a repository of commonplace assumptions.[13] He pursued visible, measurable markers of difference that he interpreted according to the standards of his age; he insisted on the "monstrosity" of social deviance.[14] Historian David Horn contends that the body of Lombroso's "female offender was constituted as a particular kind of social text: an index of present and potential risks to the larger social organism."[15] Contemporary feminist criminologists pay particular attention to these late-nineteenth- and early-twentieth-century theories because they see the theories as having a continuing influence on sociological and criminological studies. Although Lombroso's work has been discredited, it is still worthy of attention, since, as Frances M. Heidensohn has shown, "later writers rely on those sexual ideologies based on implicit assumptions about the physiological and psychological nature of women that are explicit in Lombroso."[16] The concept of a readable or marked body persisted over time and resurfaced in the 1940s in the scientific, medical, and psychiatric discourses around the prostitute and promiscuous female body. While recognizing that the marking of female bodies has a long history, I begin with the turn of the century, when particularly misogynist and racist sociobiological discourses gained currency.

Race, Gender, and Deviant Bodies

During World War II the campaign to prevent venereal disease from destroying military virility focused, in large measure, on controlling women, but they were not the only persons perceived as harboring disease. Gender ideology operated in tandem with race ideology, producing concepts that described prostitutes as "cesspools of infection" and African Americans as "sexually promiscuous."[17] Over time, then, it is possible to trace the development of multiple discourses "designed to keep an eye on those entities considered suspicious," whether germs or the persons who came to embody them.[18]

Even as one recognizes that categories of "marked bodies" are not a new phenomenon, it is difficult to comprehend the persistence of particular sexist, racist, and classist ideologies. A review of studies in criminology proves useful to this endeavor. Such studies can, for instance, provide additional insight into the ways in which both black and white female bodies and the black male body have been marked, over time, as liable to crime and other deviance. This practice is especially evident in, but not limited to, the realm of so-called sexual crimes.[19]

Current scholarship in criminology extends the exploration of the relationship between gender and deviance. Colin Sumner, for example, turns to Foucault's theory of normalization to develop an interpretation of the relationship between gender and the "censure of deviance." He posits a concept of "master censures" as an integral feature of "hegemonic ideology" and contends that "the censure of femininity is one of them." Since Sumner sees censures as "interconnected by their associated employment in ideological practices," he suggests that "most hegemonic censures of deviance are, at a minimum, coloured at a deep structural level by the master censure of femininity in connection with other master censures."[20] This analysis lends insight into the dominant discourse of the militarized state, especially in terms of its inconsistent attitudes toward women. At the same time, the notion of multiple censures allows one to rethink the interplay of race, class, and gender. Such analyses assist in uncovering the influence of race and class that are, for the most part, underreported in the World War II documents.

Early-twentieth-century prostitution studies, as well as more recent studies of prostitution and working-class forms of leisure, also assist in identifying censures based on race and class. For example, two studies of prostitution completed in the interwar years and used as references by World War II officials focused on places and persons marked as deviant. Working-class and black neighborhoods represented sites of danger, both sexual and criminal; the persons—criminals including prostitutes —who inhabited those sites embodied deviance. During World War II, many sites of surveillance fit the model described in these and other studies. Influenced by racial and class stereotypes, wartime law enforcement authorities assumed that working-class and nonwhite, especially African American, neighborhoods were inevitably ridden with vice and disease.[21] Similar stereotypes also worked to deny adequate medical services to nonwhite persons and to categorize working women as potentially sexually promiscuous.

Social Sciences and Deviant Bodies

During the Progressive Era many moral reformers focused on prostitution and prostitutes as the source of venereal infection. In the conservative period following World War I, when public discussions of venereal disease and sexual issues, in general, fell out of favor, parties such as the ASHA, the Bureau of Social Hygiene, and individual researchers conducted studies of prostitution and searched for a means to ameliorate the ravages of venereal disease. In the late 1930s, as the United States moved closer to military involvement and the issue of venereal disease prevention became of paramount importance to the defense effort, the apparatus of the state had a large body of material to draw from regarding female prostitution, promiscuity, and venereal disease.

Abraham Flexner's study of regulated prostitution in Europe is, perhaps, the most well known.[22] Following Flexner's example, Howard B. Woolston authored a major study entitled *Prostitution in the United States*, which focused on prostitution prior to World War I.[23] The final product, published in 1921, became a salient resource for World War II planners, having already served as a reference for interwar reformers such as William F. Snow, the first director of the Bureau of American Social Hygiene. These early-twentieth-century reports served as sites of a particular discourse of female sexuality that focused, in part, on a notion of an inherent female propensity to promiscuous sexuality.

Woolston claimed that since prostitutes allegedly had a 65 to 75 percent rate of venereal disease, "the great majority of prostitutes are a constant menace as a source of contamination."[24] Here we can see a source of attitudes that came to influence Charles P. Taft's 1942 claim that "prostitutes mean venereal disease, just the way a louse means typhus."[25] In line with other early-twentieth- century researchers on prostitution, Woolston opposed regulation by means of segregated districts because he believed that "lewd women" would evade control by "relocating beyond the limits of the vice districts." Female sexual vice, in his estimation, could not merely be restricted or regulated; it had to be stopped, preferably by government intervention.[26]

In addition to gender stereotypes, class and racial stereotypes emerged in Woolston's study, with its focus on so-called vice-saturated districts, generally located in lower-class areas and in neighborhoods peopled by immigrants and "Negroes." Referring to such areas as "vicious districts," Woolston contended that "girls" and more specifically "colored women" there were not only aggressive in approaching men but also apt to "suggest perversions."[27] By focusing on the populations in working-class and nonwhite neighborhoods, Woolston and other early-twentieth-century social scientists established these areas as sites of sociosexual deviance. By the 1940s, demographic changes exacerbated already existing suspicions about black and working-class areas. Ultimately such stereotypes led not only to increased surveillance in traditionally black and working-class areas but also to arrests of numerous black and white women both inside and outside so-called vice districts.[28]

Woolston, while calling himself a man of a "new era," recurred to a Lombrosian discourse of the marked body, as evidenced in his comments regarding women in prison. He described the "typical" female delinquent as "shorter and heavier than other women of her age. . . . [T]he ordinary prostitute appears to be a short stocky woman . . . characterized by a high degree of physical defectiveness of all kinds."[29] Such descriptions, which reappeared during the Second World War, can also be read as code for class, ethnicity, and possibly lesbianism, which was seldom discussed aloud. In the 1940s lesbianism did become visible in a few instances: for example, a government committee noted that some female bar patrons were characterized as having "a touch of lavender."[30]

The New York City Health Department published a chart indicating extensive female-to-female transmission of venereal disease.[31]

Woolston turned his gaze on young women. He claimed that his study found that "the most dangerous period of a girl's life [was] during her later adolescence (15–19) because her emotions overruled her judgement." He pointed to unchaperoned dates for late-night dinners, dance clubs, movies, and amusement parks, which often involved travel by automobile, as "unquestionably dangerous for young girls."[32] During the Second World War, as numerous young women frequented places of public entertainment, social concerns reemerged. Woolston's claim that automobiles could serve as "mobile dens of iniquity" had clear parallels with the later claim of "mechanized prostitution."[33] And as the SPD closed down numerous prostitution districts, the vice spotlight focused on young women typically referred to as amateurs or as having "khaki fever."[34] Absent, however, was the notion that these young women were endangered; by World War II these young women became the danger. Seen as aggressively sexual, they supposedly required new measures of control, especially since, according to the authorities, they were harder to identify. Framed by the suggestion "She may look clean . . . but . . . ," young women found themselves in an ever-expanding zone of control. Questionable statistics attributed approximately 70 percent of the venereal diseases contracted by World War II servicemen to young women who were not professional prostitutes; the men called them pickups.[35] By the time of the Second World War, then, a plethora of marked bodies had already become objects to be watched.

A decade after Woolston's study, Walter C. Reckless conducted a similar study of prostitution in Chicago. His conclusions supported prevailing notions regarding prostitution, particularly "Negro prostitution" and the "social maladjustment" that, in his view, characterized Chicago's undesirable and disorganized neighborhoods.[36] He, too, focused on working-class sites of leisure, referring to "a notable increase of cabarets and roadhouses" and other "developments in commercialized recreation and changes in life and habits of city dwellers." According to Reckless, such problems had grown steadily worse as a result of the influx of southern blacks over the preceding twenty years. He pointed out that black women, while only 7 percent of the population, represented 70 percent of the cases brought before the morals court in 1929. "The police," he said, "prepared cases mainly against the obvious, cheap Negro resorts . . . located in the poorest Negro neighborhoods." Reckless admitted, however, that blacks were more liable to arrest than whites because police officers shared in the general public opinion that they were more criminal than whites.[37] Law enforcement officials also agreed that they encountered less chance of repercussions when they arrested blacks, whereas greater care had to be exercised in arresting whites. The FBI's *Uniform Crime Reports* for 1941–45 indicate that such attitudes continued to affect African Americans adversely during the war years. Black women remained susceptible to more frequent arrests for morals offenses, and black men were more often arrested as third-party offenders—that is, as pimps or procurers.[38]

During the first three decades of the twentieth century, then, we can see that black women, some white women, and black men had been closely examined and found liable to promiscuity and sexually transmitted diseases. Moreover, a connection had been made between such persons and particular urban areas, including places of commercial entertainment. By the 1940s, however, commercial entertainment was certainly not the exclusive bailiwick of the "lower orders"; the population of the cities had undergone dramatic change as wartime migration escalated. Nonetheless, during World War II, government and social agencies found easy targets for repression by accepting preexisting stereotypes about sexuality with regard to nonwhite persons, including African Americans, Mexicans, Native Americans, and Asians, as well as members of the working class, especially women.

The U.S. Public Health Service

As the USPHS undertook the tremendous task of maintaining the nation's health during wartime, the prevention and control of venereal diseases occupied a prominent place on the agenda.[39] The USPHS trained additional personnel and placed them in state and local health departments. Assistant Surgeon General Vonderlehr proclaimed that a large increase in the venereal disease rate no longer had to be a "wartime inevitability." He pointed out that "stringent civilian control measures and the vigorous control program of the armed services" had already been instrumental in avoiding a "sharp increase in syphilis and gonorrhea among soldiers, sailors, and war workers." In addition, he pointed to practices such as finding servicemen's sources of infection, treating them, and confining them until they were "permanently noninfectious" as salient factors in the success of the program. Vonderlehr reiterated the importance of gathering information on "persons (women) who had presumably infected members of the armed forces" and reporting such information to health officers, who would then find these "suspected persons" and bring them in for examination.[40]

Who were these suspects? First and foremost, they were women, but not necessarily prostitutes. During 1940 and 1941, numerous red-light districts and houses of prostitution had been closed down. But the venereal disease rate in the military had not diminished as a result of the lack of access to prostitutes. Vonderlehr explained this puzzle by calling attention to a report by the NAPCSP regarding the spread of venereal disease.[41] The committee's report supported the idea that "promiscuous girls" had become an increasingly serious problem. This report was based on a study of 4,641 women, of whom only one-fifth were named as paid prostitutes. The noncommercial pickup to whom no fee was paid "accounted for 64 percent of the white and 45 percent of the colored sources of infection . . . with streets and taverns replacing houses of prostitution."[42] The SPD's dragnet trapped several thousand women and charged them with sexual misconduct for what might have been the proverbial one-night stand. While the USPHS aimed to control and prevent the spread of communicable diseases, the representation of women as responsible not only for spreading disease but also for initiating sexual contacts marred the control of venereal disease from the start. The approach failed to address how women became infected, and the existence of male carriers of venereal disease was absent from the discussion. The concept of diseased and aggressive women seemed to go beyond the problem of venereal disease per se and problematized just what was meant by the term *venereal disease control*.

Embodied Deviance and Disease

Gender ideology has affected perceptions of diseases in females over time; Kary L. Moss notes that "gender stereotyping continues to significantly affect the formation and implementation of public policy."[43] Cultural prescriptions regarding proper behavior for women resulted in numerous diagnoses of female deviance during the nineteenth and twentieth centuries.[44] One of the most salient examples of the interconnectedness of gender, science, and medicine occurred in the early twentieth

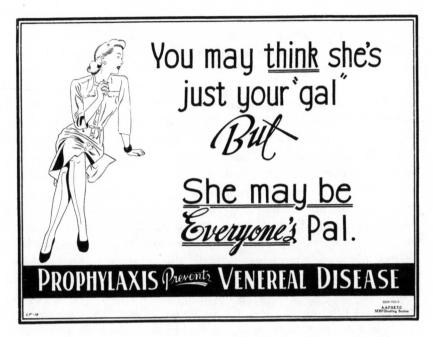

"You may think she's just your gal . . ." Poster, 1944. Social Welfare History Archives, University of Minnesota.

century in the case of Mary Mallon, better known as Typhoid Mary, who had been identified as a healthy carrier of typhus.[45] In Mallon's case one can see the construction of not only medical danger and deviance but also social danger and deviance. Mary Mallon was described by the authorities as doubly deviant. Invisible disease lurked within her body, but her visible body also suggested deviance. Medical authorities questioned Mallon's femininity by describing her appearance and actions as masculine. What purpose did such depictions of Mary Mallon serve? Judith Walzer Leavitt suggests that the experts "needed to see in her an aberrant 'other' in order to justify their actions against her."[46] In effect, the authorities claimed that they could identify hidden corruption by reading the visible body. In Mallon's case we can identify a precedent for the wartime practice of naming particular bodies as contagious. In 1940, the *Journal of Social Hygiene* coined the term *Spirochete Annie* for the "Typhoid Mary" of World War II.[47] Like Mallon, prostitutes and promiscuous women during World War II were described by some officials as healthy carriers. As Bascomb Johnson put it, prostitutes "even though they are not infected . . . are mechanical conveyors of the germs of these diseases from some of their customers to others."[48]

A local Ohio newspaper picked up on the same point and claimed that "a prostitute can transmit gonorrhea, syphilis, and other venereal diseases without becoming self-infected." This article not only presented prostitutes as mechanical carriers of disease but also depicted them as particularly disgusting individuals. It began by asserting that a prostitute does not know how to take care of herself—that is, to keep herself free of disease. Recognizing that prostitutes do have ways of cleaning up/out (douching), the article asked: "Does a prostitute ever take that much time (20 minutes) between customers?" The paper answered its own question with a resounding "NO." Continuing in the same style, the article suggested that the reader "visualize 20 to 40 men bathing in the same tub of water in one evening. The risk of disease would be less in this loathsome comparison than the risk of venereal disease to 20 to 40 men employing the same prostitute in one evening." The article concluded: "We won't use someone else's toothbrush. We would despise anyone for offering us a cud of tobacco out of someone else's mouth. But truthfully, there is far less danger and hazard involved in such detestable practices than in sexual intercourse with a prostitute or promiscuous woman."[49] Entitled "She Looked Clean—But . . . Tells Tavern Men Why Venereal Disease Control Is Important," the article did not confine itself to damning prostitutes but once again suggested that any woman could be harboring disease. In the World War II years such attitudes resulted both in health card requirements for women food handlers and in the marking of waitress and hostess bodies, among others, as at best suspicious and more likely dangerous and diseased.

Psychological Deviance

In many cases, once a woman came under the control of the authorities she also became an object to be studied by psychologists. Numerous women became multiply stigmatized: in addition to embodying sexual deviance and disease, they were classified as mentally deficient. One official defined some alleged prostitutes as constitutionally or congenitally handicapped and therefore unable to control their sexual behavior.[50] He also diagnosed many of these women as mentally defective, some as morons and imbeciles, and a significant number as psychopaths. In a similar vein, the Mid-western Center for Venereal Disease Treatment conducted a study of 500 venereally diseased women who had been apprehended by community health authorities and directed to the center. Test scores of "mental ability" of both white and black patients were "found to be well below normal." The median intelligence for 340 white women was measured as 84, with 24 percent of the full group falling in the category labeled "defective intelligence." For the 160 black women the median intelligence was measured as 70; "defective intelligence" was ascribed to 51 percent.[51] These two diagnoses were not unusual; apparently sexual activity by women was often equated with mental dullness. As previously noted, many of these statistics are problematic; some functioned as a rationale for funding, some were used to gain support for wartime repression, and many were influenced by pre-existing attitudes based on class, race, and gender. Statistics, such as those discussed above, supported the concept of biological degeneracy that had become, through the eugenics movement, a rationale for sterilization. Dorothy Roberts states that "intelligence became a shorthand for moral worth as well as cognitive capacity."[52] The psychological component of the venereal disease/prostitution campaign increased the consequences that many women faced should they run afoul of the law.

Female promiscuity also occupied the California medico-scientific establishment. Over a period of seven years, from 1941 to 1947, the Venereal Disease Division of the USPHS conducted a major psychiatric study of promiscuity. The researchers' stated goal was "to investigate the causative factors in promiscuity" in order to "prevent the promiscuity leading to [venereal] infection and reinfection."[53] When this phase of the study began on January 1, 1943, its subjects included women defined as promiscuous or as potentially promiscuous. Most patients were between the ages of eighteen and twenty-five, both black and white, and not all of them had a venereal disease. Of the 365 women in the study, 90 percent had been referred by physicians or public health nurses and 10 percent by other sources such as social agencies, hospitals, and courts. An early problem arose as the experts tried and failed to define promiscuity.

The director of the project, Dr. Benno Safier, and his associates read the female sexual body in relation to many other factors, including occupation. "Many promiscuous women," they contended, "used their employment as a situation in which to make the acquaintance of men easily and quickly."[54] This was especially true, they said, "of those who were waitresses and of the few who were usherettes, 'photo girls' in concessions, and taxi dancers."[55] While we know that many wartime women, especially black women, experienced difficulties getting industrial jobs or had child care problems that precluded such work and thus often took more casual labor, this study claimed that the "availability of war work" showed that no women actually needed to take such jobs.[56]

The experts had not yet finished their litany; they also made neuropsychiatric diagnoses and studied "personality characteristics." They noted certain common characteristics such as "uneven development in the areas of physical, intellectual, emotional and social maturity."[57] In sum, the women studied appeared to these researchers as "immature, impulsive, irresponsible, impetuous," with a tendency to blame others for any problems they might have had. Admitting that it was more difficult to find "marked deviations from the normal" with "potentially promiscuous patients," the researchers reported that while they identified only one woman as a homosexual, several others "had strong emotional attachments to other women in excess of those found in normal adolescent psychosexual development."[58]

In most cases female promiscuity was seen as resulting from "personality difficulties, intrapsychic conflict, dependency and immaturity, and as part of the maladapted behavior characteristic of the unstable patient who lacked social responsibility and self-restraint."[59] Some women were placed in more than one diagnostic category. According to the researchers, women who fell into the first four categories of promiscuity seemed to use sex as "a neurotic equivalent": that is, they tried to solve their problems through sexual encounters or relationships. More specifically, "some patients used promiscuity to attempt to overcome anxiety regarding sexual normalcy or feelings of inadequacy as women."[60] Those women who experienced inner conflict over their promiscuity were diagnosed as suffering from "masculinity-femininity conflict," which in a broad sense included "difficulties in fulfilling a feminine role." The eight patients who fell outside the four categories and "who utilized promiscuity to satisfy sexual desires without apparent conflict" were denied their desire. The researchers contended, "If these patients had been known for a longer period of time, more specific motivations would have appeared." And to complete the denial, they claimed that none of these eight could be considered "truly psychosexually mature individuals."[61]

Men were added to the study in July 1945, two and a half years after the study was begun. Illustrating the persistence of the double standard, the definition of promiscuity differed for the men. "Married women who had engaged in any extramarital sexual relations within the six months prior to registration with the service" were diagnosed as promiscuous. Men were not considered promiscuous if they had sexual relations while separated from their wives or, if unmarried, they had only one partner at a time. The study produced two more categories for female promiscuity: "single women who had engaged in sexual relations with more than one man within the six months preceding registration and single women who had engaged in sexual relations with one man more than twice in the same period." Before single or divorced men were considered promiscuous, they had to have multiple partners. "Patients (female) who did not fit the definition of promiscuity but who were considered likely to become promiscuous during a year's period following their registration were considered potentially promiscuous." How the authorities were able to diagnose this potential was, unfortunately, not explained. Promiscuity was, however, seen as "only one expression of the non-adaptability characteristic since early childhood."[62]

Another study, conducted at the Clifton, New Jersey Reformatory for Women in 1942 and entitled "The Female Psychopath," also denied female desire, concluding, in part, that "hedonism" presented as an "outstanding abnormal personality characteristic." While a diagnosis of psychopathic personality was applied more frequently to white than black women, "in both negro and white psychopaths approximately one half manifested their psychopathy in some form of abnormal libidinous activities." Even if women had been convicted of another crime, such as child neglect or a crime against property, it was "almost invariably linked" to sex by the authorities. "A hedonistic attitude" was, according to this study, "the most characteristic attitude of the female psychopath whether white or black."[63] The apparatus of the wartime state was either unwilling or unable to accept deviations from prescribed gender norms; especially difficult was the notion of sexual autonomy.

As an official network of doctors, scientists, social workers, and law enforcers apprehended or arrested more and more women, the pool of subjects to be studied increased. The *American Journal of Public Health* announced the establishment of a Psychiatric Service at the San Francisco City Venereal Disease Clinic. It was a "one-of-a-kind" special field study project based on individualized case studies. The goals of the project as stated were "to provide a reeducation and readjustment program for girls and women who offer a promiscuous sex history and who may spread or are spreading venereal disease."[64] Confirmed prostitutes were excluded from the study.

Two studies that discussed a similar group of 2,063 "girls" arrested in Seattle, Washington, during an eight-month period in 1945 illustrate the varied interpretations placed on female sexuality. A medical social worker at the Seattle Treatment Center noted that only 17.3 percent of the 2,063 women had venereal disease. She also discovered that more than 200 of the women in this group were married to soldiers or sailors (109 were navy wives; the exact number of army wives had not been tabulated, but the number was felt to be much larger).[65] This is the only study I encountered that recognized that several of these women had acquired venereal disease from their husbands. (In general, male carriers were of no interest to the authorities.) This female social worker noted that the navy provided services for wives and that the army was in the process of establishing such services. However, the Eight Point Agreement stipulated that "familial contacts with naval patients will not be reported." Once again men escaped censure, while women's bodies and sexuality were seen as threatening to the war effort.

In contrast, Captain Irene Durham of the Seattle Police Department, who developed the material on this group for a longer report, stated "that the impression of the Women's Division is that there is a large proportion of prostitutes, alcoholics, feeble-minded, and extremely unstable persons among the repeaters . . . [and] only nine patients (4 percent) gave evidence of essentially normal personalities." Many of the repeaters (those who had been arrested more than once) had appeared, according to Durham, "at one time or another before the Sanity commission."[66] In sum, many women who became enmeshed in the psychiatric medical system were diagnosed as intellectually, emotionally, or socially defective or deficient. The officials who gathered data seemed to be more interested in these psychological factors than they were in the presence or absence of venereal disease or in how the women became infected. Thus we find women, some with and some without venereal disease, being confined and quarantined.

Quarantine and Confinement

At the beginning of the wartime repression campaign, many official discussions took place regarding ways to deal with venereally diseased women. The key strategy was confinement. Thus, in addition to quarantine, numerous women served time in institutional homes, jails, prisons, reformatories, and mental institutions. Some women received short sentences, others received indeterminate sentences, and numerous others judged mentally incompetent were typically incarcerated for extensive periods.[67]

Quarantine camps and hospitals were set up and used specifically for women. In the early 1940s, the FSA acquired several CCC camps that they ultimately used to warehouse venereally diseased women. In South Carolina, two quarantine hospitals, located in former CCC camps, housed only women and were racially segregated. While neither facility provided much in the way of amenities, the camp for black women was both "more dilapidated" and "less convenient as to facilities for care of patients."[68] The white camp, which had two hundred beds, was located about fourteen miles from the capital city, Columbia; the black camp was located sixty miles from Columbia and two miles off the highway. South Carolina, having received Lanham Act funds, opened one new venereal disease hospital in December 1942. A modern two-story brick building with eighty-five beds, the hospital served the general population. The hospitals were administered by the state board of health.[69]

Women from other states were also sent to camps. For example, in 1941, a journalist wrote of seven women who, as a result of the federal government's policies regarding prostitution, were in the process of being transferred to a camp. Repeating, as he said, "the official line," the author referred to these women as the "first batch"; a local official said that at least thirty more women would soon arrive at the camp.[70] Other women were detained at the Venereal Disease Hospital in Hot Springs, Arkansas, and the Lindbergh estate in New Jersey became a center for venereally infected women.[71] Quarantine camps and the twentieth-century equivalent of lock hospitals confined numerous other women. Women neither went willingly to nor remained quietly in such confinement.[72] Official records refer almost entirely to quarantine for women but give little detail regarding life in camps. Both in the camps and hospitals women were treated for venereal disease and could be detained for indefinite periods. Men in the armed services who contracted a venereal disease received treatment and were returned to duty. Women, however, at least in the navy, were immediately discharged.[73]

The official medical-scientific network described wartime women as deviant for reasons including, but not limited to, where they worked, where they played, in what circumstances they grew up, what their sexual desires were, how closely they complied with prescriptive femininity, and, if they engaged in prostitution or promiscuous sexual activity, whether they had or were suspected of having a venereal disease. Just as class and gender stereotyping supported official policies in the beginning of the decade and continued to do so during the war years, so did race stereotyping. Placing the blame for spreading venereal disease on women and nonwhite men continued to confound the efficacy of the venereal disease campaign.

Race, Science, Medicine, and Marked Bodies

During the Second World War, racist policies plagued African Americans in the military, as well as in the larger society. They experienced discrimination in industry, housing, and opportunities for recreation. The "race" problem in the United States became, in fact, grist for the mill of Axis propaganda. These subjects have been written about at length, but the racial element of the venereal disease campaign has not been as well integrated in wartime accounts.[74]

In 1942, Henry H. Hazen (president of the D.C. Social Hygiene Society) wrote in a handbook for physicians that "a casual observer might be inclined to identify the syphilis problem in the United States with the negro race."[75] Hazen allowed that this "casual observer" could find considerable statistical evidence that would agree with Surgeon General Parran's recent statement that "syphilis occurs six times more frequently among negroes than among whites."[76] He suggested, however, that if one looked more carefully it became evident that "the problem transcends racial boundaries." Hazen pointed to areas with inadequate, inaccessible, or absent medical facilities, as well as a lack of information disseminated to the public, as primary factors in a high venereal disease rate; areas with high prevalence were invariably low–economic status areas, home to both blacks and whites.[77] For example, black migratory workers who came to New Jersey from the South were plagued with a variety of diseases. To the question of "why so many untreated illnesses," M. I. Roemer, in an article in *The Crisis*, replied, "The answer is obvious." He had heard "tale after tale of complete lack of physicians, many-mile walks to small clinics, exorbitant fees charged by private physicians for 'shots to clean up the blood,' thorough-going mis-

management . . . due more often to medical indifference than ignorance." While Roemer was referring mainly to the South, he pointed out
that there were similar problems in the North. In New Jersey, for example, the medical system did not welcome African Americans: "it was im-
possible to find a hospital bed" for a young black woman with a "florid
eruption of secondary syphilis."[78] A southern health official, while com-
menting on the "comparative apathy" regarding the use of public health
services by a "typical Negro family" in Bienville Parish, Louisiana, also
noted that the health office was forty miles away from the black district.
And although there had been a suboffice in the nearest town (six miles
distant), most families were not aware of its existence.[79]

The greater visibility of the venereal disease rate among African
Americans also stemmed from the fact that many blacks used public
clinics, while whites, especially those with venereal diseases, had more
access to private doctors.[80] And private practice physicians often did not
report venereal disease cases to the Public Health Service.[81] Even within
the military, medical care for African Americans was not always adequate. An article in *The Crisis* spoke of the "meagre facilities" that were
provided to treat black soldiers afflicted with venereal disease. In addition, white civilian nurses in a camp hospital refused to handle black patients.[82] Venereal disease in the African American community was thus
simultaneously excessively visible and invisible when it came to providing treatment. Dr. Hazen advised African Americans to use the official
statistics to their advantage by highlighting the need for services.[83]

Will the Real Spirochete Please Stand Up?

Both within and outside the realms of science and medicine, much
had been written about the syphilis "germ." Medical authorities have
pointed out that syphilis should really be referred to in the plural, since
what seems to be a single organism is actually four spirochetes that are
difficult to identify and that cause four different kinds of disease. Yaws,
for example, is caused by the spirochete *Treponema pertenue*, which is
"nonvenereal"; this disease is common in warm climates.[84] During the
1940s, yaws was common among the southern black population. Dr.
Hazen emphasized that the reliability of testing was another critical
point often left out of discussions regarding venereal disease, especially
syphilis. Referring to syphilis as a "great imitator," Hazen said that not

only could syphilis be mistaken for other diseases and vice versa but that also "some conditions even have the temerity to give serologic reactions that are identical to syphilis."[85] The medical etiology of syphilis is far more complicated than is generally known.

A story that concerns a young white serviceman bears telling to illustrate a particular problem that followed in the wake of a case of a misidentified spirochete.[86] Diagnosed as having syphilis when his Kahn blood test "went off the charts," this serviceman was not, in fact, suffering from a venereal disease. When the chief pharmacist's mate, out of curiosity, investigated possible "causes for false serological positives in the Kahn tests," he found two main causes—leprosy and yaws—and one not so common cause—"Vincent's disease," more commonly known as trench mouth. Further investigation turned up a probable cause: the patient recalled that at a prior base he and several other marines had "complained about inflammation in the mouth and bleeding." They had come to the conclusion that their problem stemmed from a practice of "using the same water to wash numerous trays in the mess hall."[87] The young white officer benefited from further investigation; others were not as fortunate. Nonetheless, during his hospital stay prior to the new diagnosis, he was criticized by medical officers for failure to meet the standards of his race and class.

Underanalyzed statistics served to maintain a stereotype of African Americans as excessively sexual as well as diseased; the medical problem of false positives and negatives was complicated by preexisting attitudes, particularly toward blacks, who were far more often assumed to be venereally diseased.[88] Given the complexity of the spirochete, it seems logical to raise some questions about the reported statistics regarding the venereal disease rate among African Americans. The authors of a 1942 serological study make several points, including the influence of malaria in producing positive serologic tests for syphilis in persons not infected with syphilis, the extensive malarial region in the United States, the large black population in that area, and the high prevalence of syphilis diagnoses based on serologic tests among blacks in the malarial region.[89] With few exceptions, however, wartime officials continued to report a high venereal disease rate among "Negroes." The statistics presented, often in popular media, were always significantly higher for blacks: for example, one study conducted in the Southwest showed a black rate of 460 per thousand and a white rate of 180 per thousand.[90]

The Black Response to the VD Campaign

In 1936, when Dr. Parran became surgeon general, the African American media responded favorably to his call for plain speaking and education about venereal diseases as well as to his recognition of a need for expanded treatment facilities. In May 1936, for example, Dr. A. W. Dumas wrote an editorial in the *Baltimore Afro-American,* arguing that poverty and ignorance in sexual and medical matters were responsible for a "high morbidity and mortality rate among blacks."[91] He reiterated the call for sex education, noting an alarming spread of venereal diseases among all classes. A lack of information regarding sexual matters was widespread: African Americans (and women) did not have, and in some cases were prevented from acquiring, the medical and scientific knowledge necessary for good health, including sexual health. While gender ideology kept many women of all races in a state of ignorance regarding sexually transmitted diseases and even sexual intercourse, racial ideology influenced the dissemination of misinformation regarding health matters to African Americans. Scientific and medical authorities used the term *bad blood* to explain a multitude of ills in the black population.[92]

The Tuskegee study, which began in 1932, involved 399 black men who were unaware that they had syphilis; they were told that they were being treated for "bad blood." In *Bad Blood: The Tuskegee Syphilis Experiment,* James H. Jones explores, in part, the persistence of a nineteenth-century scientific notion that contended that disease manifested differently in blacks than in whites.[93] This belief, as noted previously, was alive and well during the war years. Dr. James E. Moore, an active player in the World War II campaign and a respected syphilologist, had been involved in the Tuskegee experiment. In 1932, Dr. Moore made a statement that had a profound effect on the study, and I might add on more general attitudes toward venereal disease in the black population. His assertion that "syphilis in the negro is in many respects almost a different disease from syphilis in the white" lent "scientific respectability" to the proposed experiment. Dr. Taliaferro Clark (USPHS) called on Dr. Moore for advice on the planned experiment.[94] Moore, in an advisory capacity, offered numerous suggestions and exhibited preconceived ideas regarding African Americans. He continuously dehumanized the men who would be used in the experiment by referring to them as "clinical material." In the formulation of protocols for examination, testing, and related procedures of the intended subjects, his attitude toward black men became evident once again. Offering advice for taking case histories, he wrote that "when dealing with blacks . . . the mere history of a penile sore only would not be adequate [in making a diagnosis of syphilis], inasmuch as the average negro has had as many penile sores as rabbits have offspring."[95] Raymond A. Vonderlehr was appointed in October 1932 to head the Alabama study.[96] It is notable that two of the major figures involved in the wartime venereal disease campaign had a prior history with regard to African Americans and venereal disease.

African Americans had actively pursued better medical treatment and facilities for themselves long before the SPD or any other government agencies became involved in the process. National Negro Health Week, for example, inaugurated by Booker T. Washington many years earlier, had become a permanent institution. In 1936, "Health Week observance was now being advocated and encouraged by the National Government" for all people, since venereal disease affected "all classes."[97] In the same year, African Americans had set up the Commission on the Eradication of Syphilis under the auspices of the National Medical Association.[98]

Even before wartime government agencies became involved in matters of defense-related health, African Americans had responded to defense needs; in 1941 Negro Health Week was entitled "Personal Hygiene and First Aid Preparedness."[99] In 1943, African Americans in Pensacola, Florida, organized a "Negro War-Time Health Committee." Their education efforts were so successful that not only was a delegate invited to attend a statewide conference but the organizers reported that "a spirit of friendly competition has been created so that the hitherto unorganized white population is starting to climb on the venereal disease control bandwagon."[100]

But when white officials did the reporting, the long history of black self-help was often minimized.[101] For example, in 1944, Mr. Jackson of the SPD, speaking of the increased activity by African Americans and the Office of Negro Health Work as "due in large measure to the growing health consciousness of the Negro people, the interest of many persons and agencies, colored and white, and to the efforts of many professional Negro men and women," implied that it took official pressure to get the black communities mobilized.[102] Moreover, ignoring both black health initiatives and the denial of equal or adequate medical care to African Americans, the SPD continued to rely on racial stereotypes to explain a supposed lack of interest in health matters and to claim credit for prompting health awareness in black communities.[103]

Along the same lines, the SPD also felt free to interpret the black community. While nominally agreeing with those who cited low economic status, inferior education systems, and minimal access to medical services as factors in a high rate of disease and a high rate of crime in the black population, the SPD claimed that "yet Negroes as a group are apathetic and to a large degree unconcerned regarding the venereal disease problems." The SPD also claimed to understand "Negro psychology," especially their "apprehension regarding statistical data pertaining to high prevalence rates." Edward V. Taylor (SPD) contended that "Negroes" considered such data as part of "attempts to discredit them." Claiming that this body of statistics was reliable, he stated: "A discussion of the arguments that are used by many Negro leaders to refute existing data would be worthless at this time."[104] The white experts claimed the authority to read the bodies and minds of African Americans just as they read women's bodies. What was Mr. Jackson inferring when he stated that "prostitution has seldom been a problem among Negroes. . . . [I]nstead it is largely one of promiscuity . . . [with] the teenage girl furnishing much of the activity"?[105] In tandem with more general racialized discourse, such statements reinforced a stereotype of hypersexuality as characteristic of black persons, especially black women, and contributed to their overrepresentation among the women who were arrested for morals offenses during the war years.

The facts indicate that African Americans were very much interested in health issues and other issues affecting their communities. However, pervasive racial stereotyping adversely influenced public and private attitudes toward African Americans. In 1943, a conference of Negro leaders discussed many social problems, including "an attitude of defeatism toward the problems of venereal disease on the part of many white community leaders and of frustration among leaders in the Negro community."[106] Several African American leaders had pointed out on many occasions that it would have made better sense to consult with African Americans on black issues and to send them into the field to facilitate entry into black communities. In some few instances white officials accepted this advice. For example, Mr. Ragland, the only SPD representative identified as Negro, traveled extensively throughout the country serving as a liaison between local authorities (generally health authorities) and the black neighborhoods.[107] Nonetheless, education and access to health care continued to be limited not only for black civilians but also for blacks in the armed forces, whose venereal disease control programs were adversely affected by a lack of venereal disease officers and by materials that were both condescending to everyone and incomprehensible to the functionally illiterate.[108]

Racial and gender stereotypes, with deep roots in the past, continued to exert a powerful influence during the war years. Marking both black and female bodies as inherently diseased, disordered, depraved, and sexually deviant, the apparatus of the state waged only a limited war against venereal disease. Affected also by the ambiguity that surrounded the venereal diseases, scientific, medical, and other authorities could not find a single answer for the question "Are venereal diseases infectious diseases just like many others, or do they represent social, moral, or spiritual afflictions?"[109] Even as scientists engaged in research to discover the means to eradicate syphilis, they had misgivings about the effects of a quick and relatively painless cure on moral behavior.[110]

Medical and scientific authorities, like military officers and agents of the SPD, based their policies and conclusions on existing assumptions about disease, race, ethnicity, and gender. Not only did official definitions of prostitution expand to include noncommercial sexual transactions, but *promiscuity* became a blanket term used to describe a variety of female activities. A promiscuous woman could be too feminine or not feminine enough, too attractive or careless about her appearance, a waitress or a welder, white or nonwhite, lower or upper class. In the clash of medical and moral discourses, the medical was applied to men and the moral to women, particularly working-class women. While women were socially stigmatized as purveyors of venereal disease, white men were constructed as innocent victims of venereal disease in need of protection. As the authorities continued to propose programs that furthered their own special interests, their actions often seemed contradictory and ambivalent. We can see this ambivalence quite clearly when we examine military policies.

4

"A Buffer of Whores"

Military and Social Ambivalence about Sexuality and Gender

The problems emerging from the ambivalent policies surrounding wartime gender and sexuality were seldom openly addressed. However, during one of the official discussions regarding military appropriation of female sexuality to meet men's sexual needs, Dr. Sheldon Glueck posed a few difficult, but illuminating, questions. "Here are the practical issues," he said. "In the first place you prevent prostitution; in the next place you allow boys to obtain contraceptives at army stations. Therefore where will they get their sexual gratification? Are you proposing that they shall invade the non-professional classes for this sort of thing? How will you answer that very practical problem?"[1] While Dr. Glueck did not receive any direct answers, the silence signified an official acceptance both of men's need for sex and of an official right to decide which women should provide such services. With regard to the latter, however, officials found themselves caught in a dilemma: How could the state both use and control female sexuality? The answers were never clearly articulated. The state's policies created spaces of confusion, as the war against venereal disease operated on multiple levels, both ideological and material. Issues such as gender, sexuality, medicine, science, morale building and female companionship, prostitution, and promiscuity circulated through the campaign to repress and regulate prostitution in order to protect servicemen from venereal disease and to maintain morale. Because of the complexity of such issues, providing sexualized services for the military was open to misinterpretation and often stigmatized the providers and left them vulnerable to legal charges. Prostitution was illegal, promiscuity was immoral, female sexuality was dangerous, but sexual labor was essential to the war effort—a veritable catch-22.

General attitudes, policy debates, and everyday practices provide insights into many official attitudes about masculinity. Shortly before the attack on Pearl Harbor, a government official exuberantly exclaimed that America had become "magnificently male again," indicating how strongly the process of militarization was linked to gender.[2] Many scholars have pointed out connections between gendered concepts such as "real" men and war. R. W. Connell looks back to Virgil's "I sing of arms and the man" to locate an early instance of "the gender of war."[3] Leisa D. Meyer, in considering attempts to form a women's army, points out that "military service" has operated as a "critical measure of cultural masculinity."[4] Joshua S. Goldstein argues: "Cultures develop concepts of masculinity that motivate men to fight." He sees the military as "providing the main remnant of traditional manhood." In this analysis, "drill sergeants draw on the entire arsenal of patriarchal ideas . . . to turn civilian male recruits into 'soldiers.' " The military man, then, is not a "pussy, faggot, or a woman."[5]

Another body of research makes a related argument that "military cultures tend to foster attitudes that are demeaning to women through training, violent and sexist language, images, jokes, drills, chants, etc."[6] Susan Gubar graphically illustrates such claims when she quotes a cadence used to instruct marines on "how to use their instruments [gun/penis] correctly: This is my rifle, This is my gun, This is for fighting, This is for fun."[7] We have seen and will continue to see wartime constructions of femininity; but men, too, experienced gender construction "in and through war." Late-twentieth-century scholarship has produced numerous studies regarding the continuous (re)construction of masculinity as well as analyses of the intersections between war and gender.[8] Wartime men were also contained within a particular symbolic system that valued certain types of masculinity, in this case military masculinity. To safeguard the manliness of the armed services, however, "the military must camouflage its reliance on womanpower in order to maintain its self-image as a quintessentially masculine institution . . . the place where boys become men."[9] If the ideal of the heroic warrior, defender of the nation and of women and children, is to be maintained, wartime women must appear in appropriate supporting roles. During the Second World War, however, women's activities upset the balance.

As sociopolitical concerns over wartime women's roles mushroomed, the official line regarding women both reinforced those concerns and confused the issue further. The military said that efficiency demanded that the armed services be protected from potentially promiscuous women and prostitutes who could destroy military power by spreading venereal diseases. The same officials, however, claimed that masculine-military morale depended on access to "good" (i.e., disease-free) women. As Cynthia Enloe points out, "war stories" should take into account the ways that militarization affects women's lives. She not only notes that militaries "rely on women" but also argues that during wartime military and civilian officials "maneuver different groups of women and the ideas about what constitutes femininity so that each can serve military objectives."[10] This mentality constructed, for example, an image of women working in defense industries that included, indeed insisted upon, femininity.

Wartime women also volunteered to provide respectable companionship for servicemen: they wrote letters, played cards with them, and danced with them, to name a few activities. But while the pressures of wartime allowed that it might be possible for a woman to work like a man in the factory without becoming masculinized, it was far more difficult for a woman working in a public dance hall to preserve respectability. When women participated in such recreational activities, their vulnerability to charges of sexual impropriety increased. Women's wartime contributions, which constituted noticeable departures from existing social norms, were perceived on the one hand as necessary to the war effort and on the other hand as disruptive to an orderly pursuit of war. Volunteer service in morale-maintaining capacities was not always recognized as patriotism; instead, many women were labeled as victory girls, khaki-wackies, good-time Charlottes, and patriotutes.[11]

Meeting Men's Needs

When Dr. James Earle Moore testified before the Joint Army and Navy Committee on Welfare and Recreation, his statement epitomized military attitudes and assumptions regarding wartime women. He spoke first about men's, especially servicemen's, "normal desire for feminine companionship."[12] Moore reacted to a recent article in *Life* magazine about the women who volunteered in service clubs. He was most concerned with *Life*'s description of the choice of hostesses: "[T]hese hostesses will be mature women who are 'womanly but not too female.' "[13]

Dr. Moore forcefully stated his opinion that if the men were not supplied with young and attractive girls, the men would find the necessary feminine companionship elsewhere. Moore's willingness to employ *attractive* women with little regard for having placed them in a vulnerable position calls to mind Glueck's questions regarding where men will get their sexual gratification when prostitutes are no longer available. Moore reiterated the idea that men's desire was normal, and he insisted on action to ensure that their needs would be met.

The venereal disease problem could not, of course, be ignored. Dr. Moore offered his opinions on these matters, saying, "It is not enough to reduce the opportunity for potentially infectious contacts between the sexes." He contended that the repression of prostitution was a negative achievement. "The positive requirement is to furnish the soldier, sailor, and industrial worker with more normal opportunities for social contact with the opposite sex—the natural desire of young men for the companionship of young women must be recognized and met." Moore's testimony regarding the prevention and control of venereal diseases focused on the provision of adequate recreational facilities for servicemen as a way to minimize inevitable sexual contacts, particularly undesirable ones. He had the solution: "It is perfectly possible to utilize the patriotic spirit of the nation's young women, thousands of whom are anxious to do their part for the national defense, in order to recruit a splendid corps of volunteer hostesses." [14]

Moore, like officials before and after him, felt no compunction regarding the use of women for militaristic purposes. By commodifying "good women" to replace "bad women" to service men in the military, Moore and the authorities avoided addressing sexual promiscuity for either gender. Many women did volunteer to serve as hostesses; if they served at USO establishments, they retained respectability. But volunteer service in other areas of public entertainment beyond the protection of the USO did not escape suspicion. Many other women, then, entered a sexual minefield. Questions lingered. Were these women patriots or potentially promiscuous women? Posters such as "She May Look Clean . . . But . . ." made an answer even more complicated by suggesting that appearances could be deceiving. Even the iconic girl next door could be dangerous. By making inferences about the girl next door (presented as white and middle class), the official stance once again blurred the line between the good girl and the bad girl.

Negative attitudes toward wartime women, certainly due, at least in part, to the sexualized official discourse of the government and the military, emerge in several accounts of wartime women. The most well-known incident is the slander campaign against the Women's Army Corps that depicted them as either lesbians, prostitutes, or promiscuous women.[15] At the same time, however, servicewomen seemed to require protection from servicemen. The nurses' quarters on New Guinea were compounds enclosed with barbed wire and having only one entrance. When the nurses visited air corps or navy camps, they were required to have escorts. The escorts were generally officers and had to be armed; their job, as one nurse noted, was to "protect [us] from our own troops not the enemy."[16] Interestingly, one of the famous Andrews Sisters and other performers on USO tours preferred enlisted men to officers, who often "proved problematic . . . [and] expected more than a musical stage show."[17]

Within the military, servicemen dwelt in an eroticized milieu where sexuality was both suppressed and talked about constantly. Since a basic commandment in military life was "be a man," and since manly virtues equaled courage, endurance, toughness, and (hetero)sexual prowess, servicemen, in a sense, received encouragement to see sexual adventures as proof of manhood.[18] Men, as one study notes, "often act with impunity because acts of aggression (including rape) are linked to traditional images of what it is to be a warrior, because of women being seen as men's property, or because women fear to speak out."[19] In the official discourse there is no acknowledgment of women's or men's differences, their emotional or sexual feelings and needs, or their own thoughts on these matters. A former serviceman and noted author offers a glimpse of reality when he describes differences among servicemen. He tells of two young married officers who never "exhibited even the slightest interest in sex with another woman, not on rest leaves in Rome . . . Sicily . . . Cairo . . . or Alexandria." Speaking of himself, an unmarried and rather inexperienced young man, he notes that he "was the boyish and ravenous satyr."[20] Military officials did, of course, recognize that many young men would take advantage of wartime opportunities to engage in sexually promiscuous behavior. It was not, however, a fact that they wanted publicized. The armed services wanted to protect servicemen's reputations and to assure the larger society that they were "good boys."

The Military, Society, and Prostitution

In public forums and in print media, the armed services supported policies that followed the repression of prostitution, such as the Eight Point Agreement and the May Act. But the policies they proposed, as well as their actual practices, reveal only equivocal support for the repression of prostitution. Moreover, conflicted attitudes toward "woman's place and role" emerged clearly as the military met and discussed topics, including prostitution, morale, and safe sex for servicemen. In the fall of 1940, state officials met to discuss a plan that epitomizes the ambiguity of the campaign to repress prostitution. The members of a subcommittee on venereal disease control deliberated the viability of regulation, or, as they termed it, "militarized prostitution."[21] Dr. J. E. Moore pointed the committee toward a document concerning French policies for regulation during the First World War in order to facilitate the deliberations. The question of the "desirability of organizing militarized houses of prostitution" came under serious consideration.[22] Opinions varied: for example, a major in the medical corps endorsed regulation as a way to control the spread of venereal disease, while a colonel in the infantry spoke against it (but not necessarily against prostitution per se). A lively discussion followed. The participants asked questions: "In what numerical ratio to the strength of the command should prostitutes be provided? Where would they [the prostitutes] be quartered? What arrangements for price . . . flat rate or according to [military] grade? Will officers and enlisted men have different places and different types of women? Will race distinctions be made among applicants for service, or will Jim Crow be held, applied and receive official recognition?"[23] The discussion is notable for its blasé attitude regarding supplying women for prostitution, as well as for its logistical concerns about maintaining a hierarchy of race, class, and rank. As Cynthia Enloe notes, across time and place "military officials have acted as though prostitution was simultaneously a resource and a threat."[24] The discussion regarding regulated prostitution did not end here. It reemerged from time to time, and regulated prostitution was, in fact, practiced, under military control, in various locales throughout the war years. As the campaign against so-called loose women gained momentum, many segments of the military remained noncompliant regarding repression. As noted earlier, noncompliance with repression was evident from the beginning of the campaign.

In December 1940, the government undertook a survey of commercialized prostitution in the area around March Field, a sizable army base in California.[25] As government officials took to the field to investigate sexual vice and to institute repression programs when deemed necessary, they encountered different responses and reactions. The March Field survey concentrated on two cities: Riverside and San Bernardino, both of them close to the army base. The ensuing report touted Riverside as a place with an "enviable record so far as commercialized prostitution is concerned": that is, there was none.[26] San Bernardino, commonly referred to as B'Doo, however, had a long-standing reputation as a "wide-open" city.[27] A general consensus in Riverside held that when March Field reached full operation—thirty-five thousand men—things would have to change. In particular, the businessmen of Riverside contended that the "long-hairs" and their "puritanical policies" would have to go because B'Doo, which was ten miles further from March Field, would get all the business. One businessman spoke of growing support for a red-light district in Riverside for two reasons: it would be good for business, and "men need sex." The servicemen who were interviewed enthusiastically agreed. A local taxi driver supported the claim of lost business by referring to a soldier he had encountered the previous evening. "He was hot as hell for a woman," the taxi driver said, "asked every cabbie in town . . . no dice . . . the guy went to San Bernardino." As talk of repression grew louder, businessmen in San Bernardino added their voices to support for segregated districts, pointing out that "rape and seduction are bound to result if any attempt is made to close the line."[28] This challenge to repression, that the nation's choice was regulated prostitution or rape, speaks volumes regarding perceptions of male sexuality. Moreover, it highlights the marking of some female bodies as "just made for that" and endorses the view of a prostitute as "a woman reduced to her sexual utility."[29] This uncritical acceptance of prostitution in some instances supported a broader notion of "women as responsible for the sexual services of men."[30] In some places, people called openly for maintaining a "buffer of whores" to protect respectable women.[31]

The Riverside and San Bernardino study illuminates several of the themes that arose repeatedly during the campaign to repress prostitution: business interests, other than organized crime, that favored the maintenance of segregated prostitution; the fear, in many communities, that if prostitution were repressed servicemen would find sex partners one way or another, with "rape and seduction" as possibilities; and the pervasive belief that men needed sex. The author of this study, whose affiliation and name are not listed, was confused by such responses. He claimed that those who saw the coming of a prostitution district to Riverside as good for business were indulging in wishful thinking. And he denied the servicemen's eager anticipation of "changes" in Riverside, contending rather that they were "eagerly awaiting the non commercial entertainment and recreation" being planned by community groups such as the YMCA. He seemed unable to grasp the idea that the men might want both. Nor did he respond to the concerns regarding rape and seduction.[32] The SPD would claim that rape had decreased; rape had, in fact, increased during the war years.[33]

When ASHA officials conducted a survey in Monterey, California, they reported that soldiers quickly determined the location of the brothels and went there often. The soldiers contended that the "girls are clean. . . . [A]n Army doctor does exams." The soldiers spoke favorably of Monterey for another reason. It seems that many of the joints where they hung out were located in the cannery district, and "hundreds of young girls employed in the canneries are compelled to pass by the resorts going and coming from work."[34] Recall, however, that if women and girls congregated in areas full of servicemen they immediately became suspect.

In July 1941, the army issued a warning to Tacoma, Washington, by calling attention to the May Act and suggesting that the city might want to avoid federal action. After brief consultations, the mayor and city officials decided that since "the federal government meant business," Tacoma would institute a repression program. On August 21, the mayor ordered Tacoma's twenty-four houses of prostitution closed. Local businessmen vigorously but unsuccessfully protested the closings, arguing that they would result in a loss of business. In short order, city officials claimed that repression worked: the venereal disease rate was significantly lowered in Tacoma, and "civic morality" had improved greatly.[35] Neither businessmen nor local officials wanted the federal government to interfere in local affairs. While not wanting to appear unpatriotic, they certainly did not want their communities declared off limits to the military. In many cases, city officials complied only temporarily with government directives on repression. Many military officials did not always agree with the repression campaign; resistance to SPD policies began before Pearl Harbor and continued throughout the war years.

In March 1941, under government pressure, a crackdown on prostitution started in El Paso, Texas, resulting in the arrests of sixty-one women and three men.[36] Six months later the houses of prostitution in El Paso that had been closed were quietly reopening. Representatives of the SPD descended on the city. The situation in El Paso was complicated by geographical proximity to Juarez, Mexico. Both El Paso and Juarez were border cities that had developed around Fort Bliss, established at the time of the war with Mexico. Since the late 1840s, Juarez had remained a popular site for soldiers from Fort Bliss in search of "a good time."[37] El Paso, a much smaller city prior to World War II, had almost continuously maintained a segregated red-light district. Earlier attempts to close this district had met with limited success. Local politics rather than any real support of repression seemed to be behind such attempts.

SPD representatives reported that both public officials and some army authorities believed in the efficacy of a segregated district; therefore the SPD intended to take steps to convince the army to take a united stand on a program of repression. A disparity between the army's public stand and the personal opinion of some officers continued, however, and contributed to city officials' growing uncertainty regarding the viability of repression. Public officials "believed that prostitution was inevitable" and agreed that the police maintained effective control in the segregated district. The army officials at this time were generally convinced that "a segregated district with medical inspection was the answer to the problem." The army was willing to support "added protection" by means of increased attention to prophylaxis.[38] SPD representatives decided it was time for a discussion with the commanding general of the Eighth Service Command. They insisted that army officials at Fort Bliss take "a strong stand on the question of prostitution."[39] Under the threat of the May Act, repression soon became the official policy at Fort Bliss. Next, SPD officials took on the task of "selling individuals (in the city) on the program and of applying necessary pressure to get the job under way."[40]

Surveillance procedures in El Paso, as elsewhere, were carried out by vice squads. In 1941 the El Paso Police Department added a second policewoman to the force. With the addition of one male sergeant, the vice squad was ready for business. Members of the squad patrolled the streets and watched taverns and other places of amusement beginning at 8:00 p.m. each evening. The vice squad also conducted raids on those establishments suspected of serving as houses of prostitution or sites of assignation. In the first month of the repression campaign in El Paso, nine women were taken from houses of prostitution and eighteen were taken from cabarets. Any woman suspected of having venereal disease was subject to arrest and incarceration in city or county jails.[41]

The El Paso situation is representative of SPD tactics—officials threatened to use the May Act and instituted other coercive measures. The SPD always tried to mobilize local police forces to support the repression campaign. However, in spite of the presence of a nationwide and sympathetic Police Advisory Commission, city business and police officials did not always comply with federal agendas. In the case of El Paso, the local SPD representative was not quite finished; he met with the mayor of Juarez, Mexico, in an attempt to convince him to support repression. But the mayor was firmly in favor of segregation and regulation of prostitution.[42] It was neither the first nor the last time that the SPD attempted to extend its program outside the United States.

The ambivalence of the military toward prostitution emerges in a number of cases that came to the attention of state and local agencies concerned with prostitution and venereal disease. In 1941, the SPD visited the naval station at Bremerton, Washington, in response to a prior report regarding the resident medical officer, who, in their estimation, was out of step with the repression program. According to the SPD, the officer, Captain Garrison, when interviewed, "made no bones about subscribing to the inevitability of prostitution and sexual exposure and the preferability of regulation over repression." Dr. Garrison also spoke of his efforts to "secure adequate prophylaxis station set-ups." Several health officials contended that the "prostitutes in Bremerton are the pets of the local health officer." The interviewer concluded that to achieve repression in this locale, it would be necessary to secure the help of "a hobnailed pair of boots from the outside . . . [from] the Admiral's office, or Washington."[43] Nonetheless, as the SPD went forward with the campaign to repress prostitution, many military officials dealt with the prostitution question in ways they thought best for the men under their command. Many military officials supported regulated prostitution, controlled some brothels by requiring medical exams, and placed restrictions on the prostitutes' ability to move about freely in surrounding areas.[44]

In October 1941, a memo from the War Department went out to the "Commanding Generals of All Armies, Air Corps, Air Force Combat Command, Departments and Corps Areas, The Chiefs of the Armored

Forces and the Army Air Forces, and The Commanding Officers of Exempted Stations." The subject of the memo was the prohibition of prostitution within reasonable distances of military establishments. "It has been evident," the memo read, "that in some cases local commanders have not taken advantage of the provisions of War Department Circular No. 170." The recipients of the memo were "enjoined to make appropriate use of the procedure" noted in the circular.[45] The circular referred to the section of the May Act that allowed military officials to invoke the act if local conditions became dangerous to the health of their men. However, since prostitution was maintained in some areas, often with active military support, the word *exempted* (in "Exempted Stations" above) suggests that regulation was tacitly accepted military policy at least in some locales. (In Hawaii, for example, regulated prostitution lasted until late in 1944.) The extent of the failure to comply with repression became evident in the wording of a general memo issued in 1943. It stated, "Reports reaching the War Department indicate a lack of understanding of War Department policies concerning moral conditions in the vicinity of camps and stations." "By order of the Secretary of War," the memo directed the recipients to "cooperate with other authorities in enforcing laws and regulations to suppress prostitution and eliminate red-light districts."[46] Public support for repression depended, in part, on the appearance of success in eliminating the most visible forms of sexual vice and thus seeming to protect the health and well-being of the armed forces and the nation.

When government officials discovered that organized prostitution operated freely around a southern marine base, the commandant received a strongly worded warning. The Interdepartmental Committee on Venereal Disease Control sent a memorandum in November 1942 that said, in part: "The committee respectfully requests the Commandant of the Marine Corps (at Kingston, North Carolina) to make personal investigations as to the toleration of houses of prostitution in the area. . . . [T]his toleration of open and organized prostitution constitutes an open and arrogant flaunting of U.S. policy and authority." The committee urged the commandant to take immediate action or suffer the consequences. This officer must have been particularly resistant to repression, since the May Act had already been invoked in this area.[47]

As the SPD continued to exert pressure on the armed services to support fully the federal mandate on repression, some officers jumped to the task. Colonel Baldinger of Lockbourne Air Base in Ohio became so

enthusiastic about cleaning up the city of Columbus that locals started
to complain to Washington. One tavern owner even went so far as to
write to President Roosevelt. The tavern owner assured the president
that he operated "one of the finest places in the state," but the colonel
thought differently. "The colonel insists," he wrote, "that all city and
state officials follow his orders. . . . [O]therwise he threatens to invoke
the May Act. As an instance of the colonel's unreasonableness, please
note the remarks about booths [he had enclosed a newspaper clipping].
The colonel does not like booths. Therefore, all grills and places serving
liquor apparently must take out their booths." The colonel had also
proposed "a ban on dancing, earlier closing hours, and a clean-up drive
against prostitution." The letter writer primarily objected to the colonel's failure to meet and discuss matters with the local tavern owners,
his complicity in getting several businesses closed down, and his arbi-
trariness in choosing whom to harass.[48] The colonel was reprimanded
for exceeding his authority and was told in "no uncertain terms [to]
limit his activities to those pertaining to the immediate needs and functions of his station [and to] refrain from any political activity of any nature."[49] Colonel Baldinger was not the only official in Columbus censured for his policies: a local judge dismissed the charges against persons
who were "rounded-up in the vice clean-up." The judge objected to the
arresting officers' "widespread use of suspicious person" charges.[50] Legal questions regarding grounds for arrest, the need for warrants, evidence, quarantine, entrapment, broad interpretations of prostitution,
and undercover studies concerned some officials; others claimed that
war justified their policies.[51] Such diverse reactions to repression issues
are representative of the contradictions, confusions, and concerns that
existed in tandem with the repression campaign. Officials and agencies
of the state were clearly not unified in their approach to these matters.

The Prostitutes

The official who conducted the government survey in Riverside and San
Bernardino, California, also interviewed prostitutes in B'Doo who discussed not only their business expenses but also their connections with
the police department and the procedures for venereal disease examinations. Several of the women, who referred to themselves as "working
girls," talked about their "Christmas gift": they had been informed by

"D" (the police) that "the police department's general practice of intermittent pickups and fines scheduled for late December would be delayed until after the holidays." And on "periodical examinations," one woman revealed that two police officers checked cards once a month and that the women could be examined by a private doctor or at a clinic. The soldiers who were interviewed considered the "line girls" (those in the segregated district) "absolutely safe" with regard to venereal disease.[52] The interviewer made no recommendations in this early investigative study, the purpose being only to gather information on existing conditions related to prostitution. During the following year, however, the authorities cracked down on towns and cities that had redlight districts, especially those that relied on the support of police departments and physicians.

In the spring of 1942, the army air force conducted a survey of the commercialized prostitution conditions in Deadwood, South Dakota. The brief summary states: "All of Deadwood's commercialized prostitution was found centered in six openly conducted brothels which together harbor eight inmates. Persons connected with the racket claim that soldiers from Fort Mead are constant patrons of the resorts." The report indicated not only that the citizens of Deadwood had no problem with their town's reputation but that they were proud of it. One man said, "This is a real western town . . . just like the old days. Never have to worry about doing anything wrong here." One of the "oldtime madams" agreed, speaking in glowing terms of Deadwood City. She could not understand, in fact, why organized prostitution did not take advantage of Deadwood's status as "one of the few remaining wide-open communities." Several of the eight prostitutes spoke freely about their lives to the interviewer. They mentioned repression in the towns and cities where they had lived previously. A woman who had run a hotel in San Pedro, California, said that she had left when the vice squad began to make frequent raids and arrests. The only complaint of the Deadwood working women and their "landlady" (madam to the authorities) was that they needed more help. One woman, in particular, really wished that "there was another girl" working with her. Although her landlady helped out on occasion by "turning a few tricks," she said she "worked 'till she was worn out." A woman from another house talked about having to send fifty soldiers back "down those stairs" last weekend because she just could not handle them. The first women agreed that paydays could become "tiresome." It could be "awful," she said. "The boys all stand around here and keep sayin' come on I am ready. I just say well wait a while I am not." The report concluded with a prostitute's words on why the army had no problem with Deadwood's women. "This is a wonderful place. Never have to worry about getting caught. . . . No mug or fingerprints in town. . . . Just check in at the police station and get a smear and blood test. . . . All the girls are examined by Dr. D . . . an Army doctor. We get a smear every seven days . . . blood test every thirty days . . . [and] we have to have a smear just before every [army] payday. [Dr.] D charges $3.00 for each examination."[53]

This woman went on to say that all the soldiers knew that the women were regularly examined and that therefore they were not afraid to patronize them. She said that the procedure was "one thing that's mighty strict around here." If a girl was found to be diseased, she "couldn't even live in the joint until she is cured by the Doc," and this required her to visit the doctor regularly.[54] This is one of the few records of women's own voices; it is clear that they do not perceive themselves in the same terms used to describe prostitutes in the official discourse. The women talk about prostitution as one would any other job: the workload is heavy; they get tired; they provide a necessary service. The clear evidence of some sort of consensus among the citizens of Deadwood, the military, medical, police, and prostitutes, shows not only how erratic the war on prostitution could be but also how complex the whole issue was. The forty-eight states and the territories did not have uniform policies or laws; in Hawaii, for example, government-regulated brothels had a long history.

The May Act was "assiduously avoided" in Hawaii by both the police and the military.[55] Honolulu's vice district served about 250,000 men per month during the early 1940s. The men paid three dollars for three minutes with a prostitute.[56] The military, as well as many citizens, approved of the brothels for the simple reason that, given "unstoppable urges and acts,"[57] regulated prostitution kept venereal disease rates down. In addition, a newspaper article that suggested that "if the sexual desires of men are going to be satisfied," it would be much better for the men to go to regulated brothels than to turn their attention to "our young girls and women—whether by rape, seduction or the encouraging of natural tendencies."[58] For most of the war period, then, regulated prostitution was the rule in Hawaii. If this made Hawaii unique, the general consensus that men had "urges" that had to be fulfilled one way or another did not. Many military officials gave lip service to government directives regarding repression, while tolerating or actively supporting servicemen's patronizing regulated and unregulated prostitutes. Other military officers disagreed with these positions.

The Military and Venereal Disease

"Venereal disease is the most dangerous single problem [my] office has to cope with; fifty percent of the venereal disease in the navy comes from prostitution," asserted one Captain Stevenson of the U.S. Navy at a NAPCSP meeting in 1942. At that same meeting, Lieutenant Colonel Thomas B. Turner discussed the army's program, firmly stating that regulated prostitution would not work. His rationale: "Medical men know that a prostitute can be examined today and found to be free of infection, and yet within an hour she may become infected." He went on to say that she could then infect "20 or 30 in an evening."[59] Turner's argument is interesting, if incomplete, for it fails to acknowledge the source of the prostitute's infection. Turner made another common charge: that a prostitute could infect large numbers of men in one night. His estimate of twenty to thirty is rather low in comparison to some of the numbers bandied about in other meetings. Dr. Moore had claimed that "it is a not unusual record for prostitutes to service 50–75 men in a night."[60] No official comments appear regarding the men who stood in long lines in these situations.

There were, in contrast, several instances of military officers contending that suppression had the effect of making the venereal disease rate worse. A military doctor from Hawaii noted, "We're just in the early stages of another free-for-all on venereal disease control. . . . [T[he two 'stuffed shirts' in charge seemed to be ready to inflict Parran's insane notion that prostitution can be abolished in this community. Heaven help us if they make the grade! They've already done it on Maui with disastrous results. . . . Seattle did it nearly a year ago, and their v.d. situation is appalling now. Our own, up to now, has been down right admirable for the last fifteen years."[61] And as we have seen, many residents of Hawaii were concerned with the possibility of rape if prostitution was eliminated. White (*haole*) Hawaiians insisted that a "buffer of whores" was needed to protect "respectable white women."[62] Such conflicting opinions, which were not unusual, contributed to a lack of coherence in the repression campaign. The one constant seems to be that some

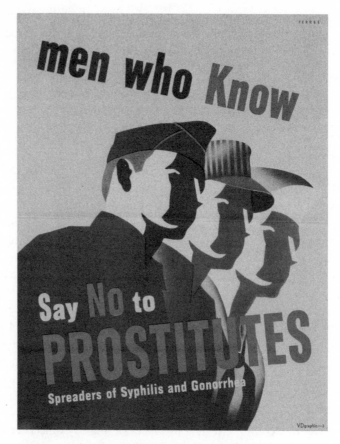

"Men who Know Say No to PROSTITUTES: Spreaders of Syphilis and Gonorrhea." Poster, 1940. Social Welfare History Archives, University of Minnesota.

women were expected to prostitute their bodies in order to protect the bodies of other women who were valued by the larger society. It bears noting that many prostitutes in Hawaii were white women from the mainland of the United States.[63]

Prophylaxis

The deeply ingrained notion that servicemen needed sex is nowhere more apparent than in the discussions regarding prophylaxis. The pre-

vention of venereal disease among servicemen through the use of condoms and chemical prophylaxis was, however, controversial. Church
groups and mothers, among others, protested against the discussion of
such ideas and practices.[64] The ASHA, in particular, included in their
booklets and pamphlets an appeal to men's better nature, the men's
"ideals, religion, or sense of duty and decency," as an alternative to prophylaxis.[65] While debate also ensued within official groups, the authorities reached a conclusion, based on the current venereal disease statistics, that sex was indeed happening. The overriding theme in their discussions became, then, that since boys would be men, they needed to
arrange for their sexual encounters to be as clean as possible. Thus the
ASHA pamphlet added advice for men "who go with prostitutes or
other loose women," including the warning to "use a protective sheath,
to wash the sex organs and the body near them with soap and water
immediately after sex contact, and to go to the nearest prophylactic
station within one hour."[66] At the "pro" stations, servicemen would
undergo both internal and external chemical cleansing. The sexual encounter was sanitized in an attempt to remove any remaining female
fluids. Both condoms and chemical prophylaxis, as Alan Brandt notes,
signified "an implicit recognition of the inability of officials to control
the troops' sexual drives."[67] The postcoital procedures maintained a
link of sex-sin-dirt-danger that not only supported the women-disease
connection but also can be seen as both deterrent and incitement to sex.

In January 1941, a committee on prophylaxis met in Washington,
D.C. Various representatives of local and national health services attended, along with Dr. W. F. Snow, at this time chairman of the Executive Committee of the ASHA. The group asked Dr. Snow to make a preliminary statement, and he began by speaking of the immediate need for
prophylactic stations in Washington, D.C. He felt that this had to be accomplished "before we could get very far in the prevention of venereal
disease in this city."[68] Dr. Leidy, the venereal disease control officer in
D.C., offered his "unofficial" views on the subject. He reported that he
had looked into the possibility of placing a prophylactic station in the
railroad and bus terminals of the city and that "the management of
both organizations state that they are willing to cooperate" but that
they first had to get approval from headquarters.[69] Considerable discussion followed regarding use of "pro stations" by civilians, with no one
quite sure what official policy would be. No one really knew what to
expect in terms of the "prophylactic load"; an army officer said that in

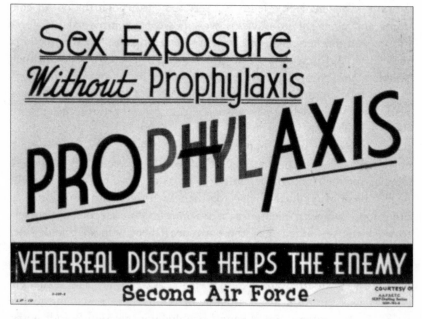

"Sex Exposure Without Prophylaxis." Poster, U.S. Army Air Forces Training Command, 1944. Courtesy of National Library of Medicine/National Institutes of Health.

nearby Virginia 359 men had reported for prophylaxis in a five-day period.[70] Throughout the war, in tacit acceptance of male sexual activity, servicemen were encouraged to use prophylaxis, and prophylactic stations became plentiful, at least for white soldiers.

The topic of prophylaxis even made it into print in *Reader's Digest.* The same article that claimed that trainloads of girls who arrived in army towns were prostitutes noted that while servicemen had been cautioned to resist sexual entrapment by aggressive women, they were also encouraged to carry condoms.[71] Military and public health officials made sure that servicemen knew where to find pro stations, and soldiers going on leave were regularly administered doses of sulfathiazole as a preventive measure against sexually transmitted diseases.[72] To publicize three new prophylactic stations in San Francisco, military and public health officials distributed five thousand lavatory placards and five hundred thousand leaflets advertising the locations.[73] Enlisted men received instruction in prophylactic use at monthly lectures and films. In Port

Clinton, Ohio, a pro station located near the gatehouse reminded the men to take their "protection" with them; prophylactic materials were distributed free to men going on liberty.[74]

Admiral Ross T. McIntire, the chief of the Navy Bureau of Medicine and Surgery, sent a bulletin to "All Ships and Stations." He was concerned that navy men were not making use of prophylaxis. Therefore, McIntire urged that officers investigate "[w]hether prophylactic heads, prophylactic packets, and condoms were available, easy to access or obtain" and whether off-base prophylactic stations were "conveniently available" and their locations matters of common knowledge. The admiral instructed his officers to make sure that "efforts have been made and are being made to inculcate into each individual a knowledge of venereal infections, and of the urgent necessity of taking prophylaxis promptly and correctly."[75] The authorities, fully expecting male sexual activity, made it possible for servicemen to indulge themselves with as little risk of disease as possible. Which brings us back to Dr. Glueck, who asked: "Are you proposing that they shall invade the non-professional classes for this sort of thing?" It seems likely that after seeing films showing venereally diseased genitals, and perhaps after a visit to a pro station, servicemen might just decide that finding a "nonprofessional" sex partner was a good idea.

Race and the Military

Ironically, given the widespread assumption by white officials that black men were promiscuous by nature, fewer prophylactic facilities served the need of black troops. The possibility of increased levels of venereal disease in the black population did not enter official discussions. As noted earlier, the designation of African Americans as a "syphilis-soaked race" clearly influenced official attitudes. Since de facto segregation prevailed across the United States, African Americans either were confined to base or had to find recreation in black communities. Unequal treatment in the area of venereal disease control once again diminished actual prevention. Dr. Hazen, chair of an interdepartmental committee on venereal disease control, stated that the authorities should make sure that several "negro" prophylactic stations were set up to avoid problems with the "race question." Dr. Zeigler of the USPHS announced that the city of Alexandria had offered a prophylactic station free of charge for the "colored troops." Black facilities in this area, as in all others, remained inferior.[76] For black men, race discrimination overshadowed gender privilege.

Racialized policies were visible in several communiqués regarding areas outside the United States. The Venereal Disease Committee made some interesting comments about the situation in Panama and the Caribbean area, where the venereal disease rates were extremely high. The committee stated: "According to recent studies by the Office of Defense Health and Welfare . . . the extensive patronage [in Panama] by white soldiers of elderly professional prostitutes, often black, and lacking in attractiveness, is one evidence of deterioration of morale."[77] The committee apparently was more concerned with whom the servicemen had sex with than with the fact that they were engaging in sex. Their comments on morale suggest that sex was all right if it occurred with an "appropriate" morale builder. The commanding officer at the Presidio in California and officials in other areas received similar memos. The race-based policies and politics of who could have sex with whom become clear in the following official correspondence. The question of prophylaxis was notably absent. Within the military there was some concern about black marines; most marines served in the Pacific theater. An officer decided that African American troops should not be sent to Polynesia because "Polynesians were delightful people, primitively romantic and their women would have sex with any comers." He also stated that it would be acceptable if white troops fathered children since "a high-class half caste would result . . . but mixing with blacks would produce a very undesirable citizen."[78] Another officer insisted on protecting American Samoans from "intimacy with blacks." He urged the marines to send Pacific-bound blacks to Micronesia where they "can do no harm"—presumably he meant "do no genetic harm."[79] Here we can see plainly military attitudes toward nonwhite women as well as toward black servicemen.

Servicemen's Morals

While the authorities focused on women's morals, concerns about servicemen's morals arose in the larger society. In late 1941, the mother of a soldier wrote to General H. H. Arnold about her sons who had enlisted in the air corps. One son stationed at Moffett Field while home on leave had told her that "just outside the gate of Moffett Field there is a dive that everyone says is 50% owned by the commanding officer." The soldier's mother also wrote about gambling, drinking, and soldiers consorting with underage girls. Her son also alleged that police protection was a factor in this milieu. The other son reported that officers and nurses on his ship got drunk while on a brief shore leave and returned to the ship and engaged in a "petting" party in the officers' stateroom. She implored General Arnold to crack down on such conditions.[80] An investigation of the shipboard incident ensued, with a decision made on December 9, 1941, that "in view of the serious emergency conditions now existing, it is recommended that no action be taken with reference to this matter at this time."[81]

In the summer of 1942, a Connecticut law firm corresponded with the War Department. Attorney Kennedy had written repeatedly in search of information on two servicemen previously stationed at Windsor Locks, Connecticut. Kennedy's clients, sisters who were seventeen and nineteen years old, had become pregnant by these men. He wrote: "We have been endeavoring to locate these soldiers for some months but all our letters have gone unanswered."[82] The lawyer made no threats but merely asked for assistance in locating the two men so that the young women could communicate with them. A brief memo from army headquarters is attached to the letter; it identified the men as noncommissioned officers currently serving outside the continental United States and recommended that "appropriate action be taken."[83] Mr. Kennedy had not been advised of this reference; "appropriate action" is not explained. However, it seems doubtful, in view of prior responses, that either the lawyers or the young women received the desired response.

Containing and Controlling Women

Prostitutes and promiscuous women and girls, viewed in a much harsher light, received very different treatment from men who indulged in sexual activity. Men could, in a sense, wash away or otherwise eliminate the germs. The case of women was different: not only did they transmit germs, but disease was perceived as embedded in their bodies, internal and hidden. Though women were constantly sexualized, they received no sex education comparable to what men in the military encountered. Many women and girls entered public spaces quite ignorant about the mechanics of sex.[84] Nonetheless, numerous women and girls were arrested, often merely for "suspicious" behavior, and held without criminal charges but still forced to undergo venereal disease testing and in many cases quarantined in a variety of punitive institutions. This is not to deny that prostitution existed during the Second World War but rather to indicate a double standard that disproportionately penalized women. Prostitutes went to jail; servicemen received sympathy and often a ride back to base if they were caught in compromising circumstances, and they were rarely charged with morals offenses.[85] Estelle Freedman points out, moreover, that male sexual offenses were underprosecuted and underreported during the war years.[86]

Military policies privileged servicemen in ways that did not apply to civilians, especially women. A navy bulletin, for example, stated that "periodic routine testing for syphilis of all personnel engaged in foodhandling is an unnecessary and unduly discriminatory procedure, since the risk of male personnel acquiring syphilis from masculine food-handlers is negligible. It is therefore recommended that the periodic serologic testing of food-handlers in the Armed services be forthwith discontinued."[87] This policy change was not intended to apply to "epidemiological testing" for women, whether prostitutes, promiscuous, or those named as contacts. In fact, waitresses could be required to provide health cards to the authorities. While many employers did not require venereal disease testing as a prerequisite for employment, the authorities could arrest a woman who failed to present a card on demand.[88] Another change in previous policy removed the onus from officers for a high venereal disease rate among their troops. "The incidence of venereal disease in a given unit of the U.S. Army or Navy," the order said, "is not necessarily an index of lax discipline in this command, but may instead depend much upon local conditions beyond the control of the unit commander."[89] By 1942, the navy removed restrictions on promotion; an enlisted man could reach warrant or commissioned rank in spite of a history of venereal disease if he "exhibits no evidence for five years and his current tests are negative."[90] Many women in the military were immediately discharged if they tested positive for venereal disease.[91] And civilian women, as we have seen, were jailed or held in quarantine camps and hospitals.

The Media and the Military

Widespread official use of posters, pamphlets, movies, and related materials that displayed prostitutes and promiscuous women (the girl next door) as dangerous and diseased resulted in provoking and producing unnecessary ambiguity over wartime women's temporary departures from traditional female roles. Suggesting that a girl or woman might not be as virtuous as she appeared obscured the line between the so-called good girls and bad girls. As official debates and discussions continued to focus on the ways in which women could be useful to the military, the military used print media to sexualize women in problematic ways. Anti–venereal disease posters such as "She May Look Clean . . . But . . ." and "Booby Trap," which pictured a "sexier" woman, as well as those that depicted prostitutes as death in a fancy dress, served to frame women as sexually available but potentially deadly.[92] The "Booby Trap" message was emblazoned on the cover of a pamphlet given to servicemen going on leave. It features a woman with the words "Booby Trap" written in large letters across the middle of her body. In the background several servicemen sit or stand, and in the corner two others are hovering around another woman. The text says, in part: "Girls who make a habit of hanging around railroad and bus stations and juke joints, waiting to be picked up, are to be avoided—just as you would avoid any other booby trap. You are badly mistaken if you think that you can tell whether or not a girl has a Venereal Disease by her looks or her clothes or by listening to her story."[93] Such representations not only cast sexual suspicion on women waiting for public transportation (and given the times, many were) but, by linking sex with danger, could have presented a subtle challenge to military men to dare the odds. At the same time, servicemen going on leave frequently heard or read, "If you can't say no, use a pro."[94] Such double messages seemed to encourage sex and point to available women, as well as those who might be available, should the man be unable to say no to his sexual urges. Servicemen could protect themselves by using condoms during a sexual encounter or by visiting a prophylactic station for treatment afterward. (Either a suggestion or a requirement, a visit to a pro station resulted in a less-than-pleasant end to sexual encounters. Chemical prophylaxis could be physically painful and reinforced the notion that sex with a woman was dirty.) Most of those who used pro stations came from the rank and file; many enlisted men viewed the entire process as a sign of manliness.[95] Officers presumably had other options. A cavalier attitude regarding servicemen who caught a venereal disease is well represented in a 1944 issue of *Newsweek*. Depicting a group of servicemen with venereal disease, who were clad in pajamas and sitting casually in a circle, the text described "an oddly mixed group . . . talking with the ease of males in the same fix."[96] That same year, *Newsweek* also carried a series of articles regarding military leaves in Calcutta, which ended with a joke about receiving a service ribbon. The DSM (Distinguished Service Medal) was adapted to mean "did or did not see Margot," a famous prostitute.[97] Such articles seemed to suggest that it was no big deal if some (white) servicemen used (nonwhite) prostitutes (outside the United States) and caught venereal diseases.

While military authorities claimed, in public, to attend to servicemen's morals and morale, in everyday life sex was ever present. The constant attention paid to sex, including safe sex, through lectures, films, pamphlets, and posters, along with the military practice of providing instruction in prophylaxis, created dissonance between any notion of male continence or sexual reserve and the stereotype of the virile, aggressive military male. Even women within the military structure were mocked and vilified as prostitutes and promiscuous women in cartoons and in military post papers.[98] Sex also intruded into technical training: soldiers in training camp learned how to read a map by using a grid placed on top of a pinup picture of Betty Grable. The positioning of the grid targeted areas of the female anatomy associated with sexuality.[99] Pinups, airplane nose art, and chants that objectified women characterized life in the military. While these practices may seem harmless on one level, on another they are representative of the pervasive subtextual linkages between military violence and sex. Men, then, came under the influence of a "masculine mystique" that prescribed certain "manly" behaviors. One can only suppose that, given the focus on sex, many men felt compelled to prove their manhood by sexual derring-do. Servicemen did, as noted earlier, visit houses of prostitution; Beth Bailey and David Farber's study of regulated prostitution in Hawaii includes a picture of numerous men lined up, waiting to enter a brothel.[100]

The SPD maintained pressure in areas of resistance, but they did not always succeed in convincing either servicemen or local and military officials that repression was in their best interests. Navy Captain Joel T. Boone's statement typified prevailing attitudes linking sexual prowess and good soldiering. "If we bear in mind," he said, "that our armed forces are sexually aggressive, that they must be if they are going to be good soldiers and sailors, an important part of our problem is solved." The remainder of the solution called for the examination of prostitutes and a requirement that the diseased ones undergo treatment. With regard to other women, military officials decided that they could not stop the amateur competition, so they encouraged their men to use condoms. The navy captain posed the question: What happens if, in spite of all the education, good advice, and easily obtained protective measures, a serviceman does get "an infection"? Then he answered the question himself: "He is not punished for having sexual desire, any more than we would punish him for having hunger or thirst."[101] Contrariwise, female sexual desire was most often denied but was punished when recognized.

Military policies in particular illuminate the paradoxes inherent both in the dual campaigns to mobilize and contain female sexuality and in attitudes toward male and female sexuality. People, in general, had differing opinions on such matters; but a sense of paradox and ambivalence regarding the role of women in wartime was particularly intense within the military. Most official discussions revealed an assumption that men required sex. Servicemen, as the "manliest" of men, not only would actively seek sex but would suffer a serious loss of morale and fighting spirit if women were unavailable. Officials of the armed forces debated the ways that they could use "good girls" to keep morale high among the troops. At the same time they discussed ways to keep the boys away from "bad," venereally diseased women and girls.

The lack of a coherent position among the various individuals and agencies that made up the apparatus of the state maintained the contradictions that were characteristic of the campaign to reduce the incidence of venereal disease through the repression of prostitution. In the next chapter, I explore the paradoxes of mobilization and control in print media by examining the ways that popular literature participated in the campaign to enlist and at the same time restrain wartime women's sexuality.

5

"Spell 'IT' to the Marines"
The Contradictory Messages of Popular Culture

During the war years, print media functioned as a site of mobilization and control where the tangled themes of sexualized morale maintenance and transgressive sexuality played out in all their complexities and ambiguities. Popular magazines, in particular, served as dispensers of wartime propaganda, including propaganda aimed specifically at women. As the media joined in the mobilization effort, magazine publishers and authors responded favorably to government encouragement to disseminate the kinds of messages that would strengthen and solidify homefront support of and participation in the war effort.[1] Magazines refrained from running photos of death in combat, using instead drawn figures to depict dead soldiers in order to downplay the horrors of war, while reinforcing the necessity to accept wartime policies and suggesting that death and destruction would result if too many women shirked their responsibilities.[2] Articles and advertisements asked female magazine readers if they were "doing their part." The *Ladies Home Journal,* for example, informed women that if they failed to take jobs in ammunition factories or other essential industries, their "menfolk fighting on distant atolls are likely to get slaughtered."[3]

While magazine literature operated, in general, to militarize the citizenry and more specifically to call upon women to meet their national obligations as wartime citizens, it simultaneously maintained and enlarged an ideology of traditional femininity. As more and more women appeared in public and entered spaces formerly defined as male, this phenomenon became a topic of frequent media discussion. The enlistment of women, while necessary to the success of the war effort, produced concerns about challenges to and changes in normative behaviors and practices. Not only did women move into previously male jobs;

they wore pants in public, frequented places of commercial entertainment unaccompanied by men, and challenged, in a variety of ways, both gender relations and existing standards of sexual morality.[4] As we have seen, in meeting their wartime obligations to labor both in the factory and in the dance hall, many women came to be viewed as dangerous individuals, in the first case too masculine and in the second too sexual. Wartime women's services were both domesticated and demonized in popular culture.

My analysis is based on two strands of sexual discourses that appeared in a variety of publications during World War II. The first strand deals with the condemnation of prostitutes, "promiscuous" women, and "female-generated venereal disease" in a wide range of periodicals, from mass-circulation popular magazines such as *Look, Life, Reader's Digest,* and *American Mercury* to professional journals such as *Probation, Federal Probation,* and the *American Journal of Public Health.* These sources provide rich detail regarding the wartime campaign in the United States, supported by the government, military, and medical institutions, to eliminate venereal disease through the suppression of so-called sexually deviant women. A discourse of female deviance emerges clearly in this literature. Prostitutes and promiscuous women become metaphors for dangerous sexuality and venereal disease.

The second strand of wartime sexual discourse consists of general portrayals of women's sexuality. For this, I examined the varied content of three different types of magazines that targeted specific groups of the population. During the war years, women of different classes and races read magazines and accepted them as a source both of up-to-date news and of female-specific advice.[5] Phyllis Palmer suggests that magazines served a textbooklike function: busy wartime women could consult them for time- and labor-saving advice as well as basic instruction in womanhood.[6] Homemakers' magazines, such as *Woman's Home Companion,* which had a wartime circulation of three million, aimed to attract white middle-class women, while romance magazines, such as *True Confessions,* were intended to appeal to working-class women. To attend to race, given the limitations of the sources—widely distributed magazines specifically aimed at black women did not appear until after the war—I used the *Negro Digest* and *The Crisis,* periodicals published by and for African Americans.[7] Both publications had high rates of circulation in the wartime black population, and both contained articles that featured black women. These varied magazines, read by middle-class and working-class white women (and men) and by female and male African Americans, contain multiple perspectives on sexuality and illustrate the competing wartime discourses of patriotic and subversive female sexuality. This sample also presents a comprehensive notion of patriotic sexuality as a female wartime obligation.[8]

I view these magazines—in their totality, including articles, stories, photographs, and advertisements—as producing multiple discourses that convey subtle messages that resonate with common perceptions of male and female nature. Viewing the magazines as a whole makes it apparent that these wartime publications reflect much of the sexual ambiguity that surrounded wartime women.[9] The traditional and familiar cultural images of women are complicated by a subtext that suggests a more fluid boundary between the good girl (patriot) and the bad girl (patriotute). The multiple discourses embedded in the texts served to mystify the spaces between patriotic and promiscuous sexuality.

Sexual display in and of itself was not unique to wartime periodicals. Successful magazines that sold well traditionally displayed women in alluring poses and included either overt or covert sexual themes.[10] During the war years, however, a significant element came into play. By presenting a close association between sexual allure and patriotism, the wartime media added to an already troublesome perception of female sexual availability. While the wartime "campaign" against prostitutes and promiscuous women generally focused on working-class and nonwhite women, many media messages also had something to say to middle-class white women. Doing their part meant protecting the homefront by guarding their respectability. The war against women who transgressed the boundaries served also as a caution for white middle-class women to police their sexual behavior. Only occasionally did they suffer the loss of freedom and involuntary rehabilitation experienced much more often by working-class women or women of color. Through this generalized, but ambiguous, sexualization of women, the wartime media reflected and reinforced ambiguities and confounded the potential impact, either positive or negative, of women's sexuality on the armed forces. Tensions mounted as women responded to the nation's call to do their part as good citizens. As women acted, in ever-growing numbers, on their prescribed national obligations, the question increasingly loomed: What would these women be like by the time the war was over?

Continuity and Change

Social and political concerns regarding female prostitution and promiscuity are not, as we have seen, without historical precedent. Commercialized prostitution and organized vice had been targeted by reformers since the late nineteenth century. The World War I campaign against venereal disease expanded to include nonprofessional girls. While such concerns led to the appointment of female protective officers and to harsher treatment of alleged sexual transgressors, the much shorter World War I campaign did not reach the level of repression that occurred in World War II. The errant woman of the earlier war, viewed by some authorities as a victim—as one acted upon rather than aggressively sexual—had a better chance of being treated as misguided rather than deviant or criminal, as occurred in later years.

In the first four decades of the twentieth century, ideas regarding female sexuality had been constantly evolving. By the 1940s U.S. society, including the media, had become increasingly eroticized. Sex had entered the marketplace in a variety of ways. Forms of commercial entertainment, such as dance halls, amusement parks, and movie theaters, patronized first by the working class and later by the middle class, brought young women and men together in new and public ways. Courtship practices moved "from front porch to backseat,"[11] that is, young women and men went on unchaperoned dates, sometimes in automobiles. By the 1920s, the figure of the flapper represented a freer sexuality, a suggestion of the female right to sexual experimentation. Many young women joined the urban workforce, enrolled in coed colleges, changed their style of dress, experimented with makeup, and enthusiastically embraced modernity. These changes in and challenges to traditional sex and gender norms, often referred to as the "first sexual revolution," were reflected in print media—novels, short stories, magazine articles, and advertisements—as well as in film.

On the one hand, it seemed as if women had been recognized as sexual beings, free to be sexual; on the other hand, a less positive political and medical discourse problematized female sexuality. Social reformers, Freud, and the sexologists often portrayed sexual women more negatively. In places such as the Greenwich Village area of New York City, they discovered lesbians, and in other urban areas, prostitutes. During the late nineteenth and early twentieth centuries, when numerous young women left the confines of home to enter the public sphere, "[o]ne result was an enlarged area of opportunity for women to choose, to play; another was the creation of new arenas for their sexual harassment."[12] And as historian Joanne J. Meyerowitz points out, "Departures from middle-class mores attracted public notice."[13] Young women's sexuality concerned not only parents but also state officials and social reformers. By midcentury, new laws, policewomen, female reformatories, and juvenile courts operated to control female sexuality.[14] As another world war loomed on the horizon, the American woman stood on contested terrain regarding her role and place in society.

During the late 1930s, when government, medical, military, and social work officials came together to plan strategies to meet the expected "woman problem," they relied on past experiences and brought preconceived and gendered notions with them. In contrast to earlier morality campaigns, for example, male continence was not considered an issue during World War II.[15] Gender relations were increasingly eroticized, especially during the 1920s, and evolved in the 1940s to a prescription for female sexuality that *obligated* wartime women to be sexually alluring and enticing. Enveloped in a discourse of sexual obligation, the wartime woman had a reciprocal duty to wartime men, especially servicemen. She had to construct herself in the prescribed manner in order to provide servicemen with both motivation and morale. In a sense, her body would repay him for risking his life in her defense.

The Media Do Their Part

Print media joined the battle on the homefront. Magazine articles, stories, and advertisements offered all kinds of normative advice to wartime women: how to dress, how to remain feminine while engaging in heavy (masculine) labor, how to act in public (especially without a male escort), and how to meet their obligations to the war effort in a variety of ways.[16] At the same time, another series of articles on the perils and evils of venereal disease focused on females as disease carriers and as dangerous and even treasonous if their contagion reached the armed forces. "Prostitution Major Wartime Threat," proclaimed *American City* in 1942. Or, as *Survey Graphic* put it the next year, "Sick Men Can't Fight."[17] Journals such as the *American Journal of Public Health* called prostitutes "Axis partners," and *Federal Probation* referred to promiscuous women as "Fifth Columnists."[18] Magazines and journals suggested diverse ways—from curfews to "camps" and federal quarantine areas—to eliminate the widespread problems of prostitutes, promiscuous women, and the danger of associating with them, namely venereal disease.

The woman-disease connection was reiterated in a variety of media organs. One could, for example, pick up almost any magazine and find a common ad for Listerine, which currently serves as a mouthwash but had wider use in the 1940s, including use as a "feminine hygiene" product. While such ads appeared most often in romance magazines, similar messages appeared in numerous widely read magazines. In many ads, wartime women were positioned at the margins of male-female activities because of some "lack of cleanliness." "Barbara" sat alone, outside the door of the party room, and "Karen" sat in a corner wearing a "Do Not Disturb" sign while a party (with servicemen) went on around her.[19] The poster "She May Look Clean . . . But . . ." presented a likeness of the proverbial "girl next door" with a clear warning that even the nicest girl could be harboring disease. "The New War against Venereal Disease," a headline article in *Look,* featured five pictures of women in a hospital setting; one picture of a seriously ill woman covered an entire page. The text read, in part, "One urgent task . . . has been to treat the numerous infected women. Most new infections today can be attributed to non-professional pick-ups."[20] Who is the woman in the large picture? Clearly, she represents one of the allegedly numerous infected (contagious) women. The source of her infection is not addressed; rather, she is depicted as possibly aggressive (picking up men) and as diseased. Numerous women, in different circumstances, attracted the attention of the authorities as possible transmitters of venereal disease, such as those already known to the police or the social welfare system, waitresses, nonwhite women, transients, and women identified as belonging to the "lower orders."[21]

Sexuality and Mental Illness

Mental incompetence soon joined disease, danger, and (sexual) deviance as a charge leveled against allegedly promiscuous women. A medical authority wrote of those "prostitutes who because of constitutional or congenital handicaps, mental deficiency or mental disorder, have little choice except to engage in repeated prostitution and other forbidden behavior." He further contended that his study, although incomplete, "already shows a large percentage of definitely diagnosed defectives and border zone cases . . . among a fair sampling of adjudicated prostitutes. The number of psychopaths is also large." He claimed that of one hundred women arrested for prostitution, "76% were defective or borderline; 65% were rated as morons or imbeciles."[22] Other instances of describing promiscuous women as having less than average intelligence or as being psychologically disturbed appeared in articles in *Probation, Federal Probation,* and the *American Journal of Public Health.* These articles, which added to an impression of rampant female sexual deviance, had echoes in popular literature. For example, a *Harper's* article mentioned the need for psychiatric assessment of some prostitutes.[23] Headlines extolled new and better treatment facilities such as the City Venereal Disease Control Clinic in San Francisco, which provided a program of reeducation and readjustment "for girls and women who offer a promiscuous sex history."[24] The characterization of some prostitutes and promiscuous women as "mentally defective" operated to contain more women and resulted in incarceration, often in a psychiatric institution.

Men and Sex

At the same time that the government, the military, and the medical establishment waged a war against prostitution and promiscuity, other voices clamored to assert men's right to sex with women. One soldier, who claimed to speak "realistically" for many other men, wrote a letter to *American Mercury's* "Open Forum," addressing the subject: "Do you welfarers wish to eliminate prostitution or sexual intercourse?" He felt that the current discussions of sex and the army followed "the conventional social-worker line," and he derided such naïveté. In his opinion, the "social ostrich" should remove its head from the sand. He wondered what would happen if the "squelching" of prostitution succeeded. According to him, there was no substitute for sex, and anyone who thought that millions of men were likely to take a vow of abstinence for the duration was sadly deluded.[25] This soldier asked several questions that the military both answered and ignored in everyday policies and practices. An article in *Reader's Digest* typified the mixed message.

Within a few lines of reading that "moral suasion" was usually sufficient to deter men from sexual promiscuity, we read that, just in case,
the men could purchase prophylactics, "which canteens sell at cost."[26]
In the *American Journal of Public Health,* the headline proclaimed:
"San Francisco Opens Three Prophylactic Stations." To draw attention
to these stations, the authorities distributed five thousand lavatory placards and half a million leaflets advertising the locations.[27] Even *Good
Housekeeping,* in a brief piece, assured its readers that one thousand
soldiers preparing to go on leave were given a "dosage of sulfathiazole"
as a preventive measure.[28] It seems clear that servicemen were not expected to take a vow of abstinence.

In 1944, U.S. Surgeon General Thomas Parran wrote an article on
the "haunting specter of venereal disease." He claimed: "The United
States Army is proving that it is preventable." Pointing out the enemy in
the homefront battle, he stated, "The noncommercial girl . . . is supplanting the prostitute as the main source of venereal infection." Such
girls (supposedly numerous) were doubly threatening because they were
"active not only around military centers where control methods are
strict, but in war boom towns, trailer towns, cities and villages where
control measures are less efficient. She is driving our national standards
of morality down."[29] In New York City, when the Social Hygiene Association reported a sizable increase in "social diseases among high school
boys and girls," the association recommended a "midnight curfew for
girls of 16 or younger."[30] As girls and women continued to be held responsible for maintaining sexual control, maintaining male morale, and
spreading venereal diseases, the military spoke of moral suasion while
dispensing prophylactics, and soldiers insisted that sex was here to stay.

Numerous articles continued to highlight a link between female sexuality and danger and disease. Titles such as "Prostitution Blamed: Suppression Near Army Camps Held Essential to the Control of Venereal
Disease" and "Public's Health: Program to Prevent Young Girls and
Women from Involvement in Prostitution and Promiscuity" represent
one strand of media treatment of "problematic" female sexuality. A recurrent theme that focused on women as the culprits in the spread of
venereal disease emerged regularly in articles such as "National Defense
vs. Venereal Disease," "War on Venereal Ills," "All Out War on Prostitution," "V.D., Menace and Challenge," "Fighting Prostitution," "Prostitution Is an Axis Partner," and "V.D. in London: Battle of Piccadilly

Circus among Our Army's Worst." Many of these articles appeared in popular magazines and reinforced a notion of dangerous and deviant women as saboteurs, traitors on the homefront.[31] If (some) women presented a clear danger to military success, the authorities claimed to be justified in the use of force to remove them from society.

Proposed Solutions

Medical and government officials suggested a variety of measures, including "a chain of small institutions—schools, hostels, farms, training centers—where these women offenders, graded according to their prospect for rehabilitation[,] may be committed." One of the purported virtues of this plan, which was proposed by a public official, was that "it offers the prospect of release when—and only when—the girl is rehabilitated. Maximum sentences would yield to truly indeterminate sentences. It would be a dynamic and flexible correctional system for the simple, realistic reason that people conform at varying pace to the effort of society to render them less troublesome."[32] Wartime women, particularly those perceived as most troublesome, could be incarcerated for as long as the authorities deemed necessary. Wartime anxiety, as reflected in media discourse, reinforced societal unease regarding these (sexually) visible and possibly dangerous women.

Popular magazines and professional journals also offered advice to eliminate the problem. One solution suggested that, to suppress prostitution wherever it was found, there had to be adequate supervision of public places. Captain Rhoda Millikin, a member of the Police Department of the District of Columbia, felt that women in law enforcement positions could be responsible for this task. Government officials called for daily surveillance of both individuals and places. "Someone must observe conditions day after day so as to be able to know which girls are causing trouble. . . . [S]ome must be arrested . . . others may just be wandering about in quest of excitement. For the latter, since they are not criminals, it would be appropriate to contain them in shelters, overnight or until individual situations can be explored."[33]

The police chief of Norfolk, Virginia, offered a suggestion that, he felt, would solve the problem. He said, "In peacetime, I believe in a segregated district for prostitution. . . . [I]n wartime we are committed to suppression. . . . I think I could come close to suppressing prostitution . . . if only I had adequate prison facilities for the women. I have asked the government to give me a concentration camp . . . large enough for two or three thousand women. If we had such a camp, we could throw every prostitute who dares enter town into it for the duration."[34] The techniques and attitudes that characterized the homefront battle against prostitutes and promiscuous women are well illustrated in the article "Norfolk—Our Worst War Town." Before the war, the red-light area of Norfolk was maintained, controlled, and tacitly accepted. The navy then ordered the town to "close the district . . . suppression for the duration."[35]

When the journalist and a local police officer toured the entertainment district, their conversation suggested an acceptance of male activities such as drinking, gambling, fighting, and picking up girls. In stark contrast are the harsh words used to describe women. Those who had venereal disease were referred to as "rotten apples," and the officer agreed with the reporter that most of the girls in the area were "sluts." The reporter viewed a place frequented by those girls who "did it" cheaply, describing the spot as "a quilt spread on the brick pavement between two garbage pails . . . an old coca-cola sign providing the only privacy." The police officer commented, "I feel sorry for the boys every time I catch one of them in a spot like that." The serviceman was then returned to his base via the shore patrol wagon. "The wench [identified as "a Negro woman"] was taken to jail."[36] While the woman involved in this situation was a prostitute, the difference in male attitudes and solutions remains striking. Both engaged in intercourse in a crude public place, but the "boy" (another innocent victim?) got compassion and a ride home; the "wench" went to jail.

On the West Coast, too, the media reported on the repression effort. The *American Journal of Public Health* stated: "Prostitution has been vigorously repressed by the law enforcement agencies and an arrangement has been worked out so that all women arrested on morals charges and who are brought to the Los Angeles County Jail are placed under legal quarantine. These suspects are held . . . until tests may be made."[37] From sea to shining sea, the media helped maintain the conflation of female promiscuity and venereal disease and supported surveillance, arrest, detention, forced venereal disease testing, and other invasive procedures to deal with women labeled as sexually transgressive.

Ambiguous Female Sexuality

The simultaneous effort to mobilize female sexuality in support of the war effort complicated the media's support for repressing prostitution and controlling "promiscuous" female sexuality. Print media, especially popular magazines, did their part by presenting female bodies engaged in and available for morale maintenance. Magazine covers regularly featured diverse women as canteen hostesses and as recreation center volunteers.[38] Many publications seemed to valorize women who met their patriotic obligation to be sexually alluring by providing entertainment for servicemen. For example, "Be the Thrill in His Furlough" and "She Makes the Wounded Wiggle" represent common media offerings. At the same time, the text complicates women's contributions by using sexually descriptive words such as *provocative, sensuous, hot,* and *sizzling,* once again blurring the line between patriotism and promiscuity.[39]

Magazines such as the *Negro Digest, The Crisis,* and *American Mercury* often featured women as entertainers and morale builders for the troops.[40] Howard Whitman of *Coronet,* for example, wrote "Johnny Get Your Fun," an article that featured female entertainers. He asserted, "The gal with the G-string, the taxi-dancer, and the chorine in the nightclub with black net stockings up to her mezzanine; in their own way they're all doing war jobs."[41] In the *Negro Digest,* articles about women most often featured entertainers, and the terms used to describe them were generally sexual. Phrases such as "moved in an insinuating manner" and "gave the impression of a hot lick" focused more on sexuality than on service, raising questions regarding women's wartime service.[42] Such textual ambiguity illuminates the ease with which the categories of patriot and prostitute could collapse into *patriotute.* Many women who did their part by working as waitresses and hostesses in roadhouses, in bars, and in the proliferating dine-and-dance tents did not receive commendations for their patriotism. Rather, they came under surveillance by law enforcement and social service personnel, who claimed that many of the girls who ultimately became involved as prostitutes started out this way.[43]

Popular literature also offered advice articles laying out the "rules" for holding on to a "good reputation," especially for women without men. *Good Housekeeping* featured "How to Behave in Public without an Escort," a hard-hitting piece of advice on the limits of acceptable public behavior. "Drinking and dancing with girlfriends" was suspect behavior at best. Conspicuous attire—"fancy duds"—could send out a clear message that one "hoped to spend the evening with a M-A-N." Generally this advice focused on the necessity of maintaining a "lady-like" demeanor.[44] An advertisement for an advice pamphlet accompanying a feature on socializing at home focused on how *not* to act in the company of men. The author particularly warned against "piling up dates that lead to entangling alliances."[45] Women who socialized in public while unattached to a specific male risked the loss of a good reputation. Women who socialized in public (or private) with too many men definitely transgressed acceptable boundaries.[46] The symbolic import of such threats (loss of a good reputation) wielded great power in the 1940s. Blaming women for any difficulties that arose in male-female encounters, Walter Lamb Newton, in *Coronet*, wrote that "a woman almost never gets into trouble with a man unless she contributes in some degree to the process."[47] By drawing attention to the boundaries of respectable behavior, the media called attention to numerous women who, if they failed to control their own sexuality, lost status as "good" women.

In an outstanding and repeated example of both sexual objectification and the blurred boundaries between prostitute and patriot, ads for Evening in Paris perfume featured a woman in provocative dress, supine, with the caption "Spell 'IT' to the Marines." The same perfume was advertised repeatedly as a product used by women who love "a soldier . . . a sailor . . . a marine."[48] A term coined in the 1920s, an "It" girl was one with sex appeal who attracted numerous male admirers.[49] Given the campaign against potentially promiscuous women, this type of ad illuminates the conflicting messages that not only wartime women but also the larger society received regarding sexuality. In many ads, articles, and stories, sexualized and militarized women appeared as patriotic in terms of their relationships with servicemen. At the same time, "victory girls" were considered too patriotic when they appeared to be sexually available—that is, promiscuous.

Articles, stories, and advertisements, particularly in women's magazines, continued to link female sexuality and the war effort via sexualized contact with servicemen. Fictional wartime women repeatedly appeared as involved in some task to improve their appearance in order to attract a man, especially a serviceman. Advertisements, in particular, valorized servicemen and portrayed women as not quite up to the standards for sexual allure. While providing specific prescriptions for improvement, ads also spoke a less obvious message. By depicting women as subject to a variety of offensive odors that would prevent them from attracting a male (serviceman), the media continued to circulate a connection between women, disease, and dirt. Men avoided, whispered about, or gazed with disgust upon the female figure. Halitosis, scalp odor, body odor, menstrual odor, and feminine hygiene were just some

"Spell 'IT' to the Marine." Advertisement, *Woman's Home Companion,* August 1943, 55.

"Be his Pin-up Girl!" Advertisement, *True Story*, June 1944, 87.

of the problems. Scarcely a body part escaped notice.[50] Other typical ads promoted a variety of beauty products as well as general advice to help attract a man, preferably a serviceman.[51]

Touting its soap, Cashmere Bouquet featured a series of ads that suggested a military-woman connection, with captions such as "6 million soldiers and here I sit," and the puzzled woman who asked: "Think 50 Cents Is Too Much?" as she tried to sell her kisses to servicemen at a bazaar.[52] The salient message told women to do whatever was necessary to disguise their defects and thereby capture the male gaze. At the same time, however, professional journals and periodicals with a more general readership carried numerous articles warning of the ease with which venereal disease could be contracted from seemingly innocent women—perhaps like those in the ads. Even if wartime women painted their nails, dyed their hair, and used skin softeners, perfume, and deodorants, they might still harbor hidden dangers. Such innocent-looking women were the same wives, girlfriends, and casual pickups that popular and social work literature blamed for more than 80 to 90 percent of the venereal disease transmissions.[53]

Married women also continued to receive a variety of messages that reinforced their obligation to maintain sexual allure by remaining the same women they had been when their husbands went to war. No matter what ensued during the period of separation, they should remain as "youthful" and attractive as they were when the men left. Wives could also meet their obligation by entering a "cheesecake" picture in contests such as the one for the "Sweetheart of the AEF" or by heeding movie star Betty Grable's advice and sending a pinup picture of themselves to their husbands. (Single women could and were urged to send a pinup picture to any serviceman.)[54] For the duration, socializing with other women in the home, preferably engaged in domestic tasks (knitting or doing some other type of wartime service), would be acceptable wartime recreation. These women, presented as keepers of the mythical norm, served as controlling images—the good women who theoretically maintained the boundaries of respectability.[55]

An excellent example of race-dependent advice to women is evident in two articles on "camp-following" wives, one in *Modern Romances,* the other in *The Crisis.* Although material on African American women is scanty, appearing only in the magazines aimed at the black community, the contrasting tone in these articles suggests the difficulty in applying a single, general standard to women of different races. *Modern Romances* criticized the wife who wanted to follow her husband both for her "jealous and mistrustful" nature and for her failure to understand her mission to "keep the home fires burning."[56] The author suggested: "Ask your soldier what he thinks of them," with the implication being that he thought that camp-following wives were unpatriotic, unable to give up sex for the duration. A completely opposite view was presented in "Negro Army Wives" in *The Crisis.* Here women who followed their husbands to camps and bases were presented as the ultimate good women: "Wives . . . are trying to maintain the morale of their soldier husbands by accompanying them wherever they are sent this side of 'over-there.' "[57] Since African American troops were segregated and refused admission to many servicemen's clubs during World War II, this advice and approval comes from an entirely different perspective. It does, however, raise questions regarding the resultant public perception of "Negro army wives" during the war years. Historically, *camp followers* was a term used to describe prostitutes. Frank Yerby used fiction to illuminate the effects of racist attitudes on black men and women in a story entitled "Health Card." In this story the military police accost the wife of a young black soldier and accuse her of prostitution, although she is walking, at the time, in the company of her husband.[58] Yerby called attention to the sociocultural assumptions that allowed white military police to assume that the black women was a prostitute and to demand that she produce her health card. During World War II, prostitutes and many waitresses were required to carry health cards that stated that they were free of venereal disease. Apparently it was not always necessary for a woman to be unescorted or to be displaying blatant sexual availability in order to be viewed with suspicion. Racial stereotypes served to stigmatize black women and men.

Girls who "flocked to public parks and places where they met and socialized with soldiers and sailors" also came under suspicion despite having been encouraged to provide companionship for servicemen. "The Girl and the Man in Uniform," an article in the journal *Probation,* claimed that "we can be sure that many of these girls became promiscuous sooner or later."[59] "Sleeping Beauty," in *Woman's Home Companion,* contained a clear warning to young women who behaved in such a fashion. Beth, a "naive" young schoolgirl, was intrigued by the local park, which had a "wooded path" that soldiers, sailors, and girls frequented. One day she opened a conversation with a redheaded soldier who sat down next to her; she hoped that the boys from school would notice her conquest. When Red became sexually threatening, she ran away but immediately felt guilty for treating a serviceman unkindly. Beth solved her dilemma by inviting the soldier to her home to meet her family. He then told her that he had thought she was one of *those girls* when he saw her at the park. Naive Beth had learned a serious lesson regarding appearances.[60] She could not freely go to a park where servicemen apparently flocked. As reparation for sending the wrong message to Red, she could bring him into her home. Prior to the war, however, respectable women and girls would not have thought it was acceptable to bring a strange male into their parents' home. Women in parks or other public spaces, then, walked the tightrope of patriot-prostitute or promiscuous woman. Beth, who came dangerously close to slipping into the latter categories, moved back to safe ground by containing herself and the serviceman within the domestic realm.

Women who refused to be contained and who continued to enter into public spaces both challenged the social order and opened themselves to challenge. *Reader's Digest,* for example, informed its readers that, on paydays, many army towns were inundated with trainloads of girls. These were the women referred to as "victory girls," and many were arrested on suspicion of soliciting.[61] At the same time, fiction and nonfiction articles in women's magazines continued to advocate the "entertainment" of the troops as women's patriotic duty. "Parties Unlimited," for example, told of an organization formed by California women that held fortnightly parties, entertaining 150 "boys." To provide female companionship for the boys, "Sorority girls from near-by colleges have been enrolled as dates and pay six dollars yearly dues."[62] Terms such as "trainloads of girls," then, could have cast suspicion on and endangered the reputations of the respectable college girls and USO hostesses who volunteered to help keep the boys' morale high.

Meanwhile, stories and articles in *Woman's Home Companion* often depicted, without disapproval, young girls who engaged in recreational activities with servicemen and frequented places that had formerly been taboo.[63] Several stories featured women on vacation (alone or with another woman) at places where servicemen abounded. Romantic involvement was always a component of these plots.[64] As mid-twentieth-century versions of "women adrift," some wartime women could avoid social stigma through marriage; "quickie" marriages became a wartime phenomenon.[65] The young women who invited servicemen into their homes to meet their approving families came closest to achieving patriotic status. One popular column in a piece entitled "How to Treat a Soldier" offered advice to young women. It urged: "[T]reat him like a man . . . do what he wants to do . . . bring him into your family life."[66] These stories, and many similar ones, suggested a patriotic homefront exchange of female (hetero)sexuality for military defense.

As women served their country by maintaining male morale, the diverse and often contradictory media images of wartime women reflected societal ambivalence regarding female sexuality. Women were sexualized in support of the war effort but were also subject to negative portrayals if they appeared to exceed the always nebulous standards of acceptability and respectability. The difficult situations that women must have found themselves in, given wartime pro-military and sexualized discourse, stood out in an article by a serviceman who was extremely annoyed by the behavior of a woman on a train. She became "insulted" when a strange man spoke to her. This army private responded that "he'd ridden 400 miles sitting opposite this type of *prissy sourpuss*" (emphasis mine).[67] He had expected her to respond favorably; she had most likely been warned against talking to or seeming friendly toward strange men.

A wartime prescription for female sexual allure was constantly promoted in popular magazines. But well before Pearl Harbor the apparatus of the state had anticipated a problem with wartime women's sexuality. Media representations of "sexy" women both supported a notion of female sexual obligation and exacerbated fears regarding overly sexual women. The state's concern about the very real problem of venereal disease quickly mutated into a conflation of female sexuality with excess, disease, and danger. But what about the actual women, the inhabitants of those alluring but dangerous bodies? In spite of the richness of the primary sources, they present several problems. Not only do they speak from a hegemonic male position, but they also lie in the realm of the specular. Women's bodies are described and their actions are interpreted by official figures; they are seldom allowed to speak for themselves. In the following chapter we will hear from some of the women who were charged with morals offenses during the Second World War.

6

Behind the Lines
The War against Women

> One of the great battles being fought today is the homefront battle
> for the health of the nation. One of the greatest enemies in that
> battle is venereal disease. But, a new problem, reported from all
> over America by the Army's venereal disease control officers, is
> making the fight harder — the problem of the noncommercial girl
> who is supplanting the prostitute as the main source of venereal in-
> fection in the armed services. It is she who is in large part responsi-
> ble for the increase of venereal disease in this country.
> —Patricia Lochridge, "VD, Menace and Challenge" (1944)

Throughout the previous chapters, women have been perceived through an official and primarily male gaze. While the authori-
tarian gaze continues to frame the narrative, this chapter also provides a
brief glimpse of the experiences of actual women ensnared by the wartime campaign. We encounter some women who overtly resisted widespread repression, as well as the more general resistance to accepting
prescribed gender boundaries. State and medical officials often saw wartime women as excessively sexual and therefore unable to perform as
responsible citizens. Women's participation in the war effort, including
their embrace of the sexual freedoms of the war years, both strengthened and challenged sociopolitical constructions of appropriate womanhood. Wartime women were everywhere, doing everything; that was a
problem. But as the officials of the state became more and more aware
that female labor was necessary for victory, and as women successfully
filled male-defined jobs and participated in other war-related activities,
the authorities suffered a cognitive crisis. Women rose to the occasion;
their response was both pleasing and confusing to state officials.

As we have seen in the preceding chapters, women joined in the war effort by supplying labor and sexualized services, but their own voices were silenced and their individuality was hidden. Women were redefined, in a sense, as war materiel. Whether they were situated in the mainstream or at the margins of respectability, their sex/gender was requisitioned in service to militarized ends. The professional women who supported the campaign, the women represented in magazines as using Ponds Cold Cream and therefore engaged to be married, the attractive (feminine) welders and WACs wearing lipstick and frilly lingerie under their mannish uniforms, and the USO volunteers, as well as the waitresses of questionable morals and promiscuous women—and, of course, prostitutes—were all absorbed into the military machine in some way. But most of these women received little recognition from their country for their conscripted services. Not only did wartime women come under intense scrutiny, but, as we have seen, they also incurred serious penalties, both material and psychological.

Both popular and official discourses described women in biological terms, reinforcing a concept of women as a monolithic group. Inevitably difference was covered over, and in theory any woman could become vulnerable to charges of inappropriate female sexuality. That women continued to cross the sex/gender boundaries served as notice that they accepted neither the prescribed roles nor the official categories. As the larger society and state and social institutions grappled with the complexities of wartime on the homefront, women continued to act in ways intended to meet their wartime obligations. Whether they chose how to respond or were, in some other sense, influenced by propaganda, numerous wartime women did answer their nation's call. Sometimes deliberately, perhaps less consciously at times, they engaged in an ever-active challenge to the traditional boundaries that circumscribed woman's role and her social space. The battle on the homefront had opposing, if unmatched, sides.

Reinterpreting Women

One strategy of control employed during wartime emerged in official language. The records of the SPD contain a litany of pejorative terms used to describe and label wartime women and girls who associated in a variety of ways with servicemen. The terms included *lewd, sex offenders, disorderly girls, vagrants, predelinquent, suspected prostitute, potentially promiscuous women, chippies, possibly foolish and immoral, disease carriers, infected persons, nonadaptable,* and *mentally deficient,* as well as the previously mentioned *promiscuous women, grass grabbers, hordes of harlots, victory girls, good-time Charlottes,* and *patriotutes.*[1] Labeling not only positioned numerous wartime women well outside the boundaries of respectability but also raised troubling questions in the public mind and reinforced suspicions regarding female sexuality.[2] Such terminology, which characterized women as potential deviants by continually focusing on sexuality, created and maintained a link between women and immorality and disease.

At the same time, wartime women were under intense pressure from the government, and also from individual men, to conform to their traditionally prescribed roles of meeting male needs. "Many a teenage girl was told that having intercourse with a soldier before he was shipped out, perhaps never to return, was a way to contribute to the war effort."[3] Even USO entertainers encountered difficulties with servicemen: one woman recalled an event during a blackout after a performance. Upon returning to their hotel, members of an all-girl band encountered "sailors . . . so drunk . . . and scared . . . that they just started grabbing any woman they could and threw her down on the ground." Another member of the band told of meeting a "boy" she knew from high school; when he asked her to go out with him, she agreed. She was shocked when he took her to an "off-limits" place, and even more so when he "tried to throw me down in a field" on the way home. She protested, saying, "I can't do that." He responded, "Yeah, but you're a good, clean girl and I'm going away."[4] One wartime woman recalled that when the hometown National Guard was called up, "immediately all the young men started to pressure the girls to have sex." This woman noted that "in those days pre-marital sex was such a taboo thing" that many women got married rather than break the taboo.[5] An impression had been created regarding female potential for sexual promiscuity that colored perceptions of wartime women. The authorities blamed women; a sociologist claimed that "girls react to the uniform. Desiring to do everything possible to please the servicemen they have been called comfort girls."[6] This was not, however, intended as a compliment. The taint of immorality extended into the women's armed services. A whispering campaign against women in the military depicted them as lesbians or camp followers (prostitutes).[7] The war on the homefront intensified.

"A Second Front against Prostitution"

In 1943 the *Journal of Social Hygiene* published an article based on a report of the NAPCSP's Committee on Enforcement. The report touted the success of the repression campaign in terms of closing down red-light districts and houses of prostitution by pointing to a reduction in military venereal disease rates. Claiming success on the prostitution front prompted official groups to declare that they were "now in a position to open a second front on the next important source of venereal disease . . . prostitution as practiced outside of the houses of prostitution."[8] SPD officials, while taking credit for closing 675 red-light districts, agreed to the necessity of expanding the repression campaign. "There is," they stated, "hardly a community in the country, near or far from military establishments, which does not contribute to the venereal disease problem and which, therefore, can be removed from the Division's interest."[9] The authorities, while still repressing prostitution, then proceeded to direct an extraordinary amount of their attention to so-called promiscuous young girls, girls who, in their opinion, "live and give lightly."[10] The promiscuous girl, as defined by the SPD, was a health menace but not "criminally motivated." She was "more likely to be a casual, fun-seeking girl, wanting male companionship; a young experimenter; someone lonely, easing her conscience for defying the social and moral codes by quixotic references to patriotism; unripe in her judgment, and disassociated from stabilizing forces such as the family and the church."[11] At the same time that the authorities described the teenage or "pick-up girl" as an amateur, they also claimed that she was "crowding out her stepsister, the professional prostitute," and becoming a "public menace, particularly in communities near military camps or war plants."[12] The amateur had quickly morphed into a dangerous girl. A USPHS consultant who visited 162 problem areas reported that the average age of girls "being picked up by vice squads had dropped to 16 from 18–20."[13] Implying that the problem was diseased teenagers, whose sexual aggressiveness decimated the ranks of fighting men, the authorities failed to note that sexual congress with underage girls was a criminal offense. Official investigators remarked with some consternation that "this pick-up girl is frequently of good [middle-class] family." They said she was "less interested in money than excitement" and that she frequently had "uniform hysteria."[14] The lure of the uniform impelled her to go where soldiers and sailors congregated. In the official analysis, she had no control; she found servicemen, she talked to them, before long she began to pick them up, and then . . . ? Constantly under surveillance by police predisposed to see sexual intent, she was picked up by them, and she entered the official records as a sex delinquent.

We can see the difficulties that many girls and women faced by noting that at the same time that the amateur, but fast-learning, young sex delinquent joined the prostitute as a danger on the homefront, the YWCA/USO was revamping plans for hostesses. It is important to note that the USO carefully investigated each candidate for hostess, accepting only those with sterling reputations, and promptly dismissed anyone who even appeared to stray outside the lines of respectability. "The original blueprint for action by the USO Division of the National YWCA did not include a specific plan for work with the young girls, 16–18. But the original plan had to be modified; as 18-year-old boys were drafted, admitting younger women to the ranks of hostesses seemed to be a viable option. Accordingly, in many communities, particularly those in which there were very young soldiers, the younger girls entered training as debutante hostesses."[15] Since, as Meghan Winchell points out, the USO was a quasi-governmental organization and the hostesses, both girls and women, were primarily white, middle class, and respectable, the organization and the volunteers were not targeted by the morals police.[16]

As the war progressed and the USO and other organizations drew more women into contact with servicemen, the opening of the second front destabilized the category of good girl for some women, particularly those of the working class. The contradictions that arose illuminate the problematic and questionable patterns in the venereal disease campaign. The authorities allowed that phase one, the repression of prostitution, involved fairly simple procedures, since a segregated district "either existed or it did not." However, the next phase would be far more difficult, as prosecuting the new front required, in their own words, "search, inquiry, and cooperation." Prostitution, the authorities claimed, "may be practiced in many different ways, few of which are outwardly apparent."[17] In other words, official agencies and individuals were going to have to work together diligently to find those numerous promiscuous girls. Descriptors such as those listed above (and there were many more) maintained the idea that sexually aggressive and most likely diseased women and girls lurked in varied social spaces, even in those spaces to which women had been lured by appeals to patriotism. In these (official) interpretations, many women could be branded suspicious individuals.

The NAPCSP's Committee on Enforcement turned its attention to the streetwalker, the call girl, the resident of upstairs side-street hotels, the hostess in the cheap saloon, the woman at a tourist camp, and the trailer girl. What did a streetwalker or a trailer girl look like; how did the authorities decide? During wartime people, in general, were on the move and roomed wherever they could. Women often took certain jobs, even in "saloons," so they could be near husbands or while they waited for a factory position to open up. Sometimes they even went for a walk and garnered the attention of authorities. Recall Frank Yerby's short story in which officials stopped a black woman walking with her serviceman-husband and demanded to see her health card. While race, as we have seen, was certainly a significant factor in who got stopped and questioned by the authorities, the widespread characterization of women, regardless of age, class, and ethnicity, as both sexually aggressive and potentially diseased theoretically allowed suspicion to fall on any woman, especially, but not limited to, those in the company of a serviceman or those in the vicinity of military establishments. What we see here is what Donna Haraway refers to as a "hardening of the category—*woman*—as always already potentially promiscuous."[18]

Men, especially servicemen, were not censured for their activities. "Whenever a soldier, sailor, or marine is found infected with a venereal disease, he is required to report the source of his infection to his VD control officer."[19] As (innocent?) victim, if he named his contact, he incurred no penalty. And if a (male) patron was discovered in a room with a "prostitute," he could make a statement and go on his way. It was not necessary for a man to testify in court in order for a woman to be charged with practicing prostitution; needless to say, this double standard privileged men. As well, the authorities claimed that businessmen such as hotel and tavern owners may have been unaware of what took place on their premises, essentially leaving them blameless. A woman, however, could be arrested "on suspicion of" by any law enforcement official as well as by an anonymous citizen making a complaint. And according to the authorities, any woman named twice as a venereal disease contact "must be stopped," for "she is more dangerous to the community than *a mad dog.*"[20]

"A National Scandal"

Problem girls seemed to be everywhere, according to J. Edgar Hoover. He claimed: "As a nation we have failed to realize the seriousness of the increase in youthful crime since the outbreak of the war. Here is a problem that is approaching a national scandal."[21] When the FBI released arrest statistics for 1942, Hoover announced that "the number of arrests of girls under 21 had increased 55.7% over 1941."[22] This figure was reported in numerous national and local newspapers, adding fuel to the fires of suspicion around wartime women. The FBI further revealed that the percentage of girls under twenty-one arrested for certain offenses showed the following increases in 1942 compared with 1941: prostitution and commercialized vice, 65 percent; other sex offenses, 105 percent; drunkenness, 40 percent; disorderly conduct, 70 percent; and vagrancy, 125 percent.[23] FBI statistics included only those women who had been arrested and fingerprinted; numerous others had been caught in the official net but were not part of these records. One must question these statistics. Did more girls and women commit crimes, or did the definition of crime expand? At this point, the latter seems to be the case.

In 1944, Mr. Pennington of the FBI, writing about female sexual promiscuity, reported that arrests for offenses against common decency showed the following increases from the previous year: for girls under twenty-one, 57 percent; for girls under nineteen, 53 percent; and for girls under eighteen, 54 percent.[24] Also during 1943, arrests of girls under twenty-one for prostitution and commercialized vice increased 75 percent. Additional statistics indicated increases of 52 percent for other sex offenses, 67 percent for disorderly conduct, 30 percent for drunkenness, and 60 percent for vagrancy.[25] Between 1940 and 1942, according to statistics released by the Children's Bureau, 25,856 girls appeared in court charged with juvenile delinquency, an increase of approximately 38 percent.

While the number of white girls was two times greater than that of black girls, "Negro children" appeared more frequently in relation to their number in the population.[26] As we have seen, women of color automatically aroused suspicion; however, the records indicate that many white women, primarily of the working class, lost race privilege.[27] The Children's Division of the Domestic Relations Court in New York City reported a 65 percent increase in charges of female juvenile delinquency in the first five months of 1943.[28] The OWI noted that while statistics could be misleading, the incidences of juvenile delinquency could be higher as well as lower than the reported numbers noted. "Expert analysts therefore caution the layman against relying altogether on statistics. But policemen on the beat and judges on the bench also warned the layman against dismissing statistics as of no importance."[29] Regardless of whether these reported numbers were higher or lower than the actual rate of arrests and court appearances, the numbers still indicate that unusually large numbers of girls and women were being drawn into legal and law enforcement systems.

Wartime Repression of Women

In spite of the richness of the primary sources documenting the repression campaign, they have significant limitations. The records speak with a hegemonic male voice. In general they lie in the realm of the specular. Women are described and interpreted by officials; they seldom get to speak for themselves. The following accounts of the campaign in one city in Texas and two in Louisiana are taken from official forms filled out by the women discussed below. These are rare recorded examples of women's own voices, and in many cases their voices were ignored by the authorities. In combination with other statistical accounts, including those from other areas of the United States, we see clearly the magnitude of the wartime campaign to control female sexuality.

In 1942, the SPD, with the cooperation of welfare and police officials, engaged in repression campaigns in Corpus Christi, Texas, and in Leesville and New Orleans, Louisiana. Along with numerous towns and cities across the United States, these cities served as sites of intense surveillance, places where the SPD conducted studies of the problems of promiscuity and prostitution. In Corpus Christi and Leesville, the authorities kept relatively detailed records, including (in some cases) occupations of women arrested.

In Corpus Christi, Texas, fourteen women arrested or apprehended on morals charges were part of a study in which they were required to fill out information forms. With regard to occupation, the group consisted of five prostitutes, one typist-riveter, three cafe workers, one domestic, one bookkeeper, and three women with no occupation.[30] While most of the existing records do not give a racial breakdown, the fourteen women in the Corpus Christi study were categorized by race. The group included ten white, two Mexican, and two Spanish American women. The ten white women came from six other states, while the nonwhite women had been residing in Texas.[31] The white women had the highest level of schooling; the Mexican women had the lowest. The ages of the women ranged from fourteen years ten months to twenty-five years, with more than half (eight) between the ages of fifteen and nineteen.[32] Of the seven women charged with prostitution, four were white, one Mexican, and two Spanish American. The investigators classified four white women and one other, not identified, as recent prostitutes and the other two as having been prostitutes for a longer period. The study also gathered statistics on marital status, age at marriage, marital status of parents, place of residence, reasons and date for leaving home (if applicable), age of "first sex experience," and "circumstances of" the first sex experience.[33] These arrests indicate some complexities of the campaign. These women held a variety of jobs; some of them, such as bookkeeper, typist, and riveter, suggest that not all of the women were necessarily from the already suspicious lower classes.

Women apprehended for or charged with morals offenses had to submit to venereal disease testing. Of the fourteen in the study, seven white women, one Mexican woman, and one Spanish American woman tested positive for gonorrhea; one white woman tested positive for syphilis; and one Mexican woman tested positive for syphilis and gonorrhea. One white woman tested negative, and for one white woman the results were not available. In the category "Sex Activity," in addition to seven "prostitutes," two white women were classified under "promiscuous," one white woman under "casual," one white woman and one Mexican woman under "limited," one white woman under "none," and one white woman under "not classified."[34] The women studied by Corpus Christi authorities were held in places such as the Corpus Christi Girls' Club, city and county jails, and the Children's Shelter.

Under what circumstances were these young women picked up by the authorities? Unnamed officials apprehended two of the youngest, ages fourteen and sixteen, at a hotel while in the company of two sailors. Perhaps the sixteen-year-old who had been arrested and jailed earlier in the summer was recognized. At that time she had run away from the Home of the Good Shepherd in San Antonio and had come to Corpus Christi in order to distance herself from her family. When welfare caseworkers arranged to send her back to Good Shepherd, she ran away again and returned to Corpus Christi. She quickly married a civilian to prevent the authorities from returning her to her hometown. This young woman informed the social worker that she had come to Texas to get away from unwelcome sexual advances on the part of her father. The younger woman had a similar history, including sexual abuse by a family member; this was her motivation for running away from Michigan to Texas. Both of these young women tested positive for gonorrhea. The younger one, who had informed the welfare interviewer that she had been sexually abused at age eight and more recently (also by a family member), was described in the following manner by the caseworker: "Denies prostitution . . . claims no sex experiences during period she was traveling to Texas . . . says she was not in Princess Louise Hotel long enough to be involved in intercourse." The interviewer stated that the young woman's story was "not true as she has recently contracted gonorrhea."[35] Even given the climate of the times, the social workers' assessments of the young women seem harsh. Moreover, the girls' allegations of sexual abuse by family members seem worthy of, if not sympathy, at least some investigation. Was it not possible that the young women contracted gonorrhea at home? Surely these girls needed some protection. As usual, no information was secured regarding the venereal disease status of the navy men in whose company they were apprehended, nor were any questions raised regarding the sailors' association with such young girls. Here we see evidence that men's sexual prerogatives permitted continuing abuse of these and many other young women.

Only in rare instances did an official figure speak to the issue of underage girls. Mr. Morrissey, president of the International Police Chiefs Association and a traveling delegate for the SPD, reported that during his recent travels he found that "it is a general opinion of the police throughout the country that something should be done from the army standpoint in controlling the companionship of their personnel with that of teen-age girls." Morrissey had recommended a joint community-military effort to establish policies for detaining servicemen who consorted with underage girls. Personally, Morrissey felt that it should not be "so easy for members of the military personnel to come into a community and have contacts with the teen-age girls and then be free to go their way unmolested." He felt that they should be prosecuted.[36] As noted previously, servicemen were consistently sent on their way and were not forced to undergo venereal disease testing, which indeed might have raised questions of who gave what to whom.

Many of the girls and young women arrested or apprehended to-tally lacked basic knowledge about sexual issues; others had too much knowledge, having been sexually abused at an early age. In this case, and in many others, the authorities acted in ways that silenced women's voices. They changed the women's self-definitions—or imposed other definitions—and incarcerated the women in a variety of penal institutions. What does *protection* mean here? Who (or what) is being protected?

In Leesville, Louisiana, women who were suspected of prostitution or promiscuity could be arrested on a variety of charges, including vagrancy, loitering, lewdness, public nuisance, disturbing the peace, and "on suspicion." One suspect, Mrs. A, was picked up while eating lunch alone. Mrs. A was a twenty-nine-year-old white woman who worked as a waitress. On the day she was arrested, she did not lunch at her place of employment but stopped to eat on her way home from work. Mrs. A said that she "only had sex with her husband." Charged with vagrancy (for dining alone?), she remained in jail for seven days until the local health department convinced her to commit herself voluntarily to the isolation hospital. Mrs. A had, however, tested negative for venereal disease.[37] As we have already seen, waitressing was "marked" employment and may have sparked suspicion regarding Mrs. A, the assumption being that she was waiting for a man. For example, out of 709 women arrested in a two-month period in the Southwest, more than 600 were waitresses.[38]

Mrs. A was not the only venereal disease-free woman whom the authorities deemed suspicious. The authorities also apprehended an eighteen-year-old white woman, B; charged her with prostitution; and confined her to the Leesville jail. She, too, signed a form requesting "voluntary" admission to the isolation hospital, but the tests indicated that she was not infected. At the time of her encounter with the law she was, with her parents' approval, working for and boarding with a friend of the family. Contrary to most official assessments of family structure, B's family was deemed stable; this did not, however, keep the family from being subjected to an expert diagnosis. Although the social worker said that B and her mother related well and that her mother was tender and protective toward her, the family's attitude toward sex was called "prudish." "If competent psychiatric service were available," the social worker said, "the client and her parents could profit by treatment for a period of a year or so."[39]

B, uninformed regarding sexual matters, was not an anomaly, but rather exactly like many other young women of the era. When she was picked up by the police and "questioned," B signed a confession and admitted to "acts of perversion." The interviewer stated that while B admitted promiscuity, "it is evident that she is ignorant of the nature of the acts to which she confessed." Since this young woman did not have venereal disease, she was released from the hospital. However, her case was turned back to the police because of the confession, and she still had to appear in court. The mother then met with the SPD representative, who advised her to "get competent assistance to follow up on the matter of the daughter's confession and to get it off the record *if it proves to be false.*"[40]

Several major contradictions and problems are evident here. The confession raises at best a lack of sensitivity for a clearly naive young woman and at worst coercion, entrapment, or other equally dubious methods of interrogation. Next, the social worker said the young woman came from a stable family, a normative family, but faulted the family for sexual prudishness. But reticence about sexual matters was fairly common in families of that time. Finally, the cavalier attitude of the SPD official belies any notion of protecting young women. Such attitudes and practices were pervasive in the official records.

C, a twenty-six-year-old black woman diagnosed as syphilitic, admitted to a previous bout with the disease. She contended that she had gotten it the first time from her first husband and this dose was from her second husband, a soldier, whose whereabouts were unknown to her. It is evident from their notes that the interviewers suspected her veracity. For example, they ended many comments with "she says" and then proceeded to ignore her replies and make their "expert" diagnosis. On the intake form, which contained no information to support this claim, C was termed a chronic alcoholic who had been emotionally disturbed since her admission to the hospital. Under the circumstances, being upset seems reasonable. One interviewer wrote that she believed that "the client entered into promiscuity much earlier than she admits." Nowhere on the form was C's marital status recognized with the title "Mrs."; nor is there indication that she admitted to promiscuity. The social worker suggested that rehabilitation would be a lengthy process and require extensive supervision.[41] Here we see a harsh diagnosis based, at least in part, on race. The treatment diagnosis is code for institutionalization, possibly for an indefinite term (a common practice at the time).

D entered the hospital voluntarily, having discovered that she had gonorrhea when she applied for a food handler's card. She was divorced and had one child and was very resistant to the charges of promiscuity. While admitting that she had sexual relations with two men, D refused to discuss her sex history to the extent that the social workers demanded. D was described as well dressed, well groomed, and self-assured. Her resistance to becoming a subject for study did not sit well with the authorities. Even though D had acted responsibly when she discovered her infection and came to get treatment, she was perceived as a subject to be controlled; the social worker claimed that D needed not only medical treatment but also additional treatment, most likely psychological.[42] D became very concerned, with good reason, that if she were to become caught in the system, her relationship with her child would be jeopardized. How many women may have neglected or avoided treatment for venereal disease if they thought the process would far exceed medical treatment for a disease?

E was picked up by state troopers on a charge of drunkenness. She listed no regular occupation on the social agency intake form, but "Prostitute" was typed by the social worker in the blank space. E, who lived locally, was known to the authorities, since her family belonged to a commune (in the utopian tradition) formed at the beginning of the century. According to the authorities, "[F]ree love was an accepted pattern in the early days of the colony and sex relations are still easy." The colony had also fallen on hard times economically, and many residents had received government relief. Many welfare recipients, then as now, were perceived as irresponsible and morally suspect; they signified potential trouble to government officials. Official attitudes become clear in a social worker's notes; she wrote that E's mother "worked at a disreputable place" and that therefore she and her daughters "are probably delinquent."[43] As we saw in chapter 3, the concept of inherited degeneracy applied to persons of the lower classes and signified a propensity for sexual delinquency.

Charles P. Taft summarized the Leesville study in a few words at a meeting of the Interdepartmental Committee on September 18, 1942. He reported that out of thirty-five subjects there were five or six professional prostitutes and eight or ten army wives who were "subnormal mentally" but that most of the others being "quite eligible for defense jobs."[44] There had been talk about job training for some of the women apprehended by the morals squad; in practice, not many women got this opportunity. In any case, as we have seen, defense work did not necessarily preclude an encounter with the morals squad, and official figures often correlated mental deficiency with promiscuity.

After Leesville, the SPD investigation moved on to New Orleans. New Orleans had two detention centers for women: Parish Prison, primarily for white women, and the House of Detention, for black women.[45] At the time of the New Orleans study, a small group held at each facility came under consideration for "redirection"—that is, rehabilitation. At Parish Prison, out of twenty-nine women, including twenty-four whites, four "Negroes," and one "Indian," the Travelers Aid Society, the agency in charge of redirection, chose thirteen women, all white, to participate in the group slated for redirection. Thirty-four black women were held at the House of Detention, overseen by the Family Service Society; fourteen were accepted for redirection.

While the New Orleans study focused on sixty-three women, a larger number had been detained.[46] According to an SPD "Report on the Repression Problem," a sizable percentage of the women held at the House of Detention were employed as domestics, more white women than black women were listed as prostitutes, and seven white women were identified as hostesses or "B" girls. Other occupations included barmaids, waitresses, cooks, laundresses, and dishwashers, as well as six factory workers and three farm workers. Discussing an increase in women admitted for venereal disease treatment between 1942 and 1943 in New Orleans, the report noted that "though no particular reason can be stated for this trend line, intensity of police pick-ups and greater efficiency in case holding and case finding should be mentioned as possible causative factors." In 1942, 157 white women and 725 black women had been admitted for venereal disease treatment. The following year, 298 white women and 845 black women were admitted. A venereal disease examination was required for all women apprehended by the New Orleans police. Those found infected were detained for treatment in a temporary isolation facility at either Parish Prison or the House of Detention. Depending upon the charge placed against the women, they stood trial after their release from quarantine; court penalties varied.[47]

Summarizing these cases, we see that they illuminate some of the preconceived notions regarding class and race that provided a rationale for apprehending lower-class women and women of color, as well as a more general rationale that rested on sex/gender stereotypes. Women who worked as waitresses were automatically suspected of immorality; many other women who were arrested in Leesville (and elsewhere) worked in some type of establishment that served food.[48] Wartime women who lived outside the normative nuclear family were also suspicious, but normativity did not necessarily provide protection. Regardless of their own explanations, there was a significant lack of consideration for women and girls who tested positive for venereal disease. Wartime women were, indeed, perceived as promiscuous and therefore reservoirs of disease. The arrests of nonwhite women in occupations such as nursing, industry, and carpentry strongly suggest suspicion based on race, since these jobs were not automatically included in the highly suspect categories. In fact, it is difficult to determine just what made a woman suspicious beyond her sex/gender, although suspicion was intensified by race, ethnicity, and class distinctions. All across the United States, as women continued to do their part, the authorities continued to monitor their activities, and more women ran afoul of the law. What began as a request that local authorities "do something" about female promiscuity took on a life of its own. In cities across the United States, tens of thousands of women spent time in penal institutions. The campaign to protect national health against debilitating venereal diseases through the repression of prostitution had evolved into a widespread effort to control female sexuality in general.

Some Consequences of Repression

When Eliot Ness and Katherine Lenroot communicated with each other about the "girl problem" in Rapid City, South Dakota, they discussed the response of local officials. Local law enforcement authorities had appointed two more policewomen to patrol streets, taverns, and places of commercial entertainment. In one month the police apprehended or arrested thirty girls. At the same time, the local army base dealt with the male venereal disease problem by opening a twenty-four-hour prophylactic station.[49] An officer of the court summed up the prevalent attitude that circulated around women who were trapped in the regulatory regime. "Certainly," he said, "one who is charged with soliciting to prostitution and one of lewd and lascivious character is one who may first be suspected of carrying such a dreadful affliction. It is most reasonable to suspect that [such persons] if carrying on the practice of prostitution are indiscriminate and promiscuous in their bodily contacts and are natural subjects and carriers of venereal disease."[50] Such attitudes and policies kept the spotlight of suspicion on women and girls, who were represented as sex delinquents and who therefore had to be kept under surveillance. As a result, law enforcement officials could and did take women off the streets at night, kept an eye on women and girls at dance halls, and defined many women in restaurants, cafes, taverns, and cocktail lounges as promiscuous girls—that is, those seeking servicemen, the so-called wrong type of girl. An unaccompanied girl getting on a hotel elevator could be questioned by the police. And any teenage girl whom the police decided was "in danger of falling into vice" could be apprehended.

In Providence, Rhode Island, the SPD convinced hotel owners to use house detectives to watch for suspicious women.[51] In Boise, Idaho, the police made periodic checks on places of commercial entertainment, and "any girl seen out with a number of different soldiers in the same night is watched and if the appearance is in any way suspicious she is booked on a vagrancy charge and detained for a physical exam."[52] Women charged with vagrancy in Boise received sentences of thirty days in jail whether or not they had venereal disease. By 1944, suspicion had reached such a point that a South Carolina police chief decided to institute a program of "close supervision of high-school dances" to prevent female sexual delinquency.[53]

The campaign had clearly escaped the bounds of repressing prostitution, as government agents were continuously searching for so-called promiscuous women. When a Chicago policeman came across a young woman asleep in a train station, he woke her with a firm rapping on the soles of her shoes. "He then grabbed her by the arm and dragged her along," saying, "you girls waiting for our boys, making a few bucks for a few minutes." In fact the young woman was the wife of a soldier, and she was on her way to join him in California. She was detained in Chicago when her train was requisitioned by the military. With no information regarding when the next train would arrive, she settled down to wait. After long hours in the waiting room, she gathered her suitcases as close as possible, put her handbag behind her head, and gave in to fatigue. When the policeman asked what she was doing, she tried to explain, but her lack of luggage raised his suspicions. Despite her protestations that the suitcases had been stolen as she slept, she was taken to the police station and questioned by the sergeant; ultimately he instructed the policeman to return her to the train station.[54] This young wife was fortunate that she was not, as so many others were, held and subjected to venereal disease testing. At this point surveillance was being directed at many young women who never expected to have encounters with law enforcement officials.

The notion that women were a potential threat to the war effort led the authorities to expand categories of deviance, creating, for example, the so-called unpaid prostitute. In this manner, many more women referred to as pickups, good-time girls, amateurs, and so on, who were, according to the authorities, still causing so much trouble, became subject to arrest and other legalistic interventions. As one commentator put it: "A much more difficult problem than the out and out professional prostitute is that of the promiscuous girl, the khaki-wacky and the girl who has become unbalanced by wartime wages and freedom. This type of girl has become as dangerous a carrier of venereal disease as the professional." "Following them," the authorities claimed, "is a public health function."[55] Such women, when named as venereal disease contacts, received a visit from a male health investigator. This investigator, working on the assumption that "the less force the better the compliance," called on the girls "with a story." The story neglected to tell them that they had been named as contacts (i.e., the source of the disease) but rather implied that they had been "in contact with a case of infectious disease."[56] This approach, intended to ensure that the women reported for an examination, was problematic on several levels. Public health officers wore uniforms, they often contacted women at their place of employment, and they misrepresented their intent. Imagine, if you will, the effects of such visits on the young women of the war years. Moreover, official investigations of women named as contacts were based on a premise that the women did transmit the venereal disease. Once women had been identified as vectors of transmission by the authorities, little or no attention was given to their risk of infection from diseased or promiscuous men. On the basis of scant information, official investigators frequently attempted to locate a specific woman: for example, one soldier gave a vague description of a girl named Betty he met in a bar. The authorities claimed to be successful in tracking down women identified in this manner.[57] Numerous women were stigmatized by such procedures. But if some women were always already unclean, then protecting their reputations had no place in the wartime plan.

Transgressing women and girls, as we have seen, were punished in numerous ways. They were diagnosed as mentally incompetent, jailed, quarantined, hospitalized, held for testing, turned over to social workers, and in general kept under surveillance. Many women incarcerated at the quarantine camps in South Carolina had been arrested on charges of loitering, disorderly conduct, drunkenness, and prostitution. A camp social worker stated that "many times such charges were placed in order to apprehend and hold girls for a health examination." The women were held in jail until the test results were received; those requiring treatment for venereal diseases were sent to the quarantine hospitals. As an "economy gesture," many women who were awaiting treatment remained in a central jail until there were enough of them "to make a load" to transport to the hospital.[58]

Upon arrival, the women were required to supply medical and other pertinent data to a record analyst and then be examined by a medical doctor. "Only a few rules applied," according to the social worker. But, in fact, numerous rules existed regarding matters such as bedtime and wake-up time, as well as restrictions on how far one could move about the grounds. The authorities censored incoming and outgoing phone calls; calls required permission. They opened all mail, removed money or checks, and credited them to the patients' accounts. Visitors were allowed only on Sundays, and then for only ten minutes. As discussed in a prior chapter, where women were segregated by race, the camp for white women was more conveniently located and in much better condition than the one for black women. White women had a recreational program; black women did not. Women were punished by confinement in the guardhouse for bad behavior such as quarreling, cursing, rejecting medical treatment, or refusing to accept work assignments. Leaving the hospital without permission generally resulted in indefinite detention in the county jail. Some of these women received industrial training; they were then pressured to complete the training and accept jobs as a patriotic duty.[59]

In El Paso, Texas, women arrested on morals charges were first held in the city jail. Due to inadequate facilities they were transferred to the county jail for diagnosis and treatment; convicted prostitutes received maximum sentences and served their time in the county jail.[60] The Civilian Military Council in Little Rock, Arkansas, conducted a study of local laws to reinforce their repression program. They found two laws, "one which made it possible to send delinquent girls under eighteen to an Industrial School" and another by which "women over eighteen . . . convicted of prostitution may be given a sentence of up to three years at the State Farm."[61]

The idea of holding women in some type of official establishment was not restricted to those who could be charged with a crime or held for venereal disease treatment. The SPD applied to the FSA for funds to "operate so-called 'service centers,' that would offer wholesome living conditions" to young women. Theoretically not places of legal deten-tion, they nonetheless provided a place to detain young women "inno-cently involved in a vice drive" and "pending return to their homes or other solutions to their problems."[62] Innocent, but clearly not free to depart if diagnosed as having psychological problems, they became sub-jects to be studied. One can see this mind-set at work in the formation of a Social Hygiene Woman's Court in San Francisco, California, in 1943. The court, located in the Health Center Building, had been estab-lished "to meet the problem of the professional prostitute, streetwalker and other sexually promiscuous women."[63] One of the objectives of the court was to "render an entirely *individualized* case study plan . . . with every effort made to refer first offenders who present a potentiality of reeducation and readjustment."[64]

"We all know," one official noted, "that too many girls who are more in need of help than of punishment are being arrested and placed in jail pending hearing. Too many girls who would benefit by sympa-thetic and understanding cooperation on the part of the local social agencies in working out plans with them are being sent to correctional institutions or sentenced to county jails and to the State Prison sys-tem."[65] While such paternalistic attitudes questioned the practice of sen-tencing women to jail or prison, they did not question the widespread use of morals charges against wartime women. With few exceptions, the authorities accepted the idea that wartime women and girls were sexu-ally promiscuous; they differed on where they should be incarcerated and who should be in charge.

In mid-1943, Marjorie Bell, a law enforcement official, addressed the National Probation Association, discussing the problem of the young girl camp follower. Many of these young women, she said, were "inex-perienced, provincial youngsters rapidly drawn into a life of prostitu-tion, beginning in careless and casual yielding to the glamour of the uni-form." She then pointed out that many of these "children" were being "indiscriminately held in many city and county jails with older women, chiefly prostitutes, a practice universally condemned, but widely practiced." Bell concluded her presentation by noting that a jail inspector for the Federal Bureau of Prisons had said that "their number runs into the *tens of thousands* annually," giving a strong indication of the immensity of campaign to repress prostitution.[66]

A more common official attitude toward prostitution, and I would argue promiscuity, emerged clearly in an article by a Los Angeles judge. "In these days all thinking begins and ends with the war," he wrote. "Few people are aware of the many subjects over which the Federal Security Agency has assumed jurisdiction, or that the elimination of prostitution is one of them." He said that during the national emergency redemption, rehabilitation, and probation were no longer options when dealing with prostitutes. Contending, moreover, that "the war has brought new and serious implications to the problem of prostitution," he noted that at meetings of judges, prosecutors, and police officials, sponsored by federal officials, it had been suggested "that unless vice-law offenders are vigorously prosecuted and punished by local authorities, an alternative may be found in the establishment of martial law."[67] The federal government asked state judges to impose maximum sentences in prostitution cases, harsh punishment being seen as a deterrent to crime. The judge quoted part of a letter he had received from Edwin James Cooley (SPD). Cooley had written that it was not enough to confine only infected prostitutes, since all prostitutes become infected. Releasing them, Cooley said, would produce "a future and certain disease menace to the community."[68] In practice, as we have seen, such penalties were not limited to prostitutes but were applied to a much broader segment of the female population.[69] SPD statistics indicated that during a six-month period approximately 7,500 women and girls had been arrested in fifteen states on charges of prostitution or on more general morals charges.[70] Although we will probably never know just how many women were arrested, apprehended, incarcerated, or unjustly accused, these partial numbers give us another clue to the vast scale of the repression effort.

Resistance and Rebellion

Wartime women resisted, in a variety of ways, the imposition of pejorative labels and the constraints imposed on their sexual and geographic mobility. Some women caught in the net of repression protested through the legal system. In 1943, a woman arrested and convicted for prostitution and found to have a venereal disease was quarantined in the health center maintained by the U.S. government at Hot Springs, Arkansas. "She filed a petition for a writ of habeas corpus, contending that the ordinances authorizing her detention were unconstitutional and void."[71] The trial court granted the writ, but the defendants—the city of Little Rock, the city health officer, and the county sheriff—appealed to the Supreme Court of Arkansas. The supreme court reversed the judgment and remanded the plaintiff to the custody of the sheriff for isolation and quarantine.

In November 1943, a case concerning two women who had filed a petition for a writ of habeas corpus reached the Supreme Court of Illinois.[72] The women had been arrested on charges of prostitution and jailed in East St. Louis on March 8, 1943. The following day the authorities filed complaints "charging that each willfully and unlawfully solicited to prostitution and willfully and unlawfully was a lewd and lascivious person in speech and character." The women were held for examination at the clinic, without bail, since, according to the judge, "It appeared that each of the petitioners may be suffering from a communicable venereal disease." While the women did not challenge the charge of prostitution, they refused to be examined "on the grounds that it was an invasion of their rights and contrary to the constitutions and statutes of the United States and the State of Illinois."[73]

On March 9, the women filed a writ of habeas corpus in the city court, but since the court held that the offense was not bailable they were returned to the custody of the chief of police. The following day the petition was filed in the circuit court, but the petition was denied. The court decreed that the women had to remain in custody until they submitted to an examination for venereal disease.[74] If they were found free from disease, bail would be set. On March 14, however, the petition was again filed and accepted in the Supreme Court of Illinois. Bail was set at $1,000 each; the women paid and were released. When the case was heard, the supreme court based its decision, in part, on public health precedents. "It has almost universally been held in this country that constitutional guarantees must yield to the enforcement of the statutes and ordinances designed to promote the public health as part of the police powers of the State. That the statute in question is a measure enacted within the police power of the State of Illinois is unquestioned."

Drawing on numerous legal arguments and on similar cases, the court concluded: "[T]he petition for discharge under the writ of habeus corpus will be denied and the petitioners remanded to the custody of the chief of police of the city of East St. Louis until they submit to an examination under the provisions of Section Four."[75] Similar decisions had been made by the supreme courts of the states of Washington and Ohio.[76]

In other instances prostitutes protested directly and publicly against the repression campaign. As Eliot Ness traveled throughout the United States speaking about the necessity to stamp out prostitution, he met with resistance from many quarters. In Peoria, Illinois, a group of prostitutes and their supporters picketed a Ness speaking engagement. They "rallied around the site of an anticrime speech by Ness . . . harassing the audience and displaying signs decrying Ness's actions as an affront to their personal liberties."[77] Prostitutes in Waikiki, Hawaii, went on strike in the summer of 1942 to protest police interference with their right to do business in the city. The women received support from the military, who supported Hawaii's system of regulated prostitution because their troops had a very low rate of venereal disease.[78]

The SPD was active in Puerto Rico, where many women escaped from extreme poverty by filling the demand from soldiers and sailors for sexual services. In May 1944, a group of women quarantined for venereal disease escaped from Troche Venereal Disease Hospital. A memo regarding this incident reads: "This must have been quite a sight—105 pajama clad women being chased through the rain by quagas and taxicabs. Dr. Quintero tells me, however, that 75 women returned of their own accord afoot."[79] A clipping from the *Puerto Rico World Journal*, Tuesday, May 30, 1944, entitled "Alleged VD Escapees Are Rounded Up," claimed that the "police succeeded in rounding up 96 women of the 105 who broke out of the Troche Venereal Disease Hospital two kilometers from here (Caguas) during torrential rains this afternoon (May 29). Nine wearing the hospital uniform are still at large. Police and hospital employees gave chase in buses and private automobiles."[80]

A venereal disease hospital in the Virgin Islands claimed to have suffered similar difficulties. The Department of Health reported that not only were most of the patients uncooperative but also "ten patients tried at one time or another to escape and we had to have the whole hospital wired like a hen house." Dr. Knudsen, the health commissioner, noted that the closing of the hospital had been "a happy event to all . . .

for the strain of keeping tabs on all those *lusty fleas* was almost more than human endurance can bear."[81]

While most women in positions of authority supported the repression campaign and all its ramifications, Eleanor Roosevelt spoke to the situation in a different vein. She described venereal disease as an ever-present problem, not just a wartime problem, and argued that "the real roots of the problem lie in the fact that we do not face our community conditions." Mrs. Roosevelt called for increased community services and for information. "I think it is a woman's business," she said, "to see that from age sixteen on there are no people who really are lacking in knowledge about sexual matters." Knowledge, according to Eleanor Roosevelt, was critical; "getting caught in something because she doesn't know the facts" would be most devastating to a young woman. She might not be able to see a way out, and then a bad situation would only get worse. Mrs. Roosevelt concluded by saying that "it is a real indictment of our intelligence when we let ignorance bring about an increase in venereal disease."[82] Eleanor Roosevelt represented a singular resistant voice in the campaign as she tried to turn the discussion in a direction that was not completely focused on repression of female sexuality. During the war years, women and girls were drawn into the public sphere; they arrived lacking the kind of knowledge that they needed to protect themselves in places already fraught with sex.

Although the records provide scant information on overt instances of resistance, it is clear that women did protest against repressive policies. Since they were fighting against the entire state apparatus, it is entirely possible that overt protests were minimal. However, as numerous women continued to claim their right to varied public spaces, they implicitly and sometimes explicitly challenged the status quo.

Imaginary Offenses

In 1947, Paul W. Tappan published a study of the New York Wayward Minor Court, examining, in particular, the years 1938 and 1942. Referring to Jeremy Bentham, he stated: "The sexual offenses now adjudicated in the Wayward Minor Court would seem to fall rather neatly into what Bentham called 'imaginary offenses.'" Such offenses, in this analysis, were defined as "acts which produce no real evil" but that were, nonetheless, regarded as offenses due to prejudice and other sociocultural factors. Tappan used Eliot Ness's definition of the sexually promiscuous girl—"not criminally motivated . . . fun-seeking . . . immature" but from a dysfunctional family—as an illustration of Bentham's thesis. Tappan discussed, among other things, the difficulty of interpreting "moral depravity" and "impending moral depravity," the great disparity in treatment by judges, a lack of clearly defined standards (for the offense one is accused of), and a lack of standard legal processing procedures. Pointing out some of the reasons for ambiguous attitudes and practices, he suggested that "sexual offenses are more liable to be misjudged by prejudice and ignorance than most other forms of criminal behavior, and bias is almost inevitable if conduct is reviewed solely in the light of narrow personal experiences and the tastes and distastes of the assessor. Sexual behavior is often assessed by persons who regard any sexual activity as perverse unless it conforms to their accustomed patterns of behavior." Tappan asserted that such factors hold true even when sociocultural norms have undergone change. Moreover, he contended that many law enforcement officials were not only "motivated by the desire to set fallen women straight" but also motivated by "the attitudes of the institutional personnel, [which] appear to be chiefly religio-moralistic and punitive-correctional." Tappan concluded that lesser offenders were often subjected to "considerably more rigorous (punitive) treatment." His analysis of women charged with sex offenses in New York is applicable to the broader repression campaign; during wartime, unknown numbers of women were charged with imaginary offenses, often based on arbitrary and ambiguous interpretations of their activities. The partial statistics that have been uncovered in this study certainly point to excessively punitive treatment of large numbers of so-called wayward girls and promiscuous women.[83]

The Paradox of Protection

Official statements on the functions of the SPD called for "the protection of women from sexual exploitation and the social rehabilitation of prostitutes and other sexually delinquent women."[84] Not only did the state apparatus fail to give many young women protection from sexual exploitation and abuse, but it incarcerated many young women on a variety of charges, and rehabilitation programs either did not exist or were based on classist ideas of normativity. As guardian of women's morals, officials of the state decided who was sexually delinquent and who needed social rehabilitation. Throughout the campaign there was much rhetoric devoted to protecting women; it was never clearly stated, however, exactly what the authorities meant by the terms *protection* and *rehabilitation*. Both male and female authorities claimed to include women and men under the rubric of protection, but as the campaign progressed it became clear that *protection* had a specific connotation when applied to women. In the wartime construction, *protection* meant that women required supervision, since the female nature implied disorderly conduct. Talk of protection was always accompanied by talk of detaining women, rehabilitating them, or confining and controlling them in some manner to be determined by medical and social officials. And while the authorities freely admitted that the country's jails were in deplorable condition and that only hardened prostitutes should be sent to reformatories and prisons, that was not the way the repression campaign played out.[85]

Most of the professional women who participated in the campaign came from a generation whose training, practice, and associations shaped their idea of protection.[86] Their belief in the incompatibility of marriage and career influenced their attitudes toward those wartime women who entered the nonprofessional workforce. In addition, many professional women brought definite strains of Progressive reform to their dealings with wartime women, strains that were influenced by classism and ethnocentrism. These and other factors allowed social workers, women in law enforcement and government agencies, and those active in other sectors of the state apparatus to classify numerous women, on the basis of ideologies of race, class, and ethnicity, as those "other" women—that is, as nonrespectable or as actual or potential deviants.

As women from both the public and private sectors served the state apparatus in varied ways, their notions of protection were consistent with positions that involved policing other women. For example, as one authority noted, "where public health nurses have been permitted to participate in the venereal disease case finding program, they have been successful assets."[87] Public health nurses, probably less threatening to women named as venereal disease contacts, were able to convince more women to report for examinations. Policewomen's roles centered on surveillance of other women, along with providing "clearance services [interview and investigation from both social and legal angles, medical examinations, and referral services] for all girls and women coming to the attention of or detained by, police or other law-enforcement agencies."[88] Policewomen, while still talking about preventing arrests and protecting women and girls, did not challenge the notion of females as potentially promiscuous. In New York, a squad of twenty policewomen and thirty-eight detectives "inspected midtown bars, dance halls and shabby hotels . . . tracked down runaways . . . and tried to get young girls out of shady places." Divided into groups of three, two detectives and one policewoman, they looked for a "girl drinking with, or in the company of, a man in a place where she should not be." The detectives interviewed the man, and "the policewoman took aside the girl and questioned her." If they told different stories, the girl was taken to the nearest police station.[89] While professional women undoubtedly acted with sincere motives, they nonetheless cooperated with the state and reinforced the double standard and the notion that for girls there were definitely forbidden spaces.

Club women, many of whom had supported the fight against syphilis that began in the late 1930s, were also recruited into the wartime repression campaign.[90] "While our boys are fighting on the battlefields in all parts of the world, disease and prostitution are depleting the strength of our army at home," wrote President Whitehurst of the General Federation of Women's Clubs in 1943. She discussed letters that the federation received from both women (mothers and wives) and other persons supporting the organization's intention "to develop public opinion against the conditions now existing" with regard to prostitution.[91] But as we have seen, the term *prostitution* applied to a broad range of female behaviors.

Male officials turned to the NWACSP when they needed supportive female voices. McNutt, Taft, and Ness spoke frequently about the assistance that women could provide to marshal public opinion in favor of the repression program. At the June 1943 meeting, Taft requested the council members to speak out in order to combat attitudes such as those recently voiced by the National Association of Broadcasters. The newspeople were, Taft claimed, "scared to death of anything regarding venereal disease and prostitution" as material for national broadcasting. When Mr. Ness asked the reason for this, the broadcasters replied: "[B]ecause the women of this country won't stand for it." Taft urged the women to be public in their support of the SPD's work in order to overcome such mistaken beliefs. He called the current prostitution problem an epidemic and reminded the women of the perils of regulated prostitution. Taft elaborated on the need to restrict prostitutes, whom he claimed serviced twenty-five to seventy men in a day. Taft also stressed the importance of cooperation with the police and other government officials.[92] The NWACSP was rarely invoked apart from times like these, when upper-class women's voices were needed to speak in support of repression. In Taft's speech, with the exception of the usual charges made against prostitutes, the language used to describe other women was less harsh than usual. Taft appealed to the notion of protection, often voiced by NWACSP women, and used an example of a group of girls at one of the quarantine hospitals to "give some kind of idea" regarding the problem of promiscuous women. He described about half of the thirty-five women who had been interviewed while under quarantine as "young and completely inexperienced—girls who found themselves caught in this kind of thing" and were anxious to get out.[93] The state apparatus needed all the support it could get to justify the campaign against not only prostitution but also female promiscuity. Since many club women, along with policewomen such as Captain Millikin, had been involved in various reform endeavors over time, he fashioned an argument that would appeal to the women attending the conference.

Eleanor Roosevelt addressed the gathering, speaking, as usual, in resistance to the dominant position on venereal disease and women. But voices such as Eleanor Roosevelt's were seldom heeded, as is evident in the topic discussed by the next speaker. Miss Castendyck of the Children's Bureau immediately returned to the problem of the "promiscuous girl." She spoke of the increase in female delinquency among teenage girls, suggesting that the problem was exacerbated by working mothers and calling for a community effort to provide a supplement for the attention, affection, and security absent from such homes. Castendyck contended that while "one does not want to exploit the war," it did provide an "opportunity to bring home to the country that the basis of juvenile delinquency lies in our family life, and in the quality of our community housekeeping and standards."[94] The contrast between Eleanor Roosevelt's position and that of Castendyck is representative of a persistent tendency on the part of many women of the professional class, like their Progressive Era counterparts, to fail to understand or to overlook the exigencies of wartime. Women, as we know, were urged to take war work; without their participation war production would not have been adequate to the task at hand. In fact, the United States considered drafting women for war work if enough women did not respond. Yet Castendyck and other professional women continued to lay the alleged rise in juvenile delinquency at the doors of working mothers and to insist that female sexual delinquency was a massive problem. In addition, by mid-1944, women's magazines featured numerous articles on juvenile delinquency, with warnings to mothers, especially working mothers.[95] As the war came closer to ending, many wartime women received frequent reminders that their service was "for the duration." But for the women caught up in the morals campaign, the end was not necessarily in sight.

One commentator summed up the wartime campaign by noting that "apparently the crusaders against venereal disease suffer from a peculiar form of one-eyed sight." He marveled at their accuracy in tracing infection to women and girls and was astounded that they ignored the male half of the equation. Referring to the crusaders as "blind vice reformers" who were incited to action by the idea of irresponsible, diseased girls, he chastised them for failing to apply the same standards to men. "Girls," he said, "have to be chased, arrested, sentenced, reformed. Men simply have to be cured, warned, handed a prophylactic kit or a sermon."[96] He summed up the campaign quite well.

Even as the war neared conclusion, the SPD maintained a focus on sexually dangerous women. Once again thousands of copies of the booklet *She Looked Clean . . . But* were distributed to taxicab companies, individual drivers, and hotel managers.[97] The constant repetition of sexualized terms, as well as the message that female appearance could be deceiving, reinforced a negative attitude toward wartime women. As more and more women continued to move beyond their traditionally assigned roles and spaces, such departures from the norm inevitably kept alive the myth of women as sexually dangerous. The question lingered on: Was she a patriot, prostitute, or patriotute?

7

Conclusion

> It took courage to face being misunderstood, suspected of servicing
> men rather than serving a country or a cause, and courage in com-
> ing home to people who could not or would not understand.
> —Shelley Saywell, *Women in War*

In the preceding chapters we have followed the workings of
a large-scale and multifaceted wartime campaign to control and prevent
venereal diseases in the armed forces through the repression of prostitution. By focusing on the apparatus of the state and, in particular, the
SPD during mobilization and wartime, we have also seen the unfolding
of another aspect of the campaign: an effort to both mobilize and control female sexuality in support of the war effort. In the beginning, officials of various state institutions focused on prostitutes as "cesspools of
infection" and instituted polices, including legal sanctions, to protect
the nation and the military from venereally diseased prostitutes who
could endanger national defense. Seemingly a straightforward task, the
campaign became complicated both by deeply embedded ideologies of
female and male sexuality and by issues of race, class, and ethnicity. As
women were called upon to do their patriotic duty, their bodies were
drafted in support of the war effort. But in sexualizing female bodies as
simultaneously appealing to men and dangerous to men and the nation,
the campaign quickly exceeded its stated purpose. (The gendered aspect of the World War II campaign to prevent venereal disease made
women's participation in the war effort all too visible in terms of dangerous sexuality and invisible in terms of service to the nation.) A look
at the past indicates that in the midst of wartime change certain persistent notions about female sexuality adversely affected numerous wartime women.

Beginning in the late nineteenth century, perceptions of the "New

Woman's" increasing independence and potential opportunity for sexual experiences escalated already mounting concerns regarding social, political, and economic changes. Literature and motion pictures featured the vamp—a devouring woman—as a symbol for sexual danger. Psychiatry and medicine conflated the nymphomaniac, the lesbian, and the prostitute. The prostitute, the potential prostitute, and other sexually deviant women became objects to be studied. Carol Groneman contends that in these decades "commentators feared the proletarianization of sexuality": that is, they feared that middle- and upper-class women who left the confines of the home would become like working-class women, "who were perceived as inordinately lustful and sexual opportunists."[1] It was, in part, precisely this concern—that the female middle-class keepers of the prescribed male/female ideology would become sexually independent and sexually adventurous—that reemerged during the Second World War and supported the campaign against many women who participated in the war effort. An "expert" body of knowledge regarding female sexuality that had accumulated over time produced a framework that supported the World War II campaign to repress, control, and use women's sexual bodies. The mobilization of women's labor power and their sexuality, seen as crucial to the war effort, unleashed deeply embedded fears regarding female sexuality.

It is not difficult to see that trouble would follow the mobilization of female sexuality, given the powerful discourses of the sexually dangerous, potentially promiscuous, and probably diseased female individual. During the Second World War, to borrow a phrase from Susan Gubar, not only were "war" and "whore" conflated, but "whore" and "woman" were merged in the person of the patriotute.[2] Terms such as *whore, prostitute,* and *promiscuous* became code words used indiscriminately to describe numerous wartime women. Their use escalated in step with women's increasingly visible participation in the war effort. Labels, particularly of a sexual nature, are nothing new as a means of repression; representations of particular women, especially nonwhite and lower-class women, as sexually deviant have served over time as controlling images. During World War II images such as the female "booby trap" and the white, middle-class girl next door who might have "looked clean . . . but" could also harbor venereal disease broadened the pool of sexually suspect women and girls. In short order a government agent or a policeman might assume that a woman waiting in a train station was a prostitute looking for a pickup. In some instances, then, gender could trump race and class. A powerful and negative concept regarding female sexuality persisted in counterpoint to changes occurring in the wartime state.

This study has examined the paradoxes inherent in an attempt to enlist women's sexuality in support of the war effort while simultaneously trying to keep women's sexuality under control. During the Second World War the campaign to repress prostitution and to control and contain "promiscuous" female sexuality conflicted with the process of mobilizing female sexuality to fulfill male desire. This dual effort created myriad problems, both institutional and individual. One woman, in reminiscing about the war years, wrote: "[T]here is no denying that there was a new sense of freedom." She also noted that young wartime women were "having a good time . . . talking to lonely soldiers and bending a few rules now and then."[3] But another young woman felt bewildered at finding herself confined in a reformatory for something she considered her own choice—dating servicemen—rather than a crime.[4] The already blurred boundary line between acceptable and transgressive female sexuality continued to fluctuate, trapping many other women in dangerous territory. Nonetheless, the fluidity of the boundary line also opened spaces for resistance. And in many wartime accounts, one finds not only a sense of freedom and adventure but also a sense of innocence that belies the official accounts of wartime women.

Preexisting tensions in the sexual realm, exacerbated by the necessities of mobilization and ultimately of war, both added to and confused questions regarding women's "proper" place. Within the World War II militarized state, such factors not only gave rise to contradictory policies but also amplified ambiguous social attitudes toward women at a time when servicemen had a "male mystique" that valorized aggressive (hetero)sexuality. Military policies, including sex education for servicemen, free contraceptives, prophylactic stations, and support of houses of prostitution, all recognized and normalized male sexual needs and desires. The normality of women's sexual desires was, however, silenced by the framing of female desire as a psychological problem or social pathology. The equation of female desire with deviance simultaneously oversexualized and desexualized many wartime women. Silences also prevailed around other issues, such as the problem of rape, the "if not prostitutes, who" question, and the dilemmas of women experiencing intense and unwanted sexual pressures from servicemen. The refusal to address such issues or to recognize that women and girls had a right to be heard allowed the same problems to create difficulties for women and girls in the postwar years.

It was, for many reasons, extraordinarily difficult to mount any kind of organized protest to repression. One consequence of the conflation of sexual ideology with both sexual and nonsexual behavior was to obscure the validity of women's numerous contributions to the war effort. Small groups of wartime women resisted repression policies by breaking out of quarantine, going on strike, picketing, and initiating legal appeals. Less obviously, other women refused to accept imposed definitions of their sexual behaviors. And numerous women took advantage of opportunities in defense work; others joined military services, and many served as volunteer hostesses. Women made choices that not only challenged gender ideology but also continuously defended their right to remain in public spaces. The possibility of more overt protest was retarded by numerous factors. Wartime women remained divided by race, class, ethnicity, and sexual orientation. Moreover, many of the professional women who had some power and public voices were enmeshed in the state apparatus and participated on behalf of the state at a variety of levels in the repression campaign. As a result, protecting women and girls often involved punitive measures. We have seen just how difficult it could be to get out of the system once you got caught in it. Recall the girl who had no idea exactly what she was accused of and who confessed to charges of sexual perversions. She had to get a lawyer even though she was found innocent of any crime. Louisiana officials determined, without clear evidence, that Mrs. C, an African American woman, was promiscuous, a chronic alcoholic, and emotionally disturbed. She was sentenced to indeterminate rehabilitation.

The debates that occurred within the government, the military, and the larger society regarding appropriate male and female sexual behavior, sex education, contraception, and related matters were shaped not only by established conceptions of gender and sexuality but also by race-based concepts and attitudes. Racism, as we have seen, influenced interpretations of and policies toward African Americans and other women of color. Racism also ensured that nonwhite men, both civilian and military, were controlled and contained in a variety of ways, both literally and figuratively. Within the segregated military, African American men and women suffered many indignities, not the least of which emerged from race-based sexual politics. In the Caribbean military officials determined that it was acceptable for white servicemen to cohabit with Polynesian women, but black servicemen were prevented from doing so because any offspring would be, according to officials, "undesirable citizens." The women, however, had no say in the matter.

In the 1940s, especially during the war years, it would have been incredibly difficult for women to organize a formal protest against charges of sexual misconduct. Many women who were swept up by overzealous officials most likely hoped that their encounters with the long arms of the state would not become public knowledge. A critical strategy of the SPD, in particular, plus the more general apparatus of the state, was to mobilize public opinion in support of repression and control of dangerous female sexuality. In the course of this campaign, many wartime women became visible as supporters of the war effort but were simultaneously tainted by suspicion for exceeding gendered boundaries. One cannot ignore the powerful discourses that constructed some women and girls as potentially dangerous individuals and resulted in mass arrests and incarcerations. At the same time that state institutions spoke incessantly about sex/sexuality, wartime discussions of sex/sexuality involved numerous silences. For example, social workers and other authorities were unwilling to talk about or even recognize sexual abuse in families. When two young runaways, girls fourteen and sixteen years of age, were apprehended in the company of two sailors, they told the social worker that they had run away to escape sexual abuse at home. Their claims were ignored, and the authorities interpreted the fact that they both had gonorrhea as evidence of sexual promiscuity. Linda Gordon, in a study of family violence, points out the process that transformed victims of incest into sexual delinquents.[5] Silence also loomed large on the issue of rape during wartime. Beth Bailey writes about "regulatory systems" that by "controlling women made women, themselves, the controllers of sex."[6] That is, women were told that they were responsible for stopping unwanted advances. We have seen a few cases when women were able to do so, but in many cases women were indeed raped. Unfortunately, wartime statistics showing that rape increased do not include specifics, and the SPD claimed, contrary to FBI statistics, that rape had decreased. It seems likely that, given the discourse of servicemen as victims and of girls and women as responsible for sexual control, many pressured sexual encounters were not defined as rape. While the fourteen- and sixteen-year-old runaways found with the sailors were described as sexual delinquents, no mention was made of possible statutory rape.

The war years might have also marked an important transition in the precocious sexualization of adolescent girls by constructing them as potentially dangerous deviants rather than innocents in need of protection.[7] In many cases the SPD claimed that girls as young as ten years of age had been apprehended on morals charges. In 1941, when policewomen observed (prewar) conditions in expanding towns and cities, they reported that girls between ages thirteen and sixteen were involved in prostitution.[8] Precocious sexualization increased in the postwar years. Magazines featured advice columns for young girls: for example, a "sub-deb" adviser in the *Ladies' Home Journal* provided dating advice to a fourteen-year-old girl.[9] Joan Jacobs Brumberg points out that "[i]n the postwar world, the budding adolescent body was big business."[10] For example, during the early 1950s, when movie stars were notable for voluptuous breasts, young girls became concerned about their physical development. Their concerns were reinforced by the advertising and marketing of products such as prepubescent triple A bras. As the twentieth century progressed, the ages of girls used in sexualized advertising decreased.

The paradoxes inherent in women's wartime service that were based on the centrality of their sexualized bodies to their wartime roles maintained persistent stereotypical and negative discourses that exerted an influence on societal perceptions regarding women. Nonetheless, wartime women negotiated their spaces in the sociopolitical arena, albeit within these structures of power. While representations of inappropriate female bodies proliferated, many of those bodies refused to accept imposed definitions. Sexuality, as Carol Vance describes it, is "simultaneously a domain of restriction, repression, and danger as well as a domain of exploration, pleasure, and agency."[11] Wartime women were neither victims nor docile bodies; they took what was available and made it work for themselves both as individuals and as members of the larger society. Numerous women agreed to do their part to support the war effort, both by working in factories and by providing support services for the military, even though they were accused of threatening the socio-sexual system and homefront stability. Wartime women learned how to negotiate many of the obstacles placed in the paths to new experiences, learned new ways to negotiate the gender system, and gained a sense of pride that lingered after the war.

Nonetheless many scholars agree that the gender order remained intact despite a series of challenges, such as the one posed by the utilization of hundreds of thousands of women for war work, including work in heavy industry. As Leila Rupp points out, while public images were adapted to resonate with the demands of wartime, basic ideas about women's place were not challenged.[12] The complex sociopolitical campaign launched by the apparatus of the state, which operated simultaneously both to mobilize and to contain female sexuality while privileging hegemonic masculinity, shows that war and gender politics are intertwined. In and through the activities of the war state, sex/gender was defined by military needs, so that men became defined as warriors and women became defined as the good women who supported them and the bad women who could unman them. While such "techniques of power" supported the efforts to control female sexuality, they also contained, as we have seen, the possibility of dissent

Building on the work of scholars who have debated the impact of the war on women, I contend that the dual discourses of female sexual mobilization and control not only operated to mitigate women's wartime gains but also had long-term consequences that emerged, in part, from a wartime reification of symbolic female roles.[13] I suggest that the constructed figure of the patriotute who supposedly hid in Rosie's overalls and the volunteer morale builders' more fashionable attire was a concept that not only devalued women's wartime service but also left a persistent trace of suspicion regarding female sexuality that complicated women's postwar status. In the postwar era, tensions between sexuality and sexual control and containment continued to bedevil women and other so-called dangerous individuals and groups, and critical factors such as class, race, and sexual orientation, often eclipsed by the wartime construct of the "dangerous woman," reemerged in full force.[14] The processes employed by the apparatus of the state to define acceptable and deviant sexual behavior for women during the Second World War enlarged the body of accumulated knowledge regarding so-called female "nature" that continued to interrupt and disrupt women's right to self definition. The postwar years were, however, more complex.

Joanne Meyerowitz notes that the postwar years were also a "time of notable change and cultural complexity."[15] We know that as a result of wartime changes many women continued to challenge the status quo. Numerous married women remained in the workforce. Others carved a place for themselves in law enforcement, and some chose careers in the military. Many women became active in politics and in the civil rights and other rights movements.[16] Others formed same-sex relationships and found community and support, but visibility produced new difficulties, such as the construction of a "postwar lesbian threat" and the re-fusion of "lesbian" and "prostitute" as a symbol of sexual excess.[17] And while a postwar discourse of illegitimate pregnancy recuperated white middle-class girls and women by medicalizing their transgression, excessive sexuality was attributed to nonwhite women, particularly African American women. Psychiatry desexualized white women's "excess" sex by renaming it neurosis, while black women, especially unmarried mothers, inherited the mantle of pathological sexuality.[18] The postwar and Cold War periods were characterized by a reassertion of male authority that required dependent (contained) women.[19] Print media featured articles that prescribed women's postwar obligations, including deference to men, especially returning servicemen.[20] Popular and professional literature supported women's return to the home by featuring many articles linking burgeoning juvenile delinquency with absentee mothers. And in 1947 Ferdinand Lundberg and Marynia Farnham, MD, wrote *Modern Woman: The Lost Sex,* a book that placed full responsibility for social discord on "neurotic" women.[21] *Neurotic,* in this case, referred to any woman who resisted her prescribed gendered role. Joanne Meyerowitz takes a more positive view of the popular culture treatment of women and states that while postwar popular culture contained "contradictions between domestic ideals and individual achievement," the latter was not overshadowed by the former. Meyerowitz also describes a "bifocal vision of women"—a vision of women as having simultaneously domestic and public roles—indicating that women's postwar lives were not tension free.[22] Many scholars contend that the tensions that characterized the war years, followed by the postwar clash between real life and prescribed and stereotypical roles (female and racial, to name two), came to a head in the movements of the 1960s. The cognitive dissonance between wartime representations of female sexuality and women's own interpretations of themselves and their wartime service coalesced in the 1960s and emerged as powerful forces not only in the ensuing women's rights movement but in numerous other struggles for equality.

Appendix 1
The Eight Point Agreement

AN AGREEMENT BY THE WAR AND NAVY DEPARTMENTS, THE
FEDERAL SECURITY AGENCY, AND STATE HEALTH DEPARTMENTS
ON MEASURES FOR THE CONTROL OF THE VENEREAL DISEASES
IN AREAS WHERE ARMED FORCES OR NATIONAL DEFENSE
EMPLOYEES ARE CONCENTRATED.[1]

It is recognized that the following services should be developed by State and local health and police authorities in cooperation with the Medical Corps of the United States Army, the Bureau of Medicine and Surgery of the United States Navy, the United States Public Health Service, and interested voluntary organizations:

1. Early diagnosis and adequate treatment by the Army and the Navy of enlisted personnel infected with the venereal diseases.
2. Early diagnosis and adequate treatment of the civilian population by the local health department.
3. When authentic information can be obtained as to the probable source of venereal disease infection of military or naval personnel,[2] the facts will be reported by medical officers of the Army or Navy to the State or local health authorities as may be required. If additional authentic information is available as to extramarital contacts with diseased military or naval personnel during the communicable stage, this should also be reported.
4. All contacts of enlisted men with infected civilians [are] to be reported to the medical officers in charge of the Army and Navy by local or State health authorities.
5. Recalcitrant infected persons with communicable syphilis or gonorrhea [are] to be forcibly isolated during the period of communicability. In civilian populations, it is the duty of the local health

authorities to obtain the assistance of the local police authorities in enforcing such isolation.

6. Decrease as far as possible the opportunity for contacts with infected persons. The local police department is responsible for the repression of commercialized and clandestine prostitution. The local health departments, the State Health Department, the Public Health Service, the Army, and the Navy will cooperate with the local police authorities in repressing prostitution.

7. An aggressive program of education both among enlisted personnel and the civilian population regarding the dangers of the venereal diseases, the methods for preventing these infections, and the steps which should be taken if a person suspects that he is infected.

8. The local police and health authorities, the State Department of Health, the Public Health Service, the Army, and the Navy desire the assistance of representatives of the American Social Hygiene Association or affiliated social hygiene societies or other voluntary welfare organizations or groups in developing and stimulating public support for the above measures.

Appendix 2
The May Act

MILITARY AND NAVAL ESTABLISHMENTS —
PROSTITUTION PROHIBITED NEAR
CHAPTER 287 — 1ST SESSION
[PUBLIC LAW 163 — 77TH CONGRESS]
[H. R. 2475]

An Act to prohibit prostitution within such reasonable distance of military and/or naval establishments as the Secretaries of War and/or Navy shall determine to be needful to the efficiency, health, and welfare of the Army and/or Navy.

Be it enacted by the Senate and House of Representatives of the United States of America in Congress assembled, That:

Until May 15, 1945, it shall be unlawful, within such reasonable distance of any military or naval camp, station, fort, post, yard, base, cantonment, training or mobilization place as the Secretaries of War and/or Navy shall determine to be needful to the efficiency, health, and welfare of the Army and/or Navy, and shall designate and publish in general orders or bulletins, to engage in prostitution or to aid or abet prostitution or to procure or solicit for the purpose of prostitution, or to keep or set up a house of ill fame, brothel or bawdy house or to receive any person for purposes of lewdness, assignation, or prostitution into any vehicle, conveyance, place, structure, or building, or to permit any person to remain for the purpose of lewdness, assignation, or prostitution in any vehicle, conveyance, place, structure, or building or to lease, or rent, or contract to lease or rent any vehicle, conveyance, place, structure, or building, or part thereof, knowing or with good reason to know that it is intended to be used for any of the purposes herein prohibited; and any person, corporation, partnership, or association violating the provisions of this act shall, unless otherwise punishable under the Articles of War or the Articles for the Government of the Navy, be deemed guilty of a misdemeanor and be punished by a fine of not more than $1,000, or by imprisonment for not more than one year, or by both such fine and imprisonment, and any person subject to military or naval law violating this Act shall be punished as provided by the Articles of War or the Articles for the Government of the Navy, and the Secretaries of War and of the Navy and the Federal Security Administrator are each hereby authorized and directed to take such steps as they deem necessary to suppress and prevent the violation thereof, and to accept the cooperation of the authorities of States and their counties, districts, and other political subdivisions in carrying out the purposes of this Act: *Provided,* That nothing is this Act shall be construed as conferring on the personnel of the War or Navy Department or the Federal Security Agency any authority to make criminal investigations, searches, seizures, or arrests of civilians charged with violations of this Act.

Approved, July 11, 1941.

Appendix 3
Federal Agencies

The Social Protection Division[1]

The SPD, established in March 1941 operated, at first, out of the Office of the Coordinator of Health, Welfare, and Related Defense Activities. After a series of reorganizations, the SPD became a division of the OCWS established within the FSA. During mobilization and wartime the OCWS operated to develop and coordinate programs to meet emergency needs in the fields of health, medical care, welfare, recreation, education, and nutrition. The specific responsibility of the OCWS and its predecessors was to meet the needs of thousands of communities experiencing large population increases or other difficulties related to defense production and war that rendered local public and private organizations inadequate to the task of providing community services.

The OCWS served as a coordinating agency by working through and with other federal, state, and local agencies, as well as with private national organizations. The federal agencies included the army, navy, Office of Civilian Defense, War Manpower Commission, Federal Works Agency, War Production Board, Federal Housing Authority, Office of Defense Transportation, USPHS, Children's Bureau, Office of Education, and War Relocation Authority. Some of the private agencies were the USO, American Red Cross, ASHA, National Recreation Association, National Parent-Teachers Association, Junior Leagues of America, and numerous Community Chests and Councils. As a rule, the OCWS asked existing agencies to continue their work, adding OCWS functions where necessary or if no appropriate agencies existed. Paul V. McNutt, the FSA administrator, served as coordinator of the Office of Health, Welfare, and Related Defense Activities and as director of the OCWS from November 1940 to April 28, 1943. Charles P. Taft served as OCWS director from April 29, 1943, to November 21, 1943. He was succeeded by Mark A. McCloskey, who served until June 30, 1945. Watson Miller then assumed the directorship, serving until the agency was terminated shortly after the end of the war.

The OCWS had two responsibilities that were not within the scope of any other federal agency: recreation and social protection. Mark A. McClosky served as the Director of the Recreation Division from its formation in January 1941. The SPD, instituted in March 1941, came under the leadership of Eliot Ness after the short term of Bascomb Johnson. Ness served as director until his resignation on September 8, 1944. The SPD was the government agency charged with checking the spread of venereal disease through the repression of prostitution.

In addition to the major federal agencies, numerous committees, some preexisting the establishment of the SPD and others that formed after the establishment of the SPD, participated in the campaign to eliminate prostitution. An Interdepartmental Committee, for example, that brought together twenty federal agencies (e.g., the FSA, SPD, Army, Navy, USPHS, FBI, and Children's Bureau) had been established by the Council of National Defense in January 1940 to assist the FSA director in relation to health and other defense-related problems. The Interdepartmental Committee met regularly to discuss emergent problems and to monitor progress in the war on prostitution.

The National Advisory Police Committee on Social Protection

Out of other umbrella committees similar to the Interdepartmental Committee, a plethora of subcommittees emerged. Ness acted quickly to pull numerous groups into the SPD's orbit. In 1942 he called together law enforcement officials from all over the United States to discuss wartime problems. Out of this meeting came the NAPCSP. The committee, appointed by Paul McNutt, consisted of twenty-one police officers from fifteen states, plus representatives from the army, navy, USPHS, FBI, and ODHWS, which included the SPD. According to the NAPCSP's statement of purpose, "[T]he Committee was formed to assist in the enforcement of the Federal government's Social Protection Program and to develop new and effective techniques of police enforcement pertaining to the repression and prevention of prostitution." Shortly after the formation of NAPCSP, the OWI released a press statement: "The National Advisory Police Committee on Social Protection today called upon police and law enforcement officials throughout the country to stamp out prostitution." In a report to McNutt, the NAPCSP acknowledged their "professional obligation" to stamp out prostitution so that the "Army, Navy, and war industries are not to be decimated by casualties due to venereal diseases." This committee became one of the most active groups in the campaign to repress prostitution and to control so-called female sexual delinquency.

The NAPCSP had numerous subcommittees, including separate committees on Prevention, Repression, Enforcement, and Cooperation, as well as the NWACSP.

Notes

NOTES TO THE INTRODUCTION

1. See, for example, Karen Anderson, *Wartime Women: Sex Roles, Family Relations, and the Status of Women during World War II* (Westport, CT: Greenwood Press, 1981); D'Ann Campbell, *Women at War with America: Private Lives in a Patriotic Era* (Cambridge, MA: Harvard University Press, 1984); William H. Chafe, *The American Woman: Her Changing Social, Economic, and Political Roles, 1920–1970* (New York: Oxford University Press, 1972); Susan M. Hartmann, *The Homefront and Beyond: American Women in the 1940s* (Boston: Twayne, 1982); Maureen Honey, *Creating Rosie the Riveter: Class, Gender, and Propaganda during World War II* (Amherst: University of Massachusetts Press, 1984); Leisa D. Meyer, *Creating GI Jane: Sexuality and Power in the Women's Army Corps during World War II* (New York: Columbia University Press, 1996); and Leila J. Rupp, *Mobilizing Women for War: German and American Propaganda, 1939–1945* (Princeton: Princeton University Press, 1978).

2. See Cynthia Enloe, *Maneuvers: The International Politics of Militarizing Women's Lives* (Berkeley: University of California Press, 2000), and Francine D'Amico and Laurie Weinstein, eds., *Gender Camouflage: Women and the U.S. Military* (New York: New York University Press, 1999).

3. NAPCSP, meeting on November 19, 1943, NA RG 215, Committee Meetings, Box 1.

4. Anderson, *Wartime Women*; Campbell, *Women at War*; Chafe, *American Woman*; Hartmann, *Homefront and Beyond*; Honey, *Creating Rosie the Riveter*; Meyer, *Creating GI Jane*; Rupp, *Mobilizing Women for War*.

5. On venereal disease, see Alan M. Brandt, *No Magic Bullet: A Social History of Venereal Disease in the United States since 1880* (New York: Oxford University Press, 1987).

6. Yoshiaki Yoshimi, *Comfort Women: Sexual Slavery in the Japanese Military during World War II*, trans. Suzanne O'Brien (New York: Columbia University Press, 1995), 9. The comfort women, most of whom were Korean, were forced into a brutal system of sexual slavery to service Japa-

nese soldiers. These women were listed in the official records as "military supplies."

7. Enloe, *Maneuvers*. See also Nanette J. Davis, ed., *Prostitution: An International Handbook on Trends, Problems, and Politics* (Westport, CT: Greenwood Press, 1993); the countries include Australia, Brazil, Canada, China, England and Wales, Germany, Italy, Japan, the Netherlands, Norway, Portugal, Singapore, Taiwan, United States, Vietnam, and Yugoslavia. Also see Vera Laska, ed., *Women in the Resistance and in the Holocaust* (Westport, CT: Greenwood Press, 1983), 7, 15–16, 23, 173.

8. Judith R. Walkowitz, *Prostitution and Victorian Society: Women, Class, and the State* (Cambridge: Cambridge University Press, 1980).

9. For Italian policies, see Davis, *Prostitution*, 161–62.

10. Nancy K. Bristow, *Making Men Moral: Social Engineering during the Great War* (New York: New York University Press, 1996), and Philippa Levine, *Prostitution, Race and Politics: Policing Venereal Disease in the British Empire* (New York: Routledge, 2003).

11. Linda K. Kerber, *No Constitutional Right to Be Ladies: Women and the Obligations of Citizenship* (New York: Hill and Wang, 1998), 236, 238.

12. Meyer, *Creating GI Jane*, 1.

13. Sarah E. Chinn, "Liberty's Life Stream': Blood, Race, and Citizenship in World War II," in *Technology and the Logic of American Racism: A Cultural History of the Body as Evidence* (New York: Continuum, 2000), 93–140. "Blood donation had been a major element of the home-front war-effort during World War II, and had shaped an array of discourses around blood, American identity, democracy and citizenship" (94).

14. Ibid.

15. Meyer, *Creating GI Jane*.

16. See, for example, Carole Pateman, *The Disorder of Women: Democracy, Feminism and Political Theory* (Stanford: Stanford University Press, 1989), 4, for an analysis of the ways in which "women are incorporated into the civil order differently from men." In particular, Pateman contends that "the process through which women have been included as citizens has been structured around women's bodily difference from men."

17. See Anderson, *Wartime Women*; Campbell, *Women at War*; Chafe, *American Woman*; Hartmann, *Homefront and Beyond*; Honey, *Creating Rosie the Riveter*; Meyer, *Creating GI Jane*; Rupp, *Mobilizing Women for War*; and Ruth Milkman, *Gender at Work: The Dynamics of Job Segregation by Sex during World War II* (Urbana: University of Illinois Press, 1987).

18. Quoted in Milkman, *Gender at Work*, 61. Popular magazines relied, in part, on conventional images of women to reassure the public that women's roles were not really changing.

19. Ad for Evening in Paris perfume in *True Romance*, December 1943, 81.

20. Meyer, *Creating GI Jane*, and Mattie E. Treadwell, *The Woman's Army Corps*, United States Army in World War II, Special Studies (Washington, DC: Office of the Chief of Military History, Department of the Army, 1954).

21. See, for example, Sherrie Tucker, *Swing Shift: "All Girl" Bands of the 1940s* (Durham: Duke University Press, 2000); Honey, *Creating Rosie the Riveter;* and Meyer, *Creating GI Jane*.

22. See, for example, "Spell 'IT' to the Marines," *Woman's Home Companion* (October 1943): 131, and "Public's Health: Program to Prevent Young Girls and Women from Involvement in Prostitution and Promiscuity," *Survey*, May 1943, 152.

23. See Marilyn E. Hegarty, "Patriot or Prostitute? Sexual Discourses, Print Media, and American Women during World War II," *Journal of Women's History* 10 (Summer 1998): 112–36.

24. Charles R. Reynolds, MD, Major General, U.S. Army (Retired), "Statement," *Federal Probation* 7 (April–June 1943): 19.

25. R. W. Connell, "The Big Picture: Masculinities in Recent World History," *Theory and Society* 22 (October 1993): 597.

26. Brandt, *No Magic Bullet*, 157.

27. Colin Gordon, "Governmental Rationality: An Introduction," in *The Foucault Effect: Studies in Governmentality*, ed. Graham Burchell, Colin Gordon, and Peter Miller (Chicago: University of Chicago Press, 1991), 4, 5.

28. The full texts of the Eight Point Agreement and the May Act, reproduced in Appendices 1 and 2 respectively, can be found in NA RG 215, General Records, Box 1, folder "Army/Navy." The May Act became law in July 1941.

29. Lauren Berlant, *The Queen of America Goes to Washington City: Essays on Sex and Citizenship* (Durham: Duke University Press, 1997), 57.

30. Ibid.

31. Edwin M. Schur, *Labeling Women Deviant: Gender, Stigma, and Social Control* (Philadelphia: Temple University Press, 1983), considers the "routine devaluation" of women through the use of labeling. He contends that "deviance defining" by the use of terms such as *masculine, aggressive,* and *promiscuous* is both materially and psychologically detrimental to women. Social stigmatization of this type can operate to evaluate and control behavior. See also Michel Foucault, "The Dangerous Individual," in *Politics, Philosophy, Culture: Interviews and Other Writings*, ed. Lawrence D. Kritzman, trans. Alan Sheridan (New York: Routledge, 1980), 125–51.

Foucault analyzes the construction of certain persons as threats to specific social structures. Kai T. Erikson, *Wayward Puritans* (New York: Wiley, 1966), suggests that "deviant" groups have served a social purpose in different historical periods.

32. On prescriptive literature and propaganda, especially during World War II, see Honey, *Creating Rosie the Riveter;* Susan M. Hartmann, "Prescriptions for Penelope: Literature on Women's Obligations to Returning World War II Veterans," *Women's Studies* 5, no. 3 (1978): 223–39; and Rupp, *Mobilizing Women for War.* On the OWI, see Allan M. Winkler, "Politics and Propaganda: The Office of War Information, 1942–1945" (PhD diss., Yale University, 1974).

33. On militarization, total mobilization, and nationalism, see D'Amico and Weinstein, *Gender Camouflage;* Jean Bethke Elshtain, *Women and War* (New York: Basic Books, 1987); Cynthia Enloe, *Does Khaki Become You? The Militarization of Women's Lives* (London: Pandora Press, 1983); and Margaret Kamester and Jo Vellacott, eds., *Militarism versus Feminism: Writings on Women and War* (London: Virago Press, 1987).

NOTES TO CHAPTER 1

1. "Preventing Prostitution, Promiscuity and Disease," Preliminary Report, Denver, NA RG 215, Publications, Box 3. For "patriotutes," see NAPCSP, meeting on November 19, 1943, NA RG 215, Committee Meetings, Box 1.

2. See Anderson, *Wartime Women;* Bristow, *Making Men Moral;* Hartmann, *Homefront and Beyond;* Meyer, *Creating GI Jane;* Rupp, *Mobilizing Women for War;* and Treadwell, *Woman's Army Corps.*

3. Enloe, *Maneuvers,* 36.

4. John D'Emilio and Estelle B. Freedman, *Intimate Matters: A History of Sexuality in America* (New York: Harper and Row, 1988), 1.

5. See, for example, Bram Dijkstra, *Evil Sisters: The Threat of Female Sexuality and the Cult of Manhood* (New York: Alfred A. Knopf, 1996). On sexuality during World War II, see, for example, Anderson, *Wartime Women;* Beth Bailey and David Farber, *The First Strange Place: The Alchemy of Race and Sex in World War II Hawaii* (New York: Free Press, 1992); Alan Berube, *Coming Out under Fire: The History of Gay Men and Women in World War II* (New York: Free Press, 1990); Brandt, *No Magic Bullet;* John Costello, *Love, Sex, and War: Changing Values, 1939–1945* (London: Collins, 1985); D'Emilio and Freedman, *Intimate Matters,* especially ch. 11; Lillian Faderman, *Odd Girls and Twilight Lovers: A History of Lesbian Life in Twentieth-Century America* (New York: Columbia University Press, 1991), especially ch. 5; Michel Foucault, *The History of Sexu-*

ality, vol. 1, *An Introduction,* trans. Robert Hurley (New York: Vintage Books, 1980); and Meyer, *Creating GI Jane.*

6. Dijkstra, *Evil Sisters.*

7. Philip S. Broughton, *Prostitution and the War: The Missing Man in the Front Line* (New York: Public Affairs Committee, 1942), 1.

8. NA RG 215, General Records, Box 1, folder "Army/Navy."

9. Ibid.

10. Ibid.

11. Organizational information is based on a five-page document that serves as a preface to the Finder's Guide for Record Group 215, Office of Community War Services.

12. Charles R. Reynolds, "Prostitution as a Source of Infection with the Venereal Diseases in the Armed Forces," *American Journal of Public Health* 30 (November 1940): 1281 (this and all other issues of the *American Journal of Public Health* cited in this book are available online at www.pubmed central.nih.gov/tocrender.fcgi?action=archive&journal=259).

13. *Annual Report of the Surgeon General of the Public Health Service of the United States for the Fiscal Year 1941* (Washington, DC: U.S. Government Printing Office, 1941) (hereafter cited as *ARSG 1941*).

14. A quote from Surgeon General Thomas Parran used on fund-raising materials, ASHA Papers, Box 116.

15. From "Remarks by Vonderlehr to Be Released to the Press on June 22, 1940," ASHA Papers, Box 114. Numerous military officials and other authorities couched discussions of venereal disease in terms of defense needs and military efficiency. In doing so they reinforced the message of the Sixth Command's campaign, entitled "Plan to Win," which equated national health with military health and envisioned winning the war by saving men, material, money, and time. The chief of staff of the Sixth Command commented that Hitler would be happy if he were as successful as venereal disease in rendering so many men "ineffective," reinforcing the idea that prostitutes and promiscuous women aided and abetted the enemy. "Plan to Win," n.d., NA RG 215, General Records, Box 6.

16. See Brandt, *No Magic Bullet,* and Claude Quetel, *History of Syphilis,* trans. Judith Braddock and Brian Pike (Baltimore: Johns Hopkins University Press, 1990).

17. *ARSG 1941,* 130.

18. See James H. Jones, *Bad Blood: The Tuskegee Syphilis Experiment,* new and expanded ed. (New York: Free Press, 1993). On women in the Women's Army Corps, see Meyer, *Creating GI Jane,* and Treadwell, *Woman's Army Corps.* Both discuss the marking of certain female bodies as sexually promiscuous.

19. See Brandt, *No Magic Bullet,* 165–66.

20. "U.S. Children's Bureau, Department of Labor," NA RG 215, Statistics and Studies, Box 2. See also Harriet S. Cory, "The Relation of National Defense to Social Hygiene," *Journal of Social Hygiene* 26 (November 1940): 358–61 (this and all other issues of the *Journal of Social Hygiene* cited in this book are available online at http://hearth.library.cornell.edu/h/hearth/browse/title/4732756.html?).

21. Enloe, *Maneuvers,* 45.

22. Meghan K. Winchell, "Good Food, Good Fun, and Good Girls: USO Hostesses and World War II" (PhD diss., University of Arizona, 2003), 8.

23. M. Jacqui Alexander, "Not Just (Any) Body Can Be a Citizen: The Politics of Law, Sexuality and Postcoloniality in Trinidad and Tobago and the Bahamas," *Feminist Review* 48 (Autumn 1994): 6.

24. Shannon Bell, *Reading, Writing and Rewriting the Prostitute Body* (Bloomington: Indiana University Press, 1994). Bell writes: "Modernity through a process of othering has produced 'the prostitute' as the other of the other: the other within the categorical other, 'woman' " (2).

25. See, for example, *ARSG 1941,* 3. The report discusses studies of prostitution conducted in defense areas by the USPHS and the ASHA before 1941.

26. See Brandt, *No Magic Bullet,* on prevalence of venereal disease during World War I, and *ARSG 1941,* 3. The surgeon general's report notes studies of prostitution conducted by the USPHS and the ASHA prior to 1941. See also Reynolds, "Prostitution as a Source."

27. For the full text of the Eight Point Agreement and the May Act, see Appendices 1 and 2.

28. ODHWS, "Notes on the Eight Point Agreement," from a statement issued in early 1941, NA RG 215, General Records, Box 4.

29. See, for example, Interdepartmental Meeting, "General Review," September 18, 1942, NA RG 215, Committee Meetings, Box 1. See also Frances Sullivan and Milton Rose, "Public Health Planning for War Needs: Order or Chaos?" *American Journal of Public Health* 32 (August 1942): 831–36. Constituent agencies of the FSA included the Office of Education, USPHS, Social Security Board, National Youth Administration, and CCC. The Interdepartmental Advisory Council of the ODHWS advised the director (Paul V. McNutt) on major policy questions. Each of the twelve geographic regions of the Social Security Board had a regional advisory council corresponding in structure and function to the federal committee. In 1942, Taft chaired the committee. The members included Ness, Turner, Stephenson, Parran, Tamm, Lenroot (affiliations in text), Snow (ASHA), and duBois of the State Department.

30. Advisory Committee on Social Protection, minutes of an all-day meeting to discuss problems and programs, June 14, 1941, NA RG 215,

Committee Meetings, Box 1. The meeting was called by the Office of Coordinator of Health, Welfare, and Related Defense Activities, SPD, and was attended by thirty-seven persons representing education, health, law enforcement, the army, the navy, welfare, the FSA, and the public.

31. Quote is from Sheriffs File: Letter to the State Attorneys General, November 18, 1942, NA RG 215, General Records, Box 1. But see also Chauncey D. Leake, Dean of the School of Medicine, University of Texas, to SPD representative, New Orleans, July 17, 1945, regarding the use of "undercover studies conducted by citizens groups," ASHA Papers, Box 128; and K. Close, "Sick Men Can't Fight," *Survey Graphic,* March 1943, 80–84, also available as reprint in NA RG 215, Publications, Box 4. Close wrote: "One of the weaknesses of the VD program in San Antonio, Texas is the slim legal structure on which the repression program stands."

32. Peter M. McWilliams, *Ain't Nobody's Business If You Do* (Santa Monica, CA: Prelude Press, 1993), 198.

33. See Sheriffs File: Letter to State Attorneys General, November 18, 1942, NA RG 215, General Records, Box 1.

34. "Repression Experience Report," February 15, 1944, NA RG 215, General Records, Box 1.

35. See Chauncey D. Leake, Dean, University of Texas, School of Medicine, to SPD representative, July 17, 1945, ASHA Papers, Box 128. See also undated memo from Adm. McIntire to Venereal Disease Subcommittee, NA RG 52, Box 2.

36. "A Brief Prepared by the War Activities Committee of the Chicago Bar Association on the Prostitute-Venereal Disease Control Program," December 1942, NA RG 215, Publications, Box 1.

37. See Brandt, *No Magic Bullet,* 167–68.

38. See Patricia Cline Cohen, *A Calculating People: The Spread of Numeracy in Early America* (Chicago: University of Chicago Press, 1982).

39. See, for example, Lt. Col. Thomas B. Turner, VD Control Branch, Preventive Medicine Division, Office of the Surgeon General, U.S. Army, "Immediate Wartime Outlook and Indicated Post-war Conditions with Respect to the Control of the Venereal Diseases," *American Journal of Public Health* 33 (November 1943): 1309–13. Turner states that between October 1942 and June 1943 over fifty-five thousand men with venereal disease had been drafted (1310). They were treated after induction.

40. In 1942 and 1943 women continued to be arrested on morals charges. See, for example, U.S. Children's Bureau, Department of Labor, NA RG 215, Statistics and Studies, Box 2. In the first six months of 1942, 1,129 women were arrested on morals charges and 483 women were arrested for prostitution. Cincinnati police arrested only those women who engaged in sex for money and who in most cases had prior convictions for prostitution.

Records of the Police Department, Cincinnati, Ohio, for January–December 1943, NA RG 215, General Records, Box 2.

41. "V.D. General Prevalence Survey, May 1940," ASHA Papers, Box 115. The newspaper mentioned in the files was the *Mt. Holly, New Jersey News* (May 16, 1940).

42. Walter Clarke to Thomas Parran, May 10, 1940, ASHA Papers, Box 115.

43. Advisory Committee on Social Protection, minutes of an all-day meeting to discuss problems and programs, June 14, 1941, NA RG 215, Committee Meetings, Box 1.

44. Ibid. Dr. Sheldon Glueck was a sociologist. Mr. Hoehler (army) commented on the failure to enforce quarantine regulations against males. Taft responded that when it was tried, "the courts in Kentucky would not make the quarantine stick."

45. Ibid.

46. These statistics were also subject to debate.

47. See, for example, Raymond F. Clapp, SPD, to Katharine Lenroot, Children's Bureau, Department of Labor, December 22, 1942, "correcting" an earlier set of statistics, and a memo from Mr. Teske, of the FSA, to Mr. Ness, director of the SPD, regarding sets of statistics that had been disseminated by the division; Teske noted that he had found "misstatements of facts in all statements that I have checked." He called attention, for example, to the El Paso report claiming that girls as young as ten had been apprehended. Teske said that the youngest was sixteen and that only twelve, not, as the SPD claimed, twenty-six, of the young women were under twenty. NA RG 215, Statistics and Studies, Box 1.

48. Advisory Committee on Social Protection, minutes of an all-day meeting to discuss problems and programs, June 14, 1941, NA RG 215, Committee Meetings, Box 1.

49. Ibid.

50. Ibid.

51. Document dated November 18, 1942 (incomplete), referring to letters from the Honorable Charles J. Hahn Jr., the executive secretary of the NSA, to various local officials (generally in the attorney general's office) regarding the "power of sheriffs" to arrest prostitutes. The main questions seemed to be, Was prostitution to be treated as a crime or as a lesser offense? and Should arrest without a warrant exclude the arresting officer from liability? Replies varied from the policy in North Carolina, where no arrest could be made unless the woman was "caught in the act," to New Mexico, where the sheriff had considerable latitude to arrest a "suspected prostitute." NA RG 215, General Records, Box 1.

52. Proceedings of the NAPCSP, New York, August 7, 1942. The NAPCSP

was formed in June 1942 under advisement by McNutt. At this meeting a Special Committee on Repression was formed to make a survey of state laws for the purpose of "unity": that is, to make all prostitution laws the same, as well as more inclusive. The special committee also aimed to convince the federal government to support construction of more detention facilities that would be needed as a result of a "vigorous repression program." NA RG 215, Committee Meetings, Box 1.

53. For immediate release, July 24, 1942, by the OWI, ODHWS, NA RG 215, Committee Meetings, Box 1. See also a resolution adopted by the NSA in September 1942 entitled "Condemning the Tolerance of Prostitution in Any County in the United States." The association urged all sheriffs and law enforcement officers to participate in the repression program. NA RG 215, Publications, Box 4.

54. OWI Bulletin no. 165, July 24, 1942, NA RG 215, Committee Meetings, Box 1.

55. Proceedings of the NAPCSP, New York, August 7, 1942.

56. Report of a meeting held August 27, 1942, called by Ness, NA RG 215, Committee Meetings, Box 1. By the spring of 1945 the NAPCSP had commenced work on a manual for policewomen. The manual was discussed at an NAPCSP meeting on May 23–24, 1945; see NA RG 215, Committee Meetings, Box 1.

57. Ibid.

58. *Does Prostitution Breed Crime?* Pamphlet prepared by the SPD and distributed by the ASHA (c. 1944–45), Records of the Ohio War History Commission, Series 1142, Box "Social Conditions," Ohio Historical Society, Columbus, Ohio.

59. Ibid.

60. Ibid.

61. Meeting of the NAPCSP, June 30, 1942, "Reports from Special Committees," NA RG 215, Committee Meetings, Box 1.

62. Ibid.

63. For example, there was widespread resistance by local and state officials, businessmen, and military officials.

64. Meeting of the NAPCSP, June 30, 1942, "Reports from Special Committees," NA RG 215, Committee Meetings, Box 1.

65. "Pro stations" were located throughout areas where servicemen congregated. They provided chemical prophylaxis.

66. NAPCSP's Committee on Enforcement, November 20, 1942, NA RG 215, Committee Meetings, Box 1.

67. Ibid.

68. Ibid. Remarks made, respectively, by Sullivan (police, Massachusetts), Souter (NSA), and Roff (police, New Jersey).

69. Ibid. for all quotations in this paragraph.

70. Ibid.

71. Ibid.

72. Quoted in Brandt, *No Magic Bullet,* 167.

73. ASHA Papers, Boxes 117 and 128; NA RG 215, Statistics and Studies, Box 1.

74. NAPCSP's Committee on Enforcement, November 20, 1942, NA RG 215, Committee Meetings, Box 1. Remarks by Chief Woods of the Norfolk, Virginia, Police.

75. Ibid.

76. Ibid. Dr. Ferree (state health commissioner of Indiana), Chief Morrissey, and Mr. Stewart (Indiana State Police representative).

77. Ibid.

78. "A Digest of the Minutes of the June 9, 1943, Social Protection Conference on 'the Woman's Role in Social Protection,'" NA RG 215, Publications, Box 1. Unfortunately, the SPD records on the NWACSP are limited. The committee makes another appearance in ch. 6.

79. Ibid.

80. Ibid.

81. Ibid.

82. See, for example, "Survey of Commercialized Prostitution Conditions, March Field, California," December 1940, NA RG 215, Committee Meetings, Box 1.

83. "A Digest of the Minutes of the June 9, 1943, Social Protection Conference on 'the Woman's Role in Social Protection,'" NA RG 215, Publications, Box 1. See also "Women's Advisory Social Protection Committee Membership Announced," National Events, *Journal of Social Hygiene* 29 (November 1943): 541, for a list of members. The Executive Committee consisted of the chairman, Mrs. Howard B. Ritchie, General Federation of Women's Clubs; Mrs. Bess N. Rosa, National Congress of Parents and Teachers; Mrs. George E. Pariseau, Girls Friendly Society; Dr. Caroline Ware, American Association of University Women; Mrs. Anna M. Strong, National Congress of Colored Parents and Teachers; Mrs. Gerson Levi, National Council of Jewish Women; and Mrs. DeForest Van Slyck, Association of Junior Leagues of America. The membership included women from the American Legion Auxiliary, American Medical Women's Association, ASHA, Associated Women of the American Farm Bureau Federation, Congress of Women's Auxiliaries of the Congress of Industrial Organizations, National Board of the YWCA, National Council of Catholic Women, National Federation of Business and Professional Women's Clubs, National Nursing Council for War Services, National Women's Trade Union League of America, United Council of Church Women, Children's Bureau, U.S. De-

partment of Labor, Bureau of Public Assistance, Social Security Board, National Travelers Aid Association, USO Director of Girls and Women's Activities, Nursing Division of the USPHS, and Joint Army and Navy Committee on Welfare and Recreation. Ultimately the National Council of Catholic Women withdrew because they objected to the lack of a moral tone in public pronouncements and publications.

84. See "Special Meeting of the Executive Committee of the NAPCSP, April 2, 1943," for topics addressed, such as hotels, taxicab companies, and the Council of Alcoholic Beverage Industries to get their cooperation in the repression of prostitution. NA RG 215, Committee Meetings, Box 1.

85. NAPCSP subcommittee meeting, March 7, 1941, NA RG 215, Committee Meetings, Box 1.

86. NAPCSP subcommittee meeting, June 30, 1942, NA RG 215, Committee Meetings, Box 1.

87. NAPCSP subcommittee meeting, March 7, 1941, NA RG 215, Committee Meetings, Box 1.

88. NAPCSP subcommittee meeting, June 30, 1942, NA RG 215, Committee Meetings, Box 1.

89. Ibid.

90. NAPCSP subcommittee meeting, March 7, 1941, NA RG 215, Committee Meetings, Box 1.

91. NAPCSP subcommittee meeting, June 30, 1942, NA RG 215, Committee Meetings, Box 1.

92. "1943 Amendments to the Public Health Laws in Georgia," News from the Field, *American Journal of Public Health* 33 (June 1943): 769.

93. Advisory Committee on Social Protection, minutes of an all-day meeting to discuss problems and programs, June 14, 1941, NA RG 215, Committee Meetings, Box 1.

94. See Eliot Ness, "The Repression of Prostitution in the Social Protection Program" (June 30, 1942), address before the NAPCSP, NA RG 215, Publications, Box 4.

95. For the text of the May Act, NA RG 215, General Records, Box 1, see Appendix 2. On September 8, 1941, a letter was sent from the commanding officer of Fort Lewis, Washington, to the commanding general of the Presidio, California, regarding memos that had been sent from headquarters almost immediately after passage of the May Act to mayors in nearby cities and towns that had unacceptable prostitution conditions. A representative of the FSA was waiting for authorization to proceed with the threat of invoking the May Act. NA RG 215, General Records, Box 1. Supporters of the May Act generally agreed that the threat of invoking it would suffice to convince many localities to support repression. The May Act will be treated more extensively in ch. 2.

96. Arthur S. Fink (associate director, SPD), "Columbus and Phenix City, Alabama," five-page report to Eliot Ness (director, SPD), November 2, 1942, NA RG 215, Statistics and Studies, Box 6.

97. Ibid.

98. All quotations in this paragraph are from ibid.

99. Ibid.

100. Ibid.

101. See memo from Navy Captain Stevenson (n.d., c. 1942), NA RG 52, Box 10.

102. Fink, "Columbus and Phenix City, Alabama."

103. Ibid.

104. Ibid. See also memos from Irving K. Furst (field representative, SPD) to Alice Clements (assistant director, SPD), April 6, 1942, and from David C. Meck Jr. (field representative, SPD) to Ness, June 14, 1943, NA RG 215, Regional Files, Box 1. The gathering of statistics provided weapons necessary to deal with the prostitution problem; in cases where the legal definition of prostitution seemed inadequate, city officials "interpreted the statutes broadly."

105. Memos from Furst to Clements, April 6, 1942, and from Meck to Ness, June 14, 1943.

106. Ibid.

107. Jones, *Bad Blood*, 27.

108. See, for example, Lester B. Granger (executive director of the National Urban League) to Dr. Walter Clarke (ASHA), January 23, 1943, ASHA Papers, Box 117. Granger was responding to a copy of the ASHA's "Proposal for a Negro Educational Project." He lodged a strong objection to several parts of the proposal, including a quote from Surgeon General Thomas Parran, which Granger called an "unfortunate choice." The quote, he said, "makes a blanket assertion regarding the rate of syphilis among Negroes which has been repeatedly challenged by competent authority." See also "Discrepancies in Negro Commercialized Prostitution Survey," memo, May 1945, ASHA Papers, Box 128.

109. See, for example, Raymond F. Clapp (SPD) to Katharine Lenroot (Children's Bureau, Department of Labor), December 22, 1942, "correcting" an earlier set of statistics. See also a memo from Mr. Teske (FSA) to Mr. Ness, director of the SPD, regarding erroneous statistics. NA RG 215, Statistics and Studies, Box 1.

110. David Klassen and Kay Flaminio, *Celebrating 80 Years* (Research Triangle Park, NC: American Social Hygiene Association, 1994), 12–13.

111. Jones, *Bad Blood*, 27.

112. Dr. Paul B. Cornley to Dr. Walter Clarke, April 22, 1942, ASHA Papers, Box 117.

113. Ibid.

114. "Repression Experiences," NA RG 215, Statistics and Studies, Box 6. As a result of the Depression and war-related problems, many women, both white and nonwhite, had contact with social agencies. For additional information on the Travelers Aid Society, see NA RG 215, General Records, Box 13; and Mildred B. Bracy, "USO Travelers Aid Service to Women and Girls in Defense Areas," *Journal of Social Hygiene* 29 (January 1943): 8–11.

115. NA RG 52, Box 10, folder "Prostitution." Files on the enforcement of the May Act are minimal and devoid of information. Reference to the *Washington Post* article is in this file.

116. Helen Hironimus, "Survey of 100 May Act Violators Committed to the Federal Reformatory for Women," *Federal Probation* 7 (April–June 1943): 31–34.

117. Ibid.

118. Handwritten note, (n.d., c. 1943), by Eliot Ness, NA RG 215, General Records, Box 1. Many papers included in the records were rough drafts of speeches or articles (working drafts).

119. Ibid.

120. Interdepartmental Meeting, "General Review," September 18, 1942, NA RG 215, Committee Meetings, Box 1.

121. Ibid.

122. These comments come from a different meeting, a few months earlier, where Tamm spoke on the same subject. Summary of minutes of meeting, NAPCSP, June 30, 1942, NA RG 215, Committee Meetings, Box 1.

123. Interdepartmental Meeting, "General Review," September 18, 1942, NA RG 215, Committee Meetings, Box 1. *Contress* refers to federal interference with states' rights.

124. See, for example, Rockefeller Papers, RG III, Box 15; Sheriffs File: Letters to the State Attorneys General, NA RG 215, General Records, Box 1; NA RG 215, General Records, Box 1; ASHA Papers, Box 128; NA RG 215, General Records, Box 7; NA RG 52, Box 2.

125. Interdepartmental Meeting, "General Review," September 18, 1942, NA RG 215, Committee Meetings, Box 1.

126. Ibid.

127. Ibid.

128. L. R. Pennington, "The Challenge to Law Enforcement," *Journal of Social Hygiene* 30 (December 1944): 530–37. "Sob sisters" is a reference to social workers, a group that law enforcement disdained.

129. Edward V. Taylor, speech delivered at Venereal Disease Conference, Second Service Command Headquarters, Governor's Island, New York, on September 18, 1944, NA RG 215, General Records, Box 7.

1. On the treatment of venereal disease, see Brandt, *No Magic Bullet,* especially 40–41 and 46.

2. Bascomb Johnson had a longtime involvement in the field of social hygiene. He was one of the original founders of the ASHA in 1914. For his 1937 publication "Prostitution in the U.S.," see ASHA Papers, Box 173. On the CTCA, see Brandt, *No Magic Bullet,* and Bristow, *Making Men Moral.* The CTCA was formed in April 1917 by order of President Wilson and was charged with controlling venereal diseases through providing moral education and appropriate recreation as prevention against venereal disease in the military. Although the commission tried to retain power through the demobilization period, it was basically out of business by July 1919.

3. See Brandt, *No Magic Bullet,* and Bristow, *Making Men Moral.*

4. Brandt, *No Magic Bullet,* 52.

5. Charles Winick and Paul M. Kinsie, *The Lively Commerce: Prostitution in the United States* (Chicago: Quadrangle Books, 1971), 245–46, 248.

6. Ibid., 248.

7. Snow (ASHA) to Rockefeller, June 25, 1940. This handwritten letter also asked to set up a one-on-one meeting. Snow wrote, "It is highly important [to] secure at this time the advice of those of you who participated in and guided the work during the World War." BSH Papers, RG III, Box 16.

8. Jean B. Pinney, "Social Hygiene a Generation Ago," *Journal of Social Hygiene* 29 (June 1943): 377.

9. Ibid.

10. See Brandt, *No Magic Bullet,* 107.

11. Among the women were Miriam Van Waters, superintendent of the Massachusetts Reformatory for Women; Rhoda Millikin, captain of the Metropolitan Police, in charge of the Women's Division, District of Columbia; Eleanor Hutzel, formerly deputy commissioner of the Detroit Police Department and director of the Women's Division, who published a policewomen's manual in 1933; Katherine Lenroot, Children's Bureau, Washington, DC; and Helen Hironimus, warden of the Federal Reformatory for Women, West Virginia. Raymond B. Fosdick, chairman of the CTCA and investigator of prostitution for the Bureau of Social Hygiene (1912–16), was still active during World War II. See, for example, "Report from the Special Committee, National Advisory Police Committee on Social Protection," June 30, 1942, NA RG 215, Committee Meetings, Box 1.

12. For significant studies of prostitution that yield insights into the race and class components of the war on women, see Abraham Flexner, *Prostitution in Europe* (1914; reprint, Montclair, NJ: Patterson Smith, 1969); George Kneeland, *Commercialized Prostitution in New York City* (1913;

reprint, Montclair, NJ: Patterson Smith, 1969); Howard B. Woolston, *Prostitution in the United States* (Montclair, NJ: Patterson Smith, 1921), and Walter C. Reckless, *Vice in Chicago* (Montclair, NJ: Patterson Smith,1933).

13. Joanne J. Meyerowitz, *Women Adrift: Independent Wage Earners in Chicago, 1880–1930* (Chicago: University of Chicago Press, 1988), xix. See also D'Emilio and Freedman, *Intimate Matters,* and Cathy Peiss, *Cheap Amusements: Working Women and Leisure in Turn-of-the-Century New York* (Philadelphia: Temple University Press, 1986).

14. Dijkstra, *Evil Sisters,* 3. See also Carl N. Degler, *In Search of Human Nature: The Decline and Revival of Darwinism in American Social Thought* (New York: Oxford University Press, 1991).

15. Janis Appier, *Policing Women: The Sexual Politics of Law Enforcement and the LAPD* (Philadelphia: Temple University Press, 1998), 22

16. Mary E. Odem, *Delinquent Daughters: Protecting and Policing Adolescent Female Sexuality in the United States, 1885–1920* (Chapel Hill: University of North Carolina Press, 1995), 1.

17. Reynolds, "Prostitution as a Source." The first three quotations are from p. 1276 and the last from p. 1281.

18. Speech by Charles Reynolds at the all-day meeting of the Advisory Committee on Social Protection, June 14, 1941, regarding venereal disease and prostitution, NA RG 215, Committee Meetings, Box 1, unpaginated.

19. On meetings, see notes on Meeting of the National Research Council, Division of Medical Sciences, on June 7, 1940, to discuss, in part, the role of the USPHS in the control of venereal disease in the civilian population adjacent to areas of military concentration. This meeting discussed the removal of penalties for men who acquired venereal diseases. (Widely employed from the beginning of the war, this policy became official in 1943.) NA RG 52, Box 9. See also a memo of January 31, 1941, to Admiral McIntire discussing venereal disease control and announcing a meeting of Dr. Hazen's committee on prophylaxis. This discussion focused on the immediate need for "pro" stations in areas with numerous servicemen. NA RG 52, Box 2. Dr. Hazen was appointed by the ASHA and the USPHS as the chairman of a Special Joint Committee (on VD). Pro stations were places that servicemen could go to get treatment after unprotected sexual activity. Condoms were widely available on base or at the pro stations. During January, March, and July 1941, the Subcommittee on VD met to discuss various subjects, such as whether to draft men who tested positive, who should be responsible for treatment in general, and other questions of coordination. See also the *Annual Report of the Surgeon General of the Public Health Service of the United States for the Fiscal Year 1941* (Washington, DC: U.S. Government Printing Office, 1941), 132. In 1941, the report said that men with "uncomplicated gonorrhea should be inducted into service

and promptly treated." Popular media took up the cause also. See, for example, F. S. Wickware, "National Defense vs. Venereal Disease," *Life*, October 13, 1941, 128–30.

20. Assistant Surgeon General Vonderlehr (USPHS) to numerous officials and agencies (form letter), January 28, 1941, and Paul V. McNutt (FSA) to Dr. Ray Lyman Wilbur (ASHA), March 26, 1941, both in BSH Papers, RG III, Box 16.

21. Unmarked single sheet, Gallup poll taken in November 1942, NA RG 215, General Records, Box 8. Regulated prostitution was fairly common in Europe. For an excellent study of regulated prostitution, see Walkowitz, *Prostitution*. Although Walkowitz studied England's Contagious Diseases Acts of the 1860s, the commonalities with the World War II campaign are striking, especially the loose definition of the prostitute and the arbitrary power of the state. While many English individuals and groups protested against the Contagious Diseases Act, in the United States during World War II protest against the similar treatment of women was minimal.

22. Thomas Parran and Raymond A. Vonderlehr, *Plain Words about Venereal Disease* (New York: Reynal and Hitchcock, 1941). Parran blamed the military for failing to take sufficient action against prostitution and accused the federal government of apathy with regard to the problem. See also Brandt, *No Magic Bullet*, 162. The congressional hearings on the May Act include discussion of the inability, or in some cases unwillingness, of local law enforcement agencies to handle a "rising tide of prostitution," especially in areas around military bases and in industrial "boom" areas.

23. Memo, March 17, 1941, for Admiral McIntire regarding a meeting held on March 14 to discuss social hygiene, NA RG 52, Box 2. At that meeting, Bascomb Johnson spoke again about policies during World War I.

24. Ibid.

25. Ibid. From the beginning of the campaign to control venereal diseases, many army and navy officers favored regulated prostitution.

26. Ibid. Turf wars plagued the groups and individuals involved in the repression campaign. Mr. Holzoff, an assistant attorney general with the Department of Justice, kept insisting, much to the annoyance of the other participants, that all arrests and investigations be handled by the FBI. Captain Millikin thought that policewomen should have the right to arrest. See also Advisory Committee on Social Protection, minutes of an all-day meeting to discuss problems and programs, June 14, 1941, NA RG 215, Committee Meetings, Box 1. Charles P. Taft presided; representatives from education, health, law enforcement, the army, the navy, welfare, the public, and the FSA were in attendance. The record of this meeting makes clear the struggles between the varied groups for control of repression and also illuminates the attitudes of the attendees toward what was to be done with pro-

miscuous women. Female promiscuity was widely accepted as a given, but social work and law enforcement differed over the mechanics of arrest, apprehension, type and place of confinement, and type and length of sentence. See also Dr. Snow (ASHA) to Mr. Rockefeller, July 1940, BSH Papers, RG 111, Box 16. In typical Rooseveltian fashion, authority had been divided among many groups, a factor that complicated operations. Snow wrote about the "opinion of many of us as to the urgent need for a coordinator . . . in Washington with the power to do the necessary work of all our health, medical welfare and protective and recreational activities correlated and functioning as a whole." But even in 1942, the problem remained. See ODHWS-SPD, Memorandum No. 12, "Relationship between the Social Protection Section [Division] and American Social Hygiene Association in Respect to Local Committees," September 1942, unpaginated, NA RG 215, Publications, Box 4, for a discussion of confusion between the ASHA and the SPD, both of which were trying to recruit local committees in the same places at the same times. Some small successes were announced: see, for example, "Notes for a Coming Broadcast: 'Are We Facing a Moral Breakdown in America?'" ASHA Papers, Box 128, which referred to a "team effort and close cooperation" among the ASHA, USPHS, and SPD in Chicago. The problem of fragmentation, duplication, and lack of cooperation continued throughout the war years. For example, in 1945, many local social workers still resisted working too closely with the police.

27. Valerie H. Parker, *Social Hygiene and the Child,* pamphlet (ASHA, 1939), ASHA Papers, Box 173.

28. In October 1945, at a regional conference on social protection, Miss Zillmer repeated her earlier cautions. She clearly felt that the military's attitude toward male sexuality during the war years would be responsible for postwar problems in the realm of sexual relations. Zillmer was the only woman at the conference. She said, "I'm sure I was 'rung in' because it was 'good policy.'" Proceedings of Conference on Social Protection, October 1945, NA RG 215, Committee Meetings, Box 3. See also the memo from Ruth F. Sadler to Arthur E. Fink, subject "National Council of Catholic Women—Tel. Conv. with Marie Duffin," July 12, 1944, discussing the withdrawal of the National Council of Catholic Women from the NWACSP because they objected to an SPD pamphlet focusing on the disease aspect of venereal disease rather than on a moral aspect. The pamphlet recommended condoms. NA RG 215, General Records, Box 2.

29. Ibid.

30. Reynolds, "Prostitution as a Source," 1281. Reynolds was a retired major general in the U.S. Army, serving at this time at the State Department of Health in Harrisburg, Pennsylvania.

31. Official statistics failed to make the point that venereal diseases had

become more visible as a result of both Selective Service testing and more extensive reporting by private physicians and health departments.

32. See the *Congressional Committee Hearings Index,* part 4, 74th–78th Cong. (1935–44), 787–88. Under its terms, prostitution became a federal offense in areas within a reasonable distance of army or navy establishments when the secretary of war or of the navy believed this step was necessary to protect the health of the men in uniform.

33. "Hearings of the House of Representatives Committee on Military Affairs," March 1941, microfiche, State Library of Ohio. Congressman May was the chairman of the House Military Affairs Committee.

34. "La Guardia Backs Camp Zoning Bill," *New York Times,* March 12, 1941, 6.

35. Hearings of the House of Representatives Committee on Military Affairs, March 1941. *Reasonable distance* was a contested term.

36. Ibid. Catholic and Protestant clergy, as well as representatives of the ASHA, USPHS, and Children's Bureau (to name a few), provided additional supportive testimony.

37. The sources indicate that there was some difficulty over funding these "undercover" investigations. The records, which tell only a partial story, suggest that there was concern over legal issues. See, for example, Medical Interests/American Social Hygiene Association, memo, May 9, 1941, BSH Papers, RG III, Box 16. This seems likely given the term *undercover.* See Chauncey D. Leake, Dean of the School of Medicine, University of Texas, to SPD Representative, New Orleans, July 17, 1945, regarding use of undercover studies conducted by citizens' groups, ASHA Papers, Box 28. From time to time concerns also arose regarding the legality of procedures used to repress female prostitution and promiscuity. For example, questions arose about entrapment and arrest without a warrant, and the constitutionality of the May Act was challenged. For concerns about parts of the Eight Point Agreement, see a letter from the Chairman of the Subcommittee on Venereal Disease Control, National Research Council, to the Committee on Health and Medicine, National Research Council, January 28, 1941, pointing out that, in places, paragraph 6 was not being interpreted as intended or in a uniform manner. NA RG 52, Box 10. For a discussion on warrants, see Sheriff's File: Letter to the State Attorneys General, November 18, 1942, NA RG 215, General Records, Box 1.

38. The ASHA also conducted 86 studies in 1940 and 425 in 1941 that focused on existing prostitution and expectations of increased prostitution. BSH Papers, RG III, Box 15. See also Walter Clarke (ASHA) to Paul V. McNutt (FSA), January 21, 1941, NA RG 215, Committee Meetings, Box 1. Clarke contended that some cities that had closed their vice districts were

"re-establishing a form of regulation contrary to law, and others tolerate very bad conditions through lack of law enforcement. The profit motive and lethargic public opinion have conspired to permit the re-establishment of the illegal business of prostitution in a surprisingly large number of American communities."

39. Ibid.

40. FBI, *Uniform Crime Reports*, NA RG 287, Box J. FBI statistics reinforced the belief that prostitution and promiscuous female sexual activity were rapidly increasing. As a result, surveillance increased in areas where so-called suspicious women congregated.

41. On recruiting young women and college girls, see "Statement of James Earle Moore, M.D., Chairman, Subcommittee on Venereal Diseases, National Research Council, before the Joint Army and Navy Committee on Welfare and Recreation," Washington, DC, February 28, 1941, NA RG 52, Box 10.

42. Winchell, "Good Food, Good Fun."

43. Records of the Ohio War History Commission, Series 1142, Box "Social Concerns," June 1941, Ohio Historical Society, Columbus.

44. Charles J. Reiger Jr., "Louisville's Welfare Director Sums Up His City's Approach to Its Defense Problems," *Public Welfare News* 9 (April 1941): 7–10.

45. See, for example, F. S. Wickware, "The Army Fights VD," *Reader's Digest*, December 1941, 14–17.

46. Ovetta Culp Hobby, "Sweethearts at Ease: Army Chooses Woman Editor to Inform You about Soldiers' Behavior in Camps," *Cincinnati Enquirer*, August 2, 1941, 2.

47. "Statement of James Earle Moore, M.D., Chairman, Subcommittee on Venereal Diseases, National Research Council, before the Joint Army and Navy Committee on Welfare and Recreation," Washington, DC, February 28, 1941, NA RG 52, Box 10. For Moore's comments at the March 1941 meeting, see memo for Admiral McIntire, March 18, 1941, regarding a meeting held by the committee headed by Mr. Osborn (War Department) on the subjects of recreation and morale, NA RG 52, Box 10. For Moore's comments on regulated prostitution, see Dr. James Earle Moore to Members of the Subcommittee on Venereal Diseases and the Committee on Therapeutics and Allied Subjects, National Research Council, August 8, 1940, NA RG 52, Box 10, on the subject of setting up militarized houses of prostitution. On the Tuskegee experiment, see Jones, *Bad Blood*, 16. The Tuskegee experiment was a forty-year study of untreated syphilis in black men conducted by the USPHS.

48. Klassen and Flaminio, *Celebrating 80 Years*, 12.

49. The poster read, "She May Look Clean . . . But . . ."

50. "Survey of Commercialized Prostitution in California," December 1940, NA RG 215, General Records, Box 1.

51. "A Year of National Defense Activities," condensed report for 1941, by Dr. Walter Clarke, Executive Director, ASHA. BSH Papers, RG III, Box 15.

52. Ibid.

53. *Public Health Report,* State of Connecticut, June 30, 1941.

54. "Detection and Management of Venereal Disease in Women Arrested on Morals Charges," Report of the Social Hygiene Division of the Detroit Department of Health, November 1940, ASHA Papers, Box 115.

55. W. C. Williams and G. Y. McGinness, "Plans for Handling Special Health and Other Problems Incident to the Army Maneuvers in Tennessee," *Public Health Report,* October 24, 1941, ASHA Papers, Box 131.

56. Charles R. Reynolds speaking on his 1940 article, "Prostitution as a Source of Infection with the Venereal Diseases in the Armed Forces," at a June 14, 1941, all-day meeting of the Advisory Committee on Social Protection that focused on venereal disease and prostitution. NA RG 215, Committee Meetings, Box 1. For additional meetings concerning venereal disease and prostitution, see, for instance, the meeting of the National Research Council's Subcommittee on Venereal Disease, on January 17, 1941, to discuss the interconnectedness of prostitution and venereal disease in the armed forces and the importance of contact tracing. NA RG 52, Box 10. See also ASHA Papers, Box 32, for a series of reports and meetings, regarding prostitution, during the period from January to March 1941. Bascomb Johnson was present at many of the meetings. Professor Maurice A. Bigelow of Columbia University served as a consultant for the ASHA and the USPHS at this time. He traveled to thirteen states and networked with military and civilian authorities regarding problems related to mobilization. See also Harriet S. Cory, "The Relation of National Defense to Social Hygiene," *Journal of Social Hygiene* 26 (November 1940): 358–61, with regard to a meeting in November, attended by more than sixty social hygiene executives and medical officers, "to consider measures aimed at abolishing commercialized prostitution." On the popular press, see, for example, "All Out War on Prostitution," *Newsweek,* September 29, 1941, 58.

57. See Reynolds, "Prostitution as a Source," For use of the term *hordes of harlots,* see the remarks made by the Honorable L. Geyer in *U.S. Congressional Record* 87 (March 17–May 20, 1941): A1233.

58. See Anderson, *Wartime Women,* on the repression campaign in Detroit, Seattle, and Baltimore. See also Meyer, *Creating GI Jane,* on the control of servicewomen's sexuality.

NOTES TO CHAPTER 3

1. On the social history of venereal disease in the United States during the late nineteenth and twentieth centuries, see Brandt, *No Magic Bullet.* On the etiology of syphilis, see Jones, *Bad Blood,* 2. Jones describes syphilis as a "highly contagious disease caused by *Treponema pallidum,* a delicate organism that is microscopic in shape and resembles a corkscrew. The disease may be acquired or congenital. In acquired syphilis, the spirochete (as the Treponema pallidum is also called) enters the body through the skin or mucous membrane, usually during sexual intercourse." See also Adora A. Adimara et al., *Sexually Transmitted Diseases: Companion Handbook,* 2nd ed. (New York: McGraw-Hill, 1994), 63. "Treponema Pallidum, the causative organism of syphilis, is one of a small group of treponemes, members of the order Spirochaetales, that are virulent for human beings. T. pallidum is indistinguishable by known morphologies, chemical, or immunologic methods from treponomes which cause yaws, pinta, or endemic syphilis." Robert S. Desowitz, *Who Gave Pinta to the Santa Maria: Torrid Diseases in a Temperate World* (New York: W. W. Norton, 1997), 56–58, also discusses this group of treponomes. "To be confusingly precise," he writes, "syphilis should be syphilises since what seems to be a single organism with four different names causes four different kinds of disease. Under the microscope or by the usual immunological tests of identity, the spirochetes cannot be distinguished one from another." (The possibility of false positives in tests for syphilis is discussed later in this chapter.) There was and is scientific debate regarding other forms of bodily contact as capable of transmitting syphilis and gonorrhea and regarding nonsexual transmission. See, for example, Adimara et al., *Sexually Transmitted Diseases,* 26, for an argument that transmission through nonsexual contact is rare and that transmission by other types of sexual contact is less well defined. In the 1940s, as in the current era of AIDS, conflicting opinions circulated regarding modes of transmission, the reliability of tests, and the actual rate of disease. For instance, the notion that syphilis or gonorrhea could be contracted from common use of blankets, towels, and glasses appears often in the 1940s and, in fact, can still be found in the 1990s. See, for example, Dr. Antonio N. Feliciano and Antonio E. Feliciano Jr., *Sexually Transmitted Diseases: You May Have One but Don't Know It* (New York: Vantage Press, 1992), especially 38–39 and 130. A medical authority has assured me that the spirochete and gonococcus have a short life span outside the body and that this was known in the earlier period; therefore such statements bear careful examination. In the case of nonsexual transmission of gonorrhea via "dirty" household goods (as mentioned above), I believe it is accurate to say that class stereo-

types influenced a belief that the lower classes had lower standards of morality and cleanliness and thus were more liable to disease. In addition, during the Second World War the campaign to prevent and control venereal disease was complicated by a definite strain of "moral purity" that promoted no sex outside marital reproductive sex. These "purists" fought vigorously against prophylaxis and perversions (i.e., oral sex) and eventually questioned the quick cure afforded by penicillin, finding it an invitation to promiscuity.

2. Paul De Kruif, *Microbe Hunters* (New York: Pocket Books, 1940), 322.

3. Thomas Parran, "A Negro Educational Project" (1943), ASHA Papers, Box 117.

4. John Duffy, "Social Impact of Disease in the Late 19th Century," in *Sickness and Health in America: Readings in the History of Medicine and Public Health*, ed. Judith Walzer Leavitt and Ronald L. Numbers (Madison: University of Wisconsin Press, 1978), 396.

5. Brandt, *No Magic Bullet*, 6.

6. Elizabeth Fee, "Venereal Disease: The Wages of Sin?" in *Passion and Power: Sexuality in History*, ed. Kathy Peiss and Christina Simmons (Philadelphia: Temple University Press, 1989), 178.

7. Elizabeth Fee, "Sin vs. Sex: Venereal Disease in Baltimore in the Twentieth Century," *Journal of the History of Medicine and Allied Sciences* 43 (April 1988): 142.

8. Charles E. Rosenberg, "Framing Disease: Illness, Society, and History," in *Framing Disease: Studies in Cultural History*, ed. Charles E. Rosenberg and Janet Golden (New Brunswick: Rutgers University Press, 1992), xiv.

9. Rosi Braidotti, "Signs of Wonder and Traces of Doubt: On Teratology and Embodied Difference," in *Between Monsters, Goddesses and Cyborgs: Feminist Confrontations with Science, Medicine and Cyberspace*, ed. Nina Lykke and Rosi Braidotti (London: Zed Books, 1996), 141.

10. Dijkstra, *Evil Sisters*. On masculine (sexual) anxiety, see Joe L. Dubbert, *A Man's Place: Masculinity in Transition* (Englewood Cliffs, NJ: Prentice Hall, 1979), and Kevin White, *The First Sexual Revolution: The Emergence of Male Heterosexuality in Modern America* (New York: New York University Press, 1993).

11. Mary Jacobus, introduction to *Body/Politics: Women and the Discourses of Science*, ed. Mary Jacobus, Evelyn Fox Keller, and Sally Shuttleworth (New York: Routledge, 1990), 2.

12. Jennifer Terry and Jacqueline Urla, "Introduction: Mapping Embodied Deviance," in *Deviant Bodies: Critical Perspectives on Difference in Science and Popular Culture*, ed. Jennifer Terry and Jacqueline Urla (Bloomington: Indiana University Press, 1995), 1.

13. Nancy Harrowitz, *Antisemitism, Misogyny, and the Logic of Cultural Difference* (Lincoln: University of Nebraska Press, 1994). On Lombroso, see also David G. Horn, "This Norm Which Is Not One: Reading the Female Body in Lombroso's Anthropology," in Terry and Urla, *Deviant Bodies*, 109–208.

14. On monstrosity and deviance, see also Rosi Braidotti, "Mothers, Monsters, and Machines," in *Writing on the Body: Female Embodiment and Feminist Theory* (New York: Columbia University Press, 1997), 59–79. Braidotti uses the theme of "monsters" to discuss "different" female bodies. For her, the category "monsters" is situated in a discourse of "the history and philosophy of the biological sciences."

15. Horn, "This Norm," 109.

16. Frances M. Heidensohn, *Women and Crime: The Life of the Female Offender* (New York: New York University Press, 1985), 147.

17. For "cesspools of infection," see Charles P. Taft, Speeches, NA RG 215, General Records, Box 13. Taft uttered this commonly used phrase. See also the equation of prostitution with "a slimy social swamp" in an FSA publication entitled "The Social Challenge of Prostitution," ASHA Papers, Box 129. For "syphilis soaked race," see Jones, *Bad Blood,* ch. 2.

18. Jennifer Terry, "The Body Invaded," *Socialist Review* 19 (March 1989): 14.

19. See, for example, J. M. Charcot and Valentine Magan, "Inversions du sens genital," *Archives de Neurologie* 3 and 4 (1882), and A. J. B. Parent-Duchalet's study of Parisian prostitutes, "De la prostitution dans la ville de Paris" (1836), cited in Walkowitz, *Prostitution,* 36–39. See also Cesare Lombroso and William Ferrero, *The Female Offender* (London: Fisher Unwin, 1895).

20. Colin Sumner, "Foucault, Gender and the Censure of Deviance," in *Feminist Perspectives in Criminology,* ed. Lorraine Gelsthorpe and Allison Morris (Philadelphia: Open University Press, 1990), 26–27.

21. On leisure and entertainment, see, for example, Meyerowitz, *Women Adrift,* and Peiss, *Cheap Amusements.* For additional insight into early-twentieth-century attitudes toward young women of the working class, see Mary E. Odem, *Delinquent Daughters: Protecting and Policing Adolescent Female Sexuality in the United States, 1885–1920* (Chapel Hill: University of North Carolina Press, 1995).

22. Flexner, *Prostitution in Europe,* and Kneeland, *Commercialized Prostitution. Regulation* refers to government control of prostitution, including registration with the local authorities, regular testing for venereal disease, a requirement to carry a health card, and residence in controlled houses and districts. Before 1970, only one city in the United States adopted regulation. Between 1870 and 1874, St. Louis licensed brothels and required medical

inspection by public health officials. Pressure from the public ended the experiment.

23. Woolston, *Prostitution*.

24. Ibid., 54.

25. Charles P. Taft, Speeches, 1942, NA RG 215, General Records, Box 13.

26. Woolston, *Prostitution*, 153, 54–58, 54, 102–3. Woolston's comments on the extension of the federal government's efforts to control sexuality into the post–World War I period foreshadowed increased government intervention into the realm of sexuality in the coming years. Woolston was not alone in favoring federal control of sexuality or in focusing on black and "lower-class" neighborhoods. See also Reckless, *Vice in Chicago*.

27. Woolston, *Prostitution*, 145.

28. While class per se is invisible in the World War II records regarding sexual control efforts, its presence as a causal factor in deciding which women were termed prostitutes or promiscuous is evident in the choice of where the watching took place: at sites of working-class recreation. See Meyerowitz, *Women Adrift*, and Peiss, *Cheap Amusements*. More recent scholarship on prostitution is helpful in tracing social and political attitudes based on gender, race, and class. See, for example, Marion S. Goldman, *Gold Diggers and Silver Miners: Prostitution and Social Life on the Comstock Lode* (Ann Arbor: University of Michigan Press, 1981); Barbara Meil Hobson, *Uneasy Virtue: The Politics of Prostitution and the American Reform Tradition* (New York: Basic Books, 1987); Ruth Rosen, *Prostitution and Victorian Society: Women, Class, and the State* (Baltimore: Johns Hopkins University Press, 1982); and Walkowitz, *Prostitution and Victorian Society*.

29. Woolston, *Prostitution*, 52–54.

30. For reference to "a touch of lavender," see "A 'Second Front' against Prostitution: Techniques for Repressing 'Unorganized' Prostitution, as Recommended by the Special Committee on Enforcement of the National Advisory Police Committee," *Journal of Social Hygiene* 29 (January 1943): 43–50. On marked bodies, see, for example, Edwin J. Lukas, "Digging at the Roots of Prostitution," *Probation* 22 (April 1944): 97–100. See also Jennifer Terry, "Anxious Slippages between 'Us' and 'Them': A Brief History of the Scientific Search for Homosexual Bodies," in Terry and Urla, *Deviant Bodies*, 129–69. On lesbianism during World War II, see Sherna B. Gluck, *Rosie the Riveter Revisited: Women, the War, and Social Change* (Boston: Twayne, 1987). On p. 250, one of the women that Gluck interviewed tells about the FBI conducting an investigation to find lesbians at Lockheed Aircraft in California. For a discussion of lesbian prostitutes, see Elizabeth

Lapovsky Kennedy and Madeline D. Davis, *Boots of Leather, Slippers of Gold: The History of a Lesbian Community* (New York: Routledge, 1993), 96–104.

31. New York City Health Department, investigation of a "Localized Outbreak of Syphilis in New York City," chart, c. 1940, ASHA Papers, Box 115.

32. Woolston, *Prostitution,* 69 and 153.

33. Ibid.

34. See, for example, "Preventing Prostitution, Promiscuity and Disease: Denver Preliminary Report," NA RG 215, Publications, Box 3. The report called for, in part, surveillance of girls at public amusement sites.

35. See NA RG 215, Regional, Box 1, for an interoffice communication from Marie Duffin (senior specialist, FSA) to Acting Director Morrissey (SPD) of August 28, 1944. Duffin and Miss March (Welfare Council, New York City) had been carrying on discussions regarding the term *pickup.* While many servicemen classified their sexual partners as pickups, with the implication that they did not pay for sex, Duffin and March felt the categories *prostitute* and *pickup* overlapped.

36. Reckless, *Vice in Chicago,* viii, 15–16. Reckless, like Woolston, favored more state control of the sexual arena. During World War II, Reckless was a professor of sociology in the School of Social Administration at Ohio State University; he continued to address prostitution. See, for example, Walter C. Reckless, "A Sociologist Looks at Prostitution," *Federal Probation* 7 (April–June 1943): 12–16.

37. Reckless, *Vice in Chicago,* xii, 28, 15.

38. FBI, *Uniform Crime Reports,* 1941–45.

39. See, for example, *Annual Report of the Surgeon General of the Public Health Service of the United States for the Fiscal Year 1941* (Washington, DC: U.S. Government Printing Office, 1941), *Annual Report of the Surgeon General of the Public Health Service of the United States for the Fiscal Years 1942–1943* (Washington, DC: U.S. Government Printing Office, 1942–43), and *Annual Report of the Surgeon General of the Public Health Service of the United States for the Fiscal Years 1944–1945* (Washington, DC: U.S. Government Printing Office, 1944–45), as published by the FSA. In terms of the venereal diseases, the USPHS had officers in the forty-eight states and in Alaska, Puerto Rico, Virgin Islands, Hawaii, Panama, and Trinidad and serving with the Anglo-American Commission. The USPHS officers served in a variety of capacities throughout the Pacific and European theaters of war. On the history of the USPHS, see John Duffy, *The Sanitarians: A History of American Public Health* (Urbana: University of Chicago Press, 1992).

40. Raymond A. Vonderlehr, "The Venereal Disease Control Act," ARSG 1943, 147. Dr. Vonderlehr was in charge of the Division of Venereal Diseases, USPHS.

41. Ibid., 148.

42. Ibid. The focus on promiscuous girls, taverns, and certain areas resonates with the themes of the earlier studies by Woolston and Reckless.

43. Kary L. Moss, ed., *Man-Made Medicine: Women's Health, Public Policy, and Reform* (Durham: Duke University Press, 1996), 2.

44. See Walkowitz, *Prostitution and Victorian Society*. Walkowitz discusses the British Contagious Diseases Acts, which in fact have remarkable similarities with the policies of World War II regarding women and disease. On mentally ill women, see, for example, Elaine Showalter, *The Female Malady: Women, Madness, and English Culture, 1830–1980* (New York: Penguin Books, 1985).

45. Judith Walzer Leavitt, "Gendered Expectations: Women and Early Twentieth-Century Public Health," in *U.S. History as Women's History: New Feminist Essays*, ed. Linda Kerber, Alice Kessler-Harris, and Kathryn Kish Sklar (Chapel Hill: University of North Carolina Press, 1995), 147–69.

46. Ibid. Mallon has been described as overly large for a woman and as apt to fight and swear. In fact she was neither large nor unattractive. George Soper, a sanitary engineer and expert epidemiologist, described Mallon as having a "determined mouth and jaw, walking like a man and as having a mind with a distinctly masculine character." Soper was not alone in questioning Mallon's femininity; a medical publication characterized her as "a perfect Amazon, weighing over 200 pounds." And Dr. S. Josephine Baker (of the New York City Health Department) focused on Mallon's "fierceness —she was like an angry lion, she was maniacal, she fought and swore." Mallon, a cook, was first incarcerated in 1907 and briefly released. She returned to food service and was apprehended again. Healthy male carriers, including those in the business of handling food, were not treated in the same manner. Mallon was incarcerated for life; men went back into society, and some men continued to work at jobs involving food preparation. Quotes on 161, 152, 156f.

47. Ray H. Everett, "Program Emphases for Preparedness Conditions," *Journal of Social Hygiene* 26 (November 1940): 366.

48. Bascomb Johnson, "Vice Prevention and the Defense Program," in *Proceedings of the Seventy-First Annual Congress of the American Prison Association* (New York: American Prison Association, 1941), 150.

49. "She Looked Clean—But . . . Tells Tavern Men Why Venereal Disease Control Is Important," *Ohio Tavern News*, July 25, 1945, 8, NA RG 215, General Records, Box 1. See also Charles P. Taft, Speeches, 1942, NA

RG 215, General Records, Box 13. Taft also speaks of the possibility of a mechanical carrier.

50. Lukas, "Digging at the Roots."

51. Robert D. Weitz and H. L. Rachlin, "The Mental Ability and Educational Attainment of 500 Venereally Infected Females," *Journal of Social Hygiene* 31 (May 1945): 300–303. A median equals the exact middle and indicates that half of the subjects had a score above 84 and half below 84. The significance of such statistics is unclear because, in part, we do not have a definition of "defective."

52. Dorothy Roberts, *Killing the Black Body: Race, Reproduction, and the Meaning of Liberty* (New York: Pantheon Books, 1997), 63. For more on the eugenics movement, see also Linda Gordon, *Woman's Body, Woman's Right: Birth Control in America* (New York: Penguin Books, 1977), and Degler, *In Search of Human Nature.*

53. See Benno Safier et al., *A Psychiatric Approach to the Treatment of Promiscuity* (New York: American Social Hygiene Association, 1949), 1. This is an amended report of a psychiatric study begun in 1941 and carried out under the auspices of the Venereal Disease Division, the USPHS, the California State Department of Public Health, and the San Francisco Department of Public Health. This part of the study was conducted between January 1943 and July 1947. For information on the early years of the study, see "An Experiment in the Psychiatric Treatment of Promiscuous Girls," NA RG 215, Publications, Box 1.

54. Safier et al., *Psychiatric Approach,* 12.

55. Ibid. A taxi dancer was a girl or woman who was employed by a dance hall or a nightclub to dance with men. The men paid a fee for each dance. They were also referred to as dime-a-dance girls.

56. Ibid. "An Experiment in the Psychiatric Treatment of Promiscuous Girls," 1941, NA RG 215, Publications, Box 1.

57. Safier et al., *Psychiatric Approach,* 19–20. This study claimed a significant incidence of "mental deficiency," while simultaneously stating (in a footnote) that the incidence of women with IQs lower than 80 was statistically insignificant (19 n.). Once again, there are many problems with the meaning of such statistics. For example, we do not know what type of IQ test was administered, a factor that would affect our reading of the results. The researchers also noted that "the sex instruction which patients had received was for the most part inadequate and unscientific" (23). Women's lack of sexual knowledge is a theme that threads throughout the records. On this topic, see also Eleanor L. Hutzel, "The Policewoman's Role in Social Protection," *Journal of Social Hygiene* 30 (1944): 538–44.

58. Safier et al., *Psychiatric Approach,* 21.

59. Ibid., 20.

60. Ibid., 28, 30.

61. Ibid., 35, 37.

62. Ibid., 3, 4.

63. J. G. Wilson, "The Female Psychopath," in *Proceedings of the Seventy-Second Annual Congress of the American Prison Association* (New York: American Prison Association, 1942), 153–59. This study was conducted at the Reformatory for Women in Clifton, New Jersey.

64. "Psychiatric Service in Venereal Disease Clinic," News from the Field, *American Journal of Public Health* 33 (February 1943): 195.

65. Arrested girls, Seattle, Washington, a report on services offered contained in the minutes of a meeting on January 5, 1945. The report discussed both studies. NA RG 215, Publications, Box 4.

66. Ibid.

67. Indeterminate sentences were supported by female law enforcement officials. An indeterminate sentence did not involve a fixed or standard time period; it allowed a woman to be held until the authorities determined that she had been rehabilitated—that is, that she would accept an appropriate female role. See, for example, *Prison World* (November–December 1943): 22; Elizabeth Munger, "Indeterminate Sentences," in *Proceedings of the Seventy-Third Annual Congress of the American Prison Association* (New York: American Prison Association, 1943): 149–50; and Paul W. Tappan, *Delinquent Girls in Court: A Study of the Wayward Minor Court of New York* (New York: Columbia University Press, 1947), 57.

68. Gertrude M. Smith, Supervisor, Medical Social Work, USO, "Digest of Report, USO Travelers Aid Service in the Three Quarantine Hospitals of South Carolina, August 1943–July 1944," NA RG 215, General Records, Box 13.

69. Ibid.

70. Jonathan Daniels, "Disease and Punishment," *Nation*, August 1941, 162.

71. "Lindbergh Home to Be V.D. Treatment Center," News from the Field, *American Journal of Public Health* 33 (February 1943): 195.

72. Women's resistance is discussed in ch. 6.

73. Memo from the Chief of the Bureau of Medicine and Surgery to All Commanding Officers, November 30, 1942, NA RG 52, Box 2.

74. See Bailey and Farber, *First Strange Place*; Meyer, *Creating GI Jane*; Gary Gerstle, *American Crucible: Race and Nation in the Twentieth Century* (Princeton: Princeton University Press, 2001), ch. 5; and Jerrold M. Packard, *American Nightmare: The History of Jim Crow* (New York: St. Martin's Press, 2002): ch. 6.

75. Henry H. Hazen, *Syphilis in the Negro: A Handbook for the General Practitioner* (Washington, DC: U.S. Government Printing Office, 1942), 57–

58. See also "What Army Blood Tests Reveal," *American Journal of Public Health* 33 (September 1943): 1137. A section on books and reports in the September 1943 issue of the *American Journal of Public Health* referred to an article in the June issue of the *Journal of the American Medical Association* entitled "Syphilis in the U.S. Primarily a Negro Problem" as an example of popular commentaries around venereal disease that were interfering with a comprehensive program of venereal disease prevention and control. On inadequate health care, see Paul B. Cornley, "Trends in Public Health Activities among Negroes in 96 Southern Counties during the Period 1930–1939," *American Journal of Public Health* 32 (October 1942): 1117–24, which discusses the lack of venereal disease clinics in rural areas populated by blacks, and Joseph W. Mountin, "Responsibility of Local Health Authorities in the War Emergency," *American Journal of Public Health* 33 (January 1943): 35–38. Dr. Mountin wrote of the extreme inadequacy of public health facilities in many areas, reporting that some had only "paper" services and others lacked medical personnel and were headed by political appointees.

76. Hazen, *Syphilis in the Negro,* vii.

77. Ibid.

78. M. I. Roemer, "Negro Migratory Workers in New Jersey," *The Crisis,* November 1942, 364.

79. A. Oppenheim, "Health Education in Action," *American Journal of Public Health* 33 (November 1943): 1338–42.

80. See Howard Whipple Green, *Cases of Syphilis under Treatment in Cuyahoga County during March 1943* (Cleveland, OH: Cleveland Health Council, 1943), for confirmation of this point. See also William A. Brumfield Jr., James H. Lade, and Louis L. Feldman, "The Epidemiology of Syphilis Based upon Five Years Experience in an Intensive Program in New York State," *American Journal of Public Health* 32 (August 1942): 793–802.

81. Green, *Cases of Syphilis.*

82. "Along the NAACP Battlefront," *The Crisis,* July 1943, 211–16. On cuts to minority services, see "U.S. Indian Medical Service Curtailed," News from the Field, *American Journal of Public Health* 32 (September 1942): 1078; it notes that the U.S. Indian Medical Service had been curtailed due to reductions in appropriations. The cut in funds resulted in closing two hospitals in New Mexico and Arizona. The position of the medical director of the Navajo area, who had supervised nine hospitals and three TB sanitariums and overseen the public health program for fifty-three thousand Navajos, was abolished. "The reason for the present retrenchment is given as a war necessity."

83. Hazen, *Syphilis in the Negro.*

84. Desowitz, *Who Gave Pinta,* 56–57.

85. Hazen, *Syphilis in the Negro*, 57–58.

86. William Styron, "A Case of the Great Pox," *New Yorker,* September 18, 1995, 62–75. On the Kahn, see also *Navy Department Bulletin,* June 1942, which discussed the test's high sensitivity and cautioned that it should be used as a "screen test . . . and must never be used for the final report on positive reactions." The Kahn test was used in mass blood testings because it was "fast and easy." In the *American Journal of Public Health* 33 (September 1943): 1130, James H. Lade reviewed a book, Reuben L. Kahn's *Serology in Syphilis Control: Principles in Sensitivity and Specificity,* that also spoke to a widespread problem with false positives and the Kahn test.

87. Styron, "Case of the Great Pox," 75.

88. See, for example, G. E. Thomas and R. W. Garrity, "Report of 10,000 Tests Made on Naval Recruits, San Diego, California, January 1941," ASHA Papers, Box 130. This report discussed twenty-six strongly positive Kahn tests that were false positives and sixteen doubtful tests that subsequently tested negative. The investigators found a possible connection in relation to cowpox vaccinations and the false positives. See also C. B. Bonner and Edgar F. Kiser, "Incidence of Syphilis in Private Practice," reprint from the *Journal of the American Medical Association,* ASHA Papers, Box 115; Connie M. Guion, Elizabeth Adams, and A. Parks McCombs, "The Blood Wassermann Reaction in 300 Private Patients," New York, February 1941, ASHA Papers, Box 115; John A. Kolmer, "The Problem of Falsely Doubtful and Positive Reactions in the Sereology of Syphilis," *American Journal of Public Health* 34 (May 1944): 510–14; L. E. Burney, J. R. S. Mays, and Albert P. Iskrant, "Results of Serologic Tests for Syphilis in Non-syphilitic Persons Innoculated with the Malaria," *American Journal of Public Health* 32 (January 1942): 39–47.

89. Burney, Mays, and Iskrant, "Results of Serological Tests."

90. Memo for Admiral McIntire from Mr. Osborne, Committee on Recreation and Morale, March 16, 1941, NA RG 52, Box 2.

91. Dr. A. W. Dumas, editorial, *Baltimore Afro-American,* February 26, 1936, as discussed in the *National Negro Health News* 4 (January–March 1936): 1, Schomberg Library, New York.

92. Jones, *Bad Blood.*

93. Ibid.

94. Quoted in ibid., 106.

95. Quoted in ibid., 105.

96. Ibid. See also when USPHS officers "denied any racial overtones to the experiment" (Jones, *Bad Blood,* 12) but the *Baltimore Afro-American* wrote: "How condescending and void of credibility are the claims that racial considerations had nothing to do with the fact that 600 [all] of the subjects were black" (quoted in ibid., 12). Many newspaper editors (in 1972,

when the experiment became known to the public) used the term *moral insensitivity* to describe the USPHS officials. The *National Negro Health News* reported frequently on the problem of venereal disease, as did the *Baltimore Afro-American* newspaper.

97. See A. W. Dumas, "National Negro Health Week Observance," *National Negro Health News* 4 (April–June 1936): 16, for an editorial reprinted from the *Journal of the National Medical Association* (May 1936) that noted, "This movement has done more to arouse interest in health matters, and has made the negro more health conscious than any other agency for the promotion of the general welfare of the negro race in America."

98. Ibid.

99. See *ARSG 1941*, 103–4.

100. M. Leider, S. Brookins, and V. McDaniel, "Biography of a Civilian Committee on Venereal Disease Control: The Negro War-Time Health Committee of Pensacola, Florida," *Journal of Social Hygiene* 30 (February 1944): 67–71.

101. Dumas, "National Negro Health Week Observance," 16.

102. Nelson C. Jackson, "Community Organization Activities among Negroes for Venereal Disease Control," *Social Forces* 23 (October 1944–May 1945): 65–70.

103. Ibid.

104. Edward V. Taylor, "The Negro Community's Share in Prevention" (September 18, 1944), 1, 2, NA RG 215, General Records, Box 7.

105. Jackson, "Community Organization Activities," 65–68.

106. "Abstract of Proceedings: Conference with Negro Leaders on War-time Problems in Venereal Disease Control," *Journal of Social Hygiene* 30 (November 1944): 80. This committee, formed by African Americans following a conference of black and white leaders to discuss social problems, including venereal disease, agreed that, in addition to economics, several other factors contributed to the high venereal disease rates among African Americans. Included was "the low level of educational advantages available to the Negro population, with resulting widespread illiteracy and near illiteracy."

107. Dr. M. Davis Elkind (USPHS) to Dr. Weiss, April 12, 1944, ASHA Papers, Box 118.

108. Paul B. Cornley, M.D., head, Department of Bacteriology, Preventive Medicine and Public Health, Howard University, to Mr. Cabot, acting director, Public Information Service, ASHA, December 1, 1943, ASHA Papers, Box 119. Cornley wrote in response to a draft of a VD pamphlet for African American servicemen, pointing out that its language was not accessible to a "low literacy group" and that prophylactic information was missing. He also noted that the "appeal to patriotism, sense of duty, etc.," was

not an effective line to take in terms of avoiding venereal disease. Cornley added that "[t]his is particularly true of the Negro soldier, whose morale, is at present quite low because of the many injustices he faces in the southern area, such as lack of recreational facilities and a decent place to eat and sleep when he is on furlough."

109. Fee, "Venereal Disease," 178.

110. See Robin Marantz Henig, "The Lessons of Syphilis in the Age of AIDS," *Civilization* 2 (November/December 1995): 36–43.

NOTES TO CHAPTER 4

1. Advisory Committee on Social Protection, minutes of an all-day meeting to discuss problems and programs, June 14, 1941, NA RG 215, Committee Meetings, Box 1. Dr. Glueck, a sociologist, is listed under "Education."

2. Dubbert, *Man's Place*, ch. 8. Dubbert is quoting Jonathan Daniels, soon to become President Roosevelt's administrative assistant.

3. Robert W. Connell, "Arms and the Man: Using the New Research on Masculinity to Understand Violence and Promote Peace in the Contemporary World," in *Male Roles, Masculinities and Violence: A Culture of Peace Perspective*, by Ingeborg Brienes, Robert Connell, and Ingrid Eid (Paris: UNESCO Publishing, 2000), 21.

4. Meyer, *Creating GI Jane*, 3. In this section, Meyer refers to Anthony Rotundo, *American Manhood: Transformations in Masculinity from the Revolution to the Modern Era* (New York: Basic Books, 1993).

5. Joshua S. Goldstein, *War and Gender* (Cambridge: Cambridge University Press, 2001), 264.

6. See, for example, Breines, Connell, and Eid, *Male Roles*, 14.

7. Susan Gubar, " 'This Is My Rifle, This Is My Gun': World War II and the Blitz on Women," in *Behind the Lines: Gender and the Two World Wars*, ed. Margaret Randolph Higonnet et al. (New Haven: Yale University Press, 1987), 227–59, esp. 252.

8. See, for example, Michael Kimmell, *Manhood in America: A Cultural History* (New York: Free Press, 1996); R. W. Connell, *Masculinities* (Berkeley: University of California Press, 1995); and Rotundo, *American Manhood*.

9. D'Amico and Weinstein, *Gender Camouflage*, 6.

10. Enloe, *Maneuvers*, x, 36.

11. On victory girls, see Anderson, *Wartime Women*; and *No Magic Bullet*.

12. Statement of Joseph Earle Moore, M.D., Chairman, Subcommittee on Venereal Diseases, National Research Council before the Joint Army and

Navy Committee on Welfare and Recreation, Washington, DC, February 28, 1941, NA RG 52, Box 10. Moore was connected with Johns Hopkins University.

13. Ibid. Moore, in this case, was challenging the practice of having senior hostesses to create a homelike/motherly setting for young servicemen as well as to serve as chaperones for junior hostesses.

14. Ibid.

15. Treadwell, *Woman's Army Corps,* and Meyer, *Creating GI Jane.*

16. Barbara Brooks Tomblin, *GI Nightingales: The Army Nurse Corps in World War II* (Lexington: University Press of Kentucky, 1996), 51.

17. Tucker, *Swing Shift,* 59.

18. See Dubbert, *Man's Place,* ch. 8. Dubbert suggests that military training aimed to standardize men and that part of this process was the elimination of a "sissified boy-scout" mentality because it "bordered on being effeminate." Dubbert also cites studies of the time that blame a lack of manliness on mothers and that then suggest that men's sexual activity was a reaction to (s)mothering. Either way, women shouldered the blame for male promiscuity. See also Paul Fussell, *Wartime: Understanding and Behavior in the Second World War* (New York: Oxford University Press, 1989), for insights into male behaviors and attitudes as influenced by the military.

19. Breines, Connell, and Eid, *Male Roles,* 14.

20. Joseph Heller, *Now and Then: A Memoir, from Coney Island to Here* (London: Simon and Schuster, 1998), 170.

21. Dr. Moore to the Committee on Venereal Disease Control, August 8, 1940, unmarked page, NA RG 52, Box 10. Part of the document he referred to may be found in Army/Navy, NA RG 215, General Records.

22. Ibid.

23. Ibid.

24. Enloe, *Maneuvers,* 52.

25. "Survey of Commercialized Prostitution Conditions, March Field, California," December 1940, NA RG 215, Committee Meetings, Box 1.

26. "Survey of Commercialized Prostitution Conditions, March Field, California," December 1940, NA RG 215, Committee Meetings, Box 1.

27. Ibid.

28. All of the above quotations are from ibid. Attitudes similar to those of state officials and businessmen discussed above were fairly common throughout the war period. See, for example, a memo from the OWI, July 1942, that referred to the "policy of regulation and toleration still practiced in some communities." NA RG 215, Committee Meetings, Box 1. And see the September 18, 1942, meeting of the Interdepartmental Committee that mentioned that some states had failed to adopt repression. NA RG 215, Committee Meetings, Box 1.

29. Kathleen Barry, *Female Sexual Slavery* (New York: New York University Press, 1979), xi, xii.

30. Ibid., 121.

31. Bailey and Farber, *First Strange Place*, 99.

32. "Survey of Commercialized Prostitution Conditions, March Field, California," December 1940, NA RG 215, Committee Meetings, Box 1.

33. See interoffice memo from Manfred Lillefors to Thomas Devine, director, SPD, March 22, 1945, advising him to stop the division's practice of releasing statements claiming that rape had decreased when houses of prostitution had been closed. Lillefors pointed out that rape had increased according to FBI records and that "someday someone [would] quote the FBI crime report" that showed the increase. NA RG 215, Statistics and Studies, Box 2. See also Estelle B. Freedman, "'Uncontrolled Desires': The Response to the Sexual Psychopath, 1930–1960," *Journal of American History* 74 (June 1987): 83–106. She points out that male sex crimes were underreported, if not deliberately suppressed, during the war years. Her contentions are supported by the FBI records discussed above stating that forcible rape had increased but that statutory rape had decreased. In fact, a number of underage girls were arrested, some in "compromising" circumstances, but servicemen were not prosecuted as they could have been for impairing the morals of a minor, if not for statutory rape. See also Dr. Ralph S. Banay's "Emotional Factors in Wartime Delinquency," *Probation* 21 (April 1943): 103, which asserted that during wartime male crimes of violence and sex were increasing. Although instances of forcible rape were suppressed, in at least one case a rape was prosecuted; the men involved were African American. See "Help Save These Soldiers," *The Crisis*, March 1943, 95; "Error in Soldier Rape Trial," June 1943, 180–81; and "Supreme Court Ruling Saves Men," July 1943, 212. Three black soldiers were accused of raping a white woman in Alexandria, Louisiana, and were quickly tried, found guilty, and sentenced to death.

34. Memo from Dr. Walter Clarke (ASHA) to Paul V. McNutt (FSA), January 21, 1941, NA RG 215, Committee Meetings, Box 1.

35. Excerpts from an (undated) article in *Survey Graphic* entitled "No War Boom in Venereal Disease," by William F. Snow, that referred to the Tacoma warning of July 1941, NA RG 215, Publications, Box 4.

36. "A Report on Repression Program in El Paso, Texas," NA RG 215, Statistics and Studies, Box 6.

37. Ibid.

38. Ibid.

39. Ibid.

40. Ibid. SPD representatives threatened recalcitrant officials with the May Act. Neither military nor public officials wanted the federal govern-

ment intervening in their areas of influence. Some level of compliance with the SPD directive seemed a better strategy. In a few instances, military officials used the threat of the May Act against private citizens such as tavern owners.

41. Ibid.

42. Ibid.

43. Memo for Admiral McIntyre, September 16, 1941, NA RG 52, Box 2.

44. Bailey and Farber, *First Strange Place,* 108–9.

45. Memo from the Adjutant General's Office, War Department, to Commanding Generals and Commanding Officers, October 10, 1941, NA RG 18. See also the file "Circular No. 170," NA RG 18 (circular was marked as "not available").

46. Memo from Major General J. A. Ulio to Commanding Generals Army Airforce, Defense Commands, Service Commands, July 31, 1943, ASHA Papers, Box 131.

47. Memo from Interdepartmental Committee on Venereal Disease Control, November 16, 1942, NA RG 215, Committee Meetings, Box 1.

48. Correspondence pertaining to the Stone Grill and other taverns in Columbus, Ohio, including a copy of a newspaper article (untitled), NA RG 18, Morals and Conduct. The letter to President Roosevelt was written by Samuel Stone, President, Stone Grill Company, August 13, 1942.

49. Ibid. The file on the Stone Grill complaint was sent to the commanding general of the Army Air Forces in Washington, D.C.; Col. Baldinger was then informed to "limit his activities."

50. Ibid. The remarks of Judge Wayne Fogel (Franklin County, Ohio) are contained in a partial (undated) reprint of a newspaper article (name of newspaper not available) entitled "Liquor, Dance Bars Asked for Action Due Today on Tavern-Keepers' Plan for Drinking, Curfew, Dancing Restrictions."

51. See, for example, Sheriffs File: Letter to the State Attorneys General, November 18, 1942, NA RG 215, General Records, Box 1. Also see legal brief, December 1942, NA RG 215, Publications, Box 1.

52. "Survey of Commercialized Prostitution Conditions, March Field, California," December 1940, NA RG 215, Committee Meetings, Box 1.

53. Ibid.

54. Ibid.

55. On prostitution and sex and race relations in World War II Hawaii, see Bailey and Farber, *First Strange Place,* 99.

56. Ibid., 95.

57. Ibid., 99.

58. Quoted in ibid.

59. NAPCSP, June 30, 1942, NA RG 215, Committee Meetings, Box 4.

60. Statement of James E. Moore, MD, Chairman of the Subcommittee on Venereal Disease, National Research Council, before the Joint Army Navy Committee on Welfare and Recreation, February 28, 1941, NA RG 52, Box 10. See also Bailey and Farber, *First Strange Place*, ch. 3. In Hawaii, where there were numerous regulated brothels, some houses operated on a schedule of three minutes per customer that would support these numbers.

61. NAPCSP, June 30, 1942, NA RG 215, Committee Meetings, Box 4.

62. "Health and Social Welfare," two pages with no other headings, dated November 1942, NA RG 52, Box 10. See also Bailey and Farber, *First Strange Place*, 99.

63. Bailey and Farber, *First Strange Place*, ch. 3.

64. See, for example, Margaret T. Lynch, executive secretary, National Council of Catholic Women, to Eliot Ness, requesting that the organization's name be removed from the pamphlet *Meet Your Enemy*, May 31, 1944. Miss Lynch informed Ness that the VD pamphlet had certain critical deficiencies, including "a lack of stress on the moral law and the formation of character." Repeated attempts to convince the council to change its mind failed. NA RG 215, General Records, Box 2. See also letters from Miss Barnett and Mrs. Barnett to General Arnold, October 15, 1940. The women asked the general to "do everything in his power to have governmental measures passed whereby no intoxicating beverages will be allowed in or near our soldiers' encampments." They said many of their friends supported their stance. The Women's Society of Christian Service, of a Methodist church in Florida, wrote a similar letter on November 4, 1940, NA RG 18, Morals and Conduct, Central Decimal Files. These women and others objected to a general lack of a moral tone in the military.

65. *So Long Boys . . . Take Care of Yourselves*, pamphlet, NA RG 215, Publications, Box 4.

66. Ibid.

67. Brandt, *No Magic Bullet*, 164.

68. Memo for Admiral McIntire, January 31, 1941, Subject: Venereal Disease Control, NA RG 52, Box 2. (Snow was the former director of the ASHA.)

69. Ibid.

70. Ibid.

71. Wickware, "Army Fights VD."

72. "Keeping Up with Medicine," *Good Housekeeping*, April 1943, 119.

73. "San Francisco Opens Three Prophylactic Stations," News from the Field, *American Journal of Public Health* 33 (February 1943): 195.

74. Navy Bureau of Medicine and Surgery, Headquarters Records, Correspondence, NA RG 52, Box 22.

75. Form letter from the Chief of the Bureau of Medicine and Surgery to All Ships and Stations, Subject: Venereal Disease Prophylaxis, August 10, 1942, NA RG 52, Box 2.

76. Memo for Admiral McIntire, January 31, 1941, Subject: Venereal Disease Control, NA RG 52, Box 2.

77. Memo from the Interdepartmental Committee on Venereal Disease Control, November 16, 1942, NA RG 215, Caribbean Records, Box 1.

78. Packard, *American Nightmare*, 194–95.

79. Ibid.

80. A Soldier's Mother to General H. H. Arnold, November 27, 1941, NA RG 18, Morals and Conduct, Central Decimal Files.

81. War Department Memo of December 9, 1941, NA RG 18, Morals and Conduct, Central Decimal Files. The ship was stationed in the Philippines; apparently the attack on Pearl Harbor influenced the decision to take no action. There are no documents addressing the alleged situation at Moffett Field.

82. Letter from the law firm of Birmingham and Kennedy, July 6, 1942, NA RG 18, Morals and Conduct.

83. Memo dated July 9, 1942, from Headquarters of the Army Air Forces, Washington, DC, to the Adjutant General, NA RG 18, Morals and Conduct.

84. See "Venereal Disease Information," January 1944, NA RG 215, General Records, Box 8. This file contains excerpts from a journal on the topic of polls and public opinion and refers to a poll of high school girls. Of the girls polled, 94 percent "suggested that sex information be incorporated in 'some related course' in school."

85. J. Blan van Urk, "Norfolk—Our Worst War Town," *American Mercury,* February 1943, 144–51. In this article, the prostitute was identified as a black woman. Black women were arrested in disproportionate numbers.

86. Freedman, "Uncontrolled Desires." See also Banay, "Emotional Factors." Susan Brownmiller, *Against Our Will: Men, Women, and Rape* (New York: Penguin Books, 1975), 64. She points out that the U.S. military did not keep rape statistics during World War II. However, correspondence between the SPD and various officials indicate that rape did increase during the war years. FBI statistics support this claim. However, articles in *The Crisis* in March, June, July 1943 ("Help Save These Soldiers," "Error in Soldier Rape Trial," and "Supreme Court Ruling Saves Men") note that several African American servicemen were accused of rape.

87. Memo from the National Research Council to the Committee on Health and Medicine, FSA, January 28, 1941. The document was signed by Dr. J. E. Moore, Chairman, Subcommittee on Venereal Diseases, National Research Council. NA RG 52, Box 10.

88. On women and health cards, see, for example, Bracy, "U.S.O. Travelers Aid Service," 10. See also Gertrude M. Smith, Supervisor of Medical Social Work, USO Travelers Aid Service, "Digest of Report Covering the Period from August 1943 to July 1944," NA RG 215, Committee Meetings, Box 1. The report refers, in part, to women who were apprehended because they did not have a health card. Routine examinations were required for civilian food handlers, especially waitresses; if the women were found free of venereal disease, they received health cards. While many employers ignored the requirement, they were not penalized for hiring women without health cards. However, if a waitress was "found to be employed without one, action was taken against her, such as arrest and forced examination."

89. Form letter from Chief of Navy Department, Bureau of Medicine and Surgery to Various Commanding Officers, Navy and Commandant, Marine Corps (March 17, 1942) regarding a change in the manual approved by the Secretary of the Navy, NA RG 52, Box 9. Withholding pay from venereally diseased servicemen was also discontinued.

90. Ibid.

91. SPD records call for immediate discharge. See also Meyer, *Creating GI Jane*, who indicates that this matter was more complex and that practices varied.

92. See Brandt, *No Magic Bullet*, ch. 5. See also Higonnet et al., *Behind the Lines*.

93. *So Long Boys*.

94. See Brandt, *No Magic Bullet*.

95. See Styron, "Case of the Great Pox."

96. Zeke Cook, "Battle Line Venereal Disease," *Newsweek*, November 20, 1944, 76–79.

97. "The Twain Do Meet: Oldest Profession Thrives in India," *Newsweek*, September, 11, 1944, 63–64, followed by "Service Ribbon," *Newsweek*, November 13, 1944, 59.

98. Treadwell, *Woman's Army Corps*, ch. 11. In fact, the mobilization of female sexuality backfired in terms of recruitment of women for military service and for military nurses. The armed services got such a bad reputation with parents, husbands, boyfriends, and brothers that many forbade their relatives to join up.

99. Robert B. Westbrook, "I Want a Girl, Just Like the Girl That Married Harry James: American Women and the Problem of Political Obligation in World War II," *American Quarterly* 42 (December 1990): 587–614.

100. Bailey and Farber, *First Strange Place*.

101. Joel T. Boone, "The Sexual Aspects of Military Personnel," *Journal of Social Hygiene* 27 (March 1941): 113–24.

NOTES TO CHAPTER 5

1. See, for example, "ASHA Defense Related Activities for the Office of Civilian Defense, 1941," ASHA Papers, Box 129, file "Military Reports," esp. "Publicity Aids," February 5, 1941. On propaganda, see Honey, *Creating Rosie the Riveter;* Hartmann, "Prescriptions for Penelope"; and Rupp, *Mobilizing Women for War.* On magazines, see James Playstead Wood, *Magazines in the United States,* 3rd ed. (New York: Ronald Press, 1971), 367. Wood suggested that wartime magazines served as a forum for government policies and programs regarding economic, social, and sometimes military problems. Media, he contended, were "immediately utilized for morale purposes and for the dissemination of war doctrine to produce concerted national action." On militarization, see Raymond Fielding, *The American Newsreel, 1911–1967* (Norman: University of Oklahoma Press, 1972), 288. Between 1942 and 1946, 80 percent of all newsreel footage was devoted to some aspect of war.

2. See George H. Roeder Jr., *The Censored War: American Visual Experience during World War II* (New Haven: Yale University Press, 1993), esp. ch. 1. See also Fielding, *The American Newsreel.* In "early newsreel footage . . . the dead and maimed were rarely shown" (292).

3. J. C. Furnas, "Women Wanted," *Ladies Home Journal,* November 1942, 20.

4. On this topic, see Anderson, *Wartime Women;* Berube, *Coming Out under Fire;* Campbell, *Women at War;* Costello, *Love, Sex, and War;* Elaine Tyler May, *Homeward Bound: American Families in the Cold War Era* (New York: Basic Books, 1988); and Meyer, *Creating GI Jane.*

5. On the use of prescriptive literature, see, for example, Honey, *Creating Rosie the Riveter;* Milkman, *Gender at Work;* and Hartmann, "Prescriptions for Penelope."

6. Phyllis Palmer, *Domesticity and Dirt: Housewives and Domestic Servants in the United States, 1920–1945* (Philadelphia: Temple University Press, 1989).

7. I reviewed all issues of *Woman's Home Companion, True Confessions, Negro Digest,* and *The Crisis* (the official magazine of the NAACP) from 1942 to 1945 and a small collection of romance magazines held at the Popular Culture Library at Bowling Green State University. The romance magazines were *Love Short Stories* (August 1944); *Modern Romances* (December 1943); *Popular Love* (November 1943); *Ranch Romances* (December 31 1943); *Secrets* (December 1943); *Street and Smith's Love Story* (January 2, 1943); *True Romances* (December 1943); and *True Story* (December 1943 and October 1944).

8. Frank Yerby, "Health Card," *Negro Digest,* July 1944, 69–76. My analysis of obligation fits with that of Westbrook, "I Want a Girl." Westbrook uses the World War II pinups to develop a sophisticated analysis of liberal theory and political obligation. According to Westbrook, it is "difficult" for the liberal state "to call upon citizens as citizens to defend their nation in time of war." Thus the fulfillment of "mutual obligations" in a liberal state (during wartime) can manifest in "unexpected places." Westbrook offers an analysis of the pinup as the "living theory" supporting a notion of "(male) protector and (female) protected and of subsequent mutual obligations" (607).

9. Here I follow Erving Goffman, *Gender Advertisements* (New York: Harper and Row, 1976). Goffman contends that print media, particularly advertisements, "depict social situations that are familiar to the reader and that affirm social arrangements and announce ultimate doctrine." See also Gaye Tuchman, Arlene Kaplan Daniels, and James Benet, introduction to *Hearth and Home: Images of Women in the Mass Media,* ed. Gaye Tuchman, Arlene Kaplan Daniels, and James Benet (New York: Oxford University Press, 1978), for an in-depth analysis of media messages aimed at women. Tuchman and her coauthors contend that "Americans learn basic lessons about social life from the mass media" (2).

10. Mark Gabor, *The Illustrated History of Girlie Magazines: From National Police Gazette to the Present* (New York: Harmony Books, 1984).

11. Beth Bailey, *From Front Porch to Backseat: Courtship in Twentieth Century America* (Baltimore: Johns Hopkins University Press, 1988).

12. Kathy Peiss, " 'Charity Girls' and City Pleasures," in *Powers of Desire: The Politics of Sexuality,* ed. Ann Snitow, Christine Stansell, and Sharon Thompson, 74–87 (New York: Monthly Review Press, 1983), 74.

13. Meyerowitz, *Women Adrift,* xix.

14. On this topic, see Odem, *Delinquent Daughters,* and Appier, *Policing Women.*

15. John C. Burnham, *Bad Habits: Drinking, Smoking, Taking Drugs, Gambling, Sexual Misbehavior, and Swearing in American History* (New York: New York University Press, 1993). Burnham contends that World War I officers advocated continence among the troops but that in World War II military leaders were "indifferent to morals" and focused on making sexual activity free of the risk of disease. Brandt, in *No Magic Bullet,* points to World War I as a time when "the U.S. War Department undertook a major campaign to make the military camps in the United States safe for the soldiers—safe from the twin threats of immorality and venereal disease." The U.S. forces would be composed of "morally upright" men (52). Brandt sees this as a logical continuation of the Progressive Era's focus on "continence, as the hallmark of all sexual prescription" (26). Sanctions against

men who became venereally diseased during World War I were not uniformly enforced, but they did occur more often than during World War II.

16. See Florence Howitt, "How to Behave in Public without an Escort," *Good Housekeeping*, September 1943, 40; E. Gorham, "Lonely Wife," *Life*, December 21, 1942, 75–77; and Walter Lamb Newton, "Bums, Burglars, and Blackouts," *Coronet*, March 1942, 5–7, for examples of such advice.

17. "Prostitution Major Wartime Threat," *American City*, February 1942, 71; Close, "Sick Men Can't Fight."

18. "Prostitution Is an Axis Partner," *American Journal of Public Health* 38 (January 1942): 85. According to Reynolds, "Statement," 19, "Prostitution must be recognized as a Fifth Columnist (traitor) within our midst to be dealt with accordingly."

19. See ads in *Woman's Home Companion*, February 1943, 3, and *True Story*, October 1944, 3.

20. Thomas Parran, "The New War against Venereal Disease," *Look*, May 16, 1944, 72–73. Here we can see a way that government officials made use of the media; Parran was the surgeon general of the USPHS. In contrast, see Cook, "Battle Line Venereal Disease," 76–79. This article, by the correspondent in France, pictures a group of pajama-clad syphilitic men, relaxed and casual, sitting in a circle. The text refers to a "mixed group . . . talking with the ease of males in the same fix."

21. It is not readily apparent in the archival records (such as those of the SPD and ASHA) what marked a woman as suspicious. It is apparent, however, that certain occupations, certain geographic locations—especially the "wrong side of the tracks" and "Negro" neighborhoods—and previous contact with social or legal authorities (not necessarily for sex offenses) were grounds for suspicion.

22. Lukas, "Digging at the Roots." The medicalization and criminalization of women (and men) had its roots in an earlier period. For a discussion of feeblemindedness, intelligence testing, race, and studies that related mental deficiency and criminality in the early twentieth century, see Degler, *In Search of Human Nature*, 139–86. See also Mark Thomas Connelly, *The Response to Prostitution in the Progressive Era* (Chapel Hill: University of North Carolina Press, 1980), 41–44. Connelly discusses the "linking of prostitution and feeblemindedness" by eugenicists and psychologists in the first two decades of the twentieth century, and he points out a tendency to equate hereditary defects and antisocial behaviors. Also see Linda Gordon, *Heroes of Their Own Lives: The Politics and History of Family Violence, Boston, 1880–1960* (New York: Viking, 1988), 220. Gordon also discusses feeblemindedness as a category used to classify female victims of sexual assault (they could not protect themselves and were incapable of

moral judgment). According to Gordon, these "victims" became "villains" during World War II.

23. Helen J. Tooker, "Venereal Disease, Far from Beaten," *Harper's*, November 1944, 545–53. See Berube, *Coming Out under Fire*, for a discussion of how psychiatry gained professional prominence during World War II. Psychiatric and psychological theories also began to influence interpretations of deviance in women. As social workers adopted such theories, their attitudes toward female prostitution and promiscuity changed, hardening considerably. Gordon, *Heroes*, points out that during crisis periods social services reified the (hetero) "family unit."

24. "San Francisco Opens Three Prophylactic Stations," 195. I consider it noteworthy that these prophylactic stations were identifiable by their *green lights*.

25. "A Soldier on Sex," *American Mercury*, January 1943, 123.

26. Wickware, "Army Fights V.D."

27. "San Francisco Opens Three Prophylactic Stations."

28. "Keeping Up with Medicine," *Good Housekeeping*, April 1943, 119.

29. See P. Lochridge, "V.D. Menace and Challenge," *Woman's Home Companion*, March 1944, 34. Lochridge mentions Parran's message.

30. Parran, "New War," 72–73. On curfews, see *True Confessions*, March 1943, 7.

31. "Prostitution Blamed; Suppression Near Army Camps Held Essential to the Control of Venereal Disease," *Science News Letter* 8 (October 31, 1942): 278; "Public's Health," 152; Wickware, "National Defense"; F. S. Wickware, "War on Venereal Ills," *Science News Letter* 7 (September 1942): 300; Lochridge, "V.D. Menace"; J. C. Colcord, "Fighting Prostitution," *Survey*, August 1942, 214–15; "All Out War," 58; "Prostitution Is an Axis Partner," 85; A. Newman, "V.D. in London: Battle of Piccadilly Circus among Our Army's Worst," *Newsweek*, June 14, 1943, 60.

32. Lukas, "Digging at the Roots," 110, 112. For additional solutions and policies, see also Hironimus, "Survey"; Daniels, "Disease and Punishment," 162; and Thomas B. Turner, "The Suppression of Prostitution in Relation to Venereal Disease Control in the Army," *Federal Probation* 7 (April–June 1943): 8–11.

33. Rhoda J. Millikin, "The Role of the Police Women's Bureau in Combating Prostitution," *Federal Probation* 7 (April–June 1943): 20–22. This entire issue concentrated on prostitutes, promiscuous women, and venereal disease. In it see also Eliot Ness, "The Federal Government's Program in Attacking the Problem of Prostitution," 17–19.

34. van Urk, "Norfolk—Our Worst War Town."

35. Ibid.

36. Ibid.

37. "War and the Health Department," *American Journal of Public Health* 33 (January 1943): 23–24. Any woman arrested or apprehended for a variety of reasons had to submit to venereal disease testing.

38. "Canteen Hostess," *The Crisis,* June 1943, cover. See Mary Helen Washington, *Invented Lives: Narratives of Black Women, 1860–1960* (New York: Anchor Books/Doubleday, 1987), who claims that "like other popular black magazines of the 1940s and 1950s, *The Crisis* featured glamorous photos of beauty queens on its covers and sponsored cover girl contests that depicted women in provocative poses and various stages of undress" (301).

39. "Be the Thrill in His Furlough," *True Story,* June 1944, 2; Michael Carter, "She Makes the Wounded Wiggle," *Negro Digest,* April 1945, 67–69. See also "Plan to Land a Marine," *Modern Romances,* December 1943, 104, and "Just How Do You Land a Marine?" *Woman's Home Companion,* June 1944, 45.

40. For example, "She Made Jive Respectable," *Negro Digest,* November 1942, 7–8, and "Broad Street, Pa., USO," *The Crisis,* May 1943, 149.

41. Howard Whitman, "Johnny Get Your Fun," *Coronet,* March 1943, 169–73. Women doing these kinds of war jobs were, however, marked by those jobs as suspicious, or at best "potentially promiscuous," individuals.

42. See "She Made Jive Respectable" and Carter, "She Makes the Wounded Wiggle." Katherine Dunham, an African American performer, challenged the sexualization and objectification of female performers by the media.

43. Richard A. Anthony, "The Girl and the Man in Uniform," *Probation* 21 (February 1943): 78–88.

44. Howitt, "How to Behave in Public." Ladylike behavior is a component of the "mythical norm."

45. Gorham, "Lonely Wife."

46. Ibid.

47. Newton, "Bums, Burglars, and Blackouts."

48. See, for example, the ads in *Woman's Home Companion,* October 1943, 131, and December 1943, 61, and *True Romance,* December 1943, 81 and also the inside front cover for "one girl loves a soldier . . . one a sailor . . . one a marine."

49. Elinor Glyn, author of romance novels and movie scripts, coined the phrase in 1927. It was first used to describe the actress Clara Bow.

50. The opening pages of most issues of *Woman's Home Companion* featured ads for Listerine. See, for example, *Woman's Home Companion,* February 1943, 3, March 1943, 45, and May 1943, 40; *True Story,* December 1943, 13, and June 1944, 96; *True Confessions,* December 1943, 13, 63,

and June 1944, 96; and *True Romances,* December 1943, 9, for "serious" feminine hygiene problems.

51. For appearance improvement, see advertisement in *The Crisis,* December 1942, 393. For an ad for Palmer's Skin Success Ointment, see *Woman's Home Companion,* January 1944, 1. *True Confessions,* December 1943, 12, and *True Romances,* December 1943, 7, contain examples of the popular ad for Toushay, later called Trushay, for soft hands. (Toushay ads are also illustrative of the practice of fragmenting women's bodies.) In addition, see any Ponds ad (She's Lovely . . . She's Engaged . . . She Uses Ponds). The ads appear in most magazines; *she* is always soft, smooth, and ultra-feminine, and he is often a serviceman. These types of ads proliferated in white magazines. *Negro Digest* did not carry ads; ads began to appear in *The Crisis* in 1942. While they only featured African American companies and products, they also delivered a message that attractiveness was important and that most women generally needed help to achieve it.

52. See the ad in *Woman's Home Companion,* May 1943, 99. Cashmere Bouquet ads appeared in nearly all issues of this magazine from 1940 to 1945.

53. E. W. Norris, "Venereal Disease Epidemiology Third Service Command: An Analysis of 4,641 Contact Reports," *American Journal of Public Health* 33 (September 1943): 1065–72.

54. Westbrook, "I Want a Girl."

55. Eleanor Early, "A Soldier's Wife," *True Confessions,* December 1943, 26–27ff., and Gorham, "Lonely Wife." Married women epitomized the themes of sexual mobilization, exploitation, control, and containment. Perceived in prior times as the moral guardians of the homefront, they were now simultaneously sexualized and forbidden sex; moreover, they were subtly urged to be "understanding" toward their husbands' need for relaxation and recreation, which included female companionship. For example, see F. Hugh Herbert, "Tell Her the Score," *Woman's Home Companion,* July 1943, 20–21+. The Second World War was characterized by an unusual number of married women in the workforce; many more volunteered to be hostesses or worked in dance halls. Wives, too, were arrested on suspicion, some having been listed by their husbands as a contact, i.e., as the recipient of or source of the venereal infection.

56. "Camp Following Wives: Ask Your Soldier What He Thinks of Them," *Modern Romances,* December 1943, 32–33+.

57. Thelma Thurston Gorham, "Negro Army Wives," *The Crisis,* January 1943, 21–22.

58. Yerby, "Health Card."

59. Anthony, "Girl and the Man."

60. Rebecca Shallit, "Sleeping Beauty," *Woman's Home Companion,* October 1944, 26+.

61. Wickware, "Army Fights V.D."

62. "Parties Unlimited," Keeping Up with Hollywood, *Woman's Home Companion,* March 1942, 33–35. The campaign to mobilize women to entertain the troops was extensive enough that even the *Daily Worker,* a newspaper that generally had nothing positive to say about the war (e.g., "War Production Board Was Headed by a Dictator"), featured an ad from the American Labor Party on January 29, 1942, that issued a call for women to act as "hostesses."

63. For example, Harriet Ripperger, "A Date with New York," *Woman's Home Companion,* February 1943, 17+.; "When Love Catches Up with You," *True Story,* December 1943, 36–37; and F. Hugh Herbert and Hazel Rawson Cades, "OK with the Boys," *Woman's Home Companion,* July 1944, 32–33, on "junior hostesses" (sixteen-year-olds) to entertain servicemen.

64. For example, B. J. Chute, "Matchmaker," *Woman's Home Companion,* February 1943, 13+., and Frances Shields, "Love Is a Man Trap," *Woman's Home Companion,* March 1943, 13+.

65. See Meyerowitz, *Women Adrift.*

66. "How to Treat a Soldier," Keeping Up with Hollywood, *Woman's Home Companion,* March 1942, 33–35. See also Marjorie Brastow Greenbie, "Steps to Victory," *Woman's Home Companion,* May 1942, 22–23+, and "Keep Up with Your Soldier," *Woman's Home Companion,* November 1943, 12–13+.

67. See Greenbie, "Keep Up with Your Soldier."

NOTES TO CHAPTER 6

1. Many of these terms come from an undated, untitled rough draft by a Mr. Cooley of the SPD, NA RG 215, Publications, Box 3. See also the remarks of Thomas Devine (SPD) on November 16, 1945, at a meeting of the National Advisory Committee on Social Protection and Venereal Disease. NA RG 215, Committee Meetings, Box 3, and NA RG 215, Publications, Boxes 1–4, passim.

2. Many scholars agree with this point. See, for example, Schur, *Labeling Women Deviant.* See also Shannon Bell, *Reading, Writing.* Bell analyzes, in part, the discursive construction of the prostitute body over time. She traces a process that resulted (in modernity) in the conflation of prostitute and woman. And see Lorraine Gamman and Margaret Marshment, eds., *The Female Gaze: Women as Viewers of Popular Culture* (Seattle: Real Comet

Press, 1989), 2. The editors refer to mechanisms (in popular culture) by which women's experience is "subordinated to the categories and codes through which it is articulated." Also see Christine Overall, "What's Wrong with Prostitution: Evaluating Sex Work," *Signs* 17 (Summer 1992): 705–24, esp. 719.

3. Campbell, *Women at War,* 208.

4. Tucker, *Swing Shift,* 275, 277.

5. Mark Jonathan Harris, Franklin Mitchell, and Steven J. Schecter, *The Homefront: America during World War II* (New York: G. P. Putnam's Sons, 1984), 58.

6. Banay, "Emotional Factors," 106.

7. See Meyer, *Creating GI Jane;* and Treadwell, *Woman's Army Corps.*

8. " 'Second Front' against Prostitution," 44.

9. "Sex Delinquency as a Social Hazard," NA RG 215, Publications, Box 4. Marked "not to be released," this five-page undated document was based on a speech delivered in Cleveland, Ohio, in May 1944.

10. Ibid.

11. Ibid.

12. Ibid.

13. OWI, "Report on Juvenile Delinquency," NA RG 215, Committee Meetings, Box 2. Parts of this report were scheduled for release to Sunday newspapers on October 10, 1943. The statistics on female juvenile delinquency came from several agencies, including those of the Children's Bureau, which reported that 10,865 girls were brought to court in 1941and 14,991 in 1942, with the vast majority charged with sexual offenses. On the media and juvenile delinquency, see also Tappan, *Delinquent Girls in Court,* 3 n. 2. Tappan advises, "For the increase in delinquency during the war, particularly in the sex offenses of girls, see the *New York Times* for March 21, 1943, September 17, 1943, October 7, 1943, October 10, 1943, April 12, 1944, May 15, 1944, July 9, 1944, and December 11, 1945. The newspapers reported that there had been an apparent increase of nearly 200 percent in female delinquency and an increase of more than 100 percent in venereal disease."

14. OWI, "Report on Juvenile Delinquency."

15. Ibid. See also Florence Williams, "A New Kind of Army," *Women's Press,* June 1943, 248–49. YWCA Papers, Ohio Historical Society, Columbus. The *Women's Press* is the national magazine of the YWCA. This article discusses the rules and regulations for hostesses.

16. Winchell, "Good Food, Good Fun."

17. See " 'Second Front' against Prostitution."

18. Donna Haraway, *Modest_Witness@Second_Millenium. FemaleMan©_*

Meets_OncoMouse™: Feminism and Technoscience (New York: Routledge, 1997), 131.

19. See " 'Second Front' against Prostitution."

20. Ibid.

21. FBI, *Uniform Crime Reports,* NA RG 287, Box J. Statistics for 1942 were reported on February 18, 1943. See also NA RG 215, General Records, Box 1. Some of the same statistics were included in an SPD report entitled "Study on Youth Problems in Wartime." See also NA RG 215, Publications, Box 4, which included parts of the same report. Charles L. Chute, "Juvenile Delinquency in Wartime," *Probation* 21 (June 1943): 129–34, provides a somewhat more balanced view of these statistics. While not denying female sexual delinquency, he does point out that print media sensationalized the topic.

22. FBI, *Uniform Crime Reports,* and "Study on Youth Problems."

23. FBI, *Uniform Crime Reports,* and "Study on Youth Problems."

24. Pennington, "Challenge to Law Enforcement."

25. Ibid.

26. Ibid.

27. See, for example, "The Myth of the 'Bad' Black Woman," and "A Colored Woman, However Respectable Is Lower Than the White Prostitute," in *Black Women in White America: A Documentary History,* ed. Gerda Lerner (New York: Vintage Books, 1973), 163–64 and 166–69.

28. "Examples of Published Statements on the Extent of Juvenile Delinquency, 1943," NA RG 215, Publications, Box 4.

29. See OWI, "Report on Juvenile Delinquency."

30. "Corpus Christi Study," July 1942, NA RG 215, Statistics and Studies, Box 6.

31. Ibid. The authorities were particularly interested in "transients." Despite general population mobility, women who moved around came under suspicion as probable prostitutes. The white women came (one each) from Maine, Pennsylvania, Kentucky, Indiana, Kansas, and Louisiana.

32. Ibid. The fourteen-year-old was white. Of the women between ages fifteen and nineteen, four were white, two were Mexican, and two were South American.

33. Ibid. Typically, social workers asked these types of questions. Broken homes, or more specifically, single or working mothers, loomed large in their concerns as factors contributing to sexual delinquency.

34. Ibid.

35. Ibid.

36. Special meeting of the NAPCSP on November 19, 1943, to review and discuss a proposed police record system, NA RG 215, Committee

Meetings, Box 1. Discussion revolved around subjects such as how to treat first offenders, problems involved in holding persons (female) under guard in prison wards, and other problems arising from the extensive apprehensions and arrests of prostitutes and other suspicious women.

37. "Special Study—Miscellaneous Data," NA RG 215, Statistics and Studies, Box 7. This file is composed of numerous loose pages on lined ledger sheets and is clearly a rough draft. There are no markings regarding date. See also "Leesville Study," NA RG 215, Statistics and Studies, Box 6.

38. Interdepartmental Meeting, "General Review," September 18, 1942, NA RG 215, Committee Meetings, Box 1.

39. See "Special Study—Miscellaneous Data," NA RG 215, Statistics and Studies, Box 7, and "Leesville Study," NA RG 215, Statistics and Studies, Box 6.

40. Ibid.

41. Ibid.

42. Ibid.

43. Ibid.

44. Interdepartmental Meeting, "General Review," September 18, 1942, NA RG 215, Committee Meetings, Box 1.

45. SPD, "Report on the Repression Problem in New Orleans," 1943, NA RG 215, Statistics and Studies, Box 6. See also "New Orleans Study," 1942, NA RG 215, Statistics and Studies, Box 1.

46. SPD, "Report on the Repression Problem."

47. Ibid.

48. See "Leesville Study," NA RG 215, Statistics and Studies, Box 6.

49. Letter K. Lenroot to E. Ness, late 1942. NA RG 215, Statistics and Studies, Box 2.

50. Supreme Court File, NA RG 215, Publications, Box 3.

51. "Repression Experience: Region One," NA RG 215, Statistics and Studies, Box 6.

52. Ibid.

53. Ibid.

54. Stella Suberman, *When It Was Our War: A Soldier's Wife on the Home Front* (Chapel Hill, NC: Algonquin Books, 2003), 114–16.

55. "Address by Alan James Lowe, President of the Cleveland Hotel Association," October 30, 1944, NA RG 215, General Records, Box 1. See also Lawrence M. Friedman and Stewart Macauley, *Law and the Behavioral Sciences* (Indianapolis: Bobbs-Merrill, 1969), 99–121, for factors influencing the basis (charges) for arrest, including decisions to arrest for purposes other than prosecution and strategies for arresting prostitutes.

56. One page of a disorganized and incomplete file stamped "Report for Social Security Board," 1943, NA RG 215, Committee Meetings, Box 1.

See "Address by Alan James Lowe, President of the Cleveland Hotel Association," October 30, 1944, NA RG 215, General Records, Box 1, on cooperation of the Sanitary Unit of the Cleveland Police, the PHS, and military officers to track down women reported as venereal disease contacts.

57. Cleveland Visit, 1944, NA RG 215, General Records, Box 1. See also Close, "Sick Men Can't Fight," 6, for discussion of special investigators and an ingenious cross-file system developed by an army officer to facilitate contact tracing. If all else failed, servicemen were escorted into the city to try and identify their contact.

58. "Digest of a Report Prepared by Miss Gertrude M. Smith, Supervisor of Medical Social Work, USO Travelers Aid Service," August 1943–July 1944, 2, 3, 4. NA RG 215, General Records, Box 13.

59. Ibid.

60. "Report on Repression Program in El Paso," NA RG 215, General Records, Box 13.

61. "News from the 48 Fronts," *Journal of Social Hygiene* 27 (May 1941): 257.

62. "Recent Developments in Washington," *Public Welfare News* 9 (October 1941): 4.

63. "San Francisco Opens Social Hygiene Woman's Court," News from the Field, *American Journal of Public Health* 33 (July 1943): 921.

64. Health Department Classifications, May 16, 1944, NA RG 215, Regional Files, Box 1.

65. Mrs. W. T. Bost, "The Welfare Worker's Recent Problem—the Camp Follower," *Jail Association Journal* 4 (November–December 1942): 20.

66. Marjorie Bell, "In Times Like These," *Probation* 21 (June 1943): 140–42.

67. Wilbur C. Curtis, "The Prostitute before the Court," *Federal Probation* 7 (April–June 1943): 34–37.

68. Quoted in ibid.

69. Ibid.

70. Ness to Lenroot, December 1942. The statistics were drawn from reports of SPD representatives. NA RG 215, Statistics and Studies, Box 2.

71. "Polls and Public Opinions," NA RG 215, General Records, Box 8.

72. Opinion of the Supreme Court of Illinois, March 13, 1944, NA RG 215, Publications, Box 4. The statute in question, "An Act to Enable Counties or Cities to Segregate and Treat Persons Suffering from Certain Communicable Diseases," had been approved on June 28, 1919. Section 4 states: "When it appears to any judge or justice of the peace from the evidence or otherwise that any person coming before him on any criminal charge may be suffering from any communicable venereal disease, it shall be the duty of such judge or justice of the peace to refer such person to the director of

such hospital, sanitarium, or clinic, or to such officer as shall be selected or appointed for the purpose of examining the accused person, and if such person is found to be suffering from any communicable venereal disease he or she may by order of the court, be sent for treatment to a hospital, sanitarium or clinic if any be available and if necessary to be segregated for such term as the court may impose at such hospital, sanitarium or clinic."

73. Opinion of the Supreme Court of Illinois, March 13, 1944.

74. Ibid.

75. Ibid.

76. Ibid. While the records offer no insight into how or where these women got the expertise and money to pursue their case, they do mention that the women did not challenge the charge of prostitution. Two possibilities emerge: they were prostitutes with an organization behind them, or their case was argued as a test case.

77. Steven Nickel, *Torso: The Story of Eliot Ness and the Search for a Psychopathic Killer* (Winston-Salem, NC: John F. Blau, 1989), 193. The date is not given, but newspapers from Ohio and Illinois apparently ran the story, probably in 1943. Paul W. Heimel, *Eliot Ness: The Real Story* (Coudersport, PA: Knox Books, 1997), 171.

78. See Bailey and Farber, *First Strange Place,* ch. 3.

79. Office memo, U.S. Government, June 15, 1944, NA RG 215, Records Relating to Caribbean Area, 1943–1945, Box 1.

80. Clipping attached to ibid.

81. "Government of the Virgin Islands of the United States, Department of Health," June 19, 1944, NA RG 215, Caribbean Records, Box 1.

82. "A Digest of the Minutes of the June 9, 1943, Social Protection Conference on the 'Woman's Role in Social Protection,'" NA RG 215, Publications, Box 1.

83. Tappan, *Delinquent Girls in Court,* 13, 14, 32, 35, 36, 48, 69, 70, 72, 81, 86, 87, 90, 91, 103. See also Nicole Hahn Rafter, "The More Things Change . . . (Women's Prison System)," *Women's Review of Books* 14 (July 1997): 3–4. This special issue on women in jails and prisons discussed attitudes toward women prisoners: for example, that women were deemed harder to reform than men because they were more childlike and therefore needed more help. Thus, "in the name of helping them, women were put in state prisons for quite minor crimes, like promiscuity, that men never went to state prison for." Meda Chesney-Lind, in "Equity with a Vengeance," points out that in general "women were much less likely than men to be imprisoned unless the female offender did not fit the stereotypical female role, for example, if she was a bad mother" (5). Also see Lawrence M. Friedman, *Crime and Punishment in American History* (New York: Basic Books, 1993).

84. See Eliot Ness, "Rehabilitation in the Social Protection Program," NA RG 215, Publications, Box 4, for a 1942 summary of the SPD's position on protecting women. See also "Meeting of a Subcommittee of the Advisory Committee on Social Protection, March 7, 1942," NA RG 215, Committee Meetings, Box 1. Many professional women attended this meeting, and the discussion revolved around the lack of detention facilities.

85. Eliot Ness, "Rehabilitation in the Social Protection Program," NA RG 215, Publications, Box 4.

86. Sonya Michel, "American Women and the Discourse of the Democratic Family in World War II," in Higonnet et al., *Behind the Lines,* 154–67.

87. M. A. Burke, "Improvement of Present Methods for Extrafamilial Contact Tracing," *American Journal of Public Health* 34 (May 1944): 548.

88. Millikin, "Role of the Police Woman's Bureau," 21. See also Imra Wann Buwalda, "The Policewoman—Yesterday, Today and Tomorrow," *Journal of Social Hygiene* 31 (May 1945): 290–93; Hutzel, "Policewoman's Role." See also Ethel Bogardus, "50 Policewomen Patrol Nightclubs," subtitled "If Parents Can't Control Children, Law Will," *San Francisco News* (March 30, 1944), copy of article in NA RG 215, General Records, Box 8. Policewoman Kathlyn Sullivan had deputized fifty social workers to assist in the control program.

89. "Police Hunting Runaway Girls after 41% Rise," *Herald Tribune,* February 15, 1944. The girls did not have to be reported as "missing persons" to be classified as runaways. Copy of article in NA RG 215, General Records, Box 8.

90. On involvement of women's organizations in the social hygiene movement, see Eleanor Shenehon, "Fourth National Social Hygiene Day—February 1, 1940," *Journal of Social Hygiene* 26 (April 1940): 176–83. Mentioned in the article are the General Federation of Women's Clubs, the League of Women Voters, and the Women's Christian Temperance Union. (Prior to the war emergency, the focus of social hygiene was not limited to prostitution.)

91. Sara A. Whitehurst, "Venereal Diseases and Prostitution Must Be Eradicated," *Journal of Social Hygiene* 29 (January 1943): 26, 27.

92. "Social Protection Conference on 'The Woman's Role in Social Protection,'" June 9, 1943, NA RG 215, General Records, Box 3, and "A Digest of the Minutes of the June 9, 1943, Social Protection Conference on the 'Woman's Role in Social Protection,'" NA RG 215, Publications, Box 1.

93. Ibid. On young and inexperienced girls, see also Hutzel, "Policewoman's Role." Hutzel referred to young girls as lacking experience and therefore unable to protect themselves.

94. Ibid.

95. See Sarah Fishman, *The Battle for Children: World War II, Youth Crime, and Juvenile Justice in Twentieth-Century France* (Cambridge, MA: Harvard University Press, 2002), on juvenile delinquency in Europe during World War II.

96. Dyson Carter, *Sin and Science* (New York: Heck-Cattell, 1947), 9, 104, 105. Carter also noted that since the army's objective was to control venereal disease among the troops during the period of hostilities, it was successful. He points out that the "measure of the army's success" could be determined by "counting how many of its freely supplied prophylactics were taken by the men." The figure," he said, "was enormous and unbelievable . . . fifty million prophylactics each month in 1945." Brandt, *No Magic Bullet*, 164, reports the same figure.

97. Letter, June 14, 1945, signed by Thomas E. Connelley (SPD representative). The letter stated, in part, that the pamphlet *"She Looked Clean . . . But* has already been placed in the hands of thousands of workers in restaurants, bars, and bowling alleys." ASHA Papers, Box 128.

NOTES TO CHAPTER 7

1. Carol Groneman, "Nymphomania: The Historical Construction of Female Sexuality," *Signs* 19 (Winter 1994): 337–67.

2. Gubar, "This Is My Rifle."

3. See the oral history project directed by Dr. Sharon H. Hartman Strom and Linda P. Wood, "What Did You Do in the War Grandma," September 1997, www.stg.brown.edu/projects/WWII_Women/tocCS.html (accessed January 20, 2007).

4. Helen Hironimus, "Survey of 100 May Act Violators Committed to the Federal Reformatory for Women," *Federal Probation* 7 (April–June 1943): 31–34, discussed in ch. 1; anecdote here is on 33.

5. Gordon, *Heroes*, ch. 7.

6. Beth L. Bailey, *From Front Porch*, 87.

7. See ibid.

8. See Advisory Committee on Social Protection, minutes of an all-day meeting to discuss problems and programs, June 14, 1941, NA RG 215, Committee Meetings, Box 1.

9. Bailey, *From Front Porch*, 58, 60.

10. Joan Jacobs Brumberg, *The Body Project: An Intimate History of American Girls* (New York: Random House, 1997), 115.

11. Carol S. Vance, "Pleasure and Danger: Toward a Politics of Sexuality," in *Pleasure and Danger: Exploring Female Sexuality*, ed. Carole S. Vance (Boston: Routledge and Kegan Paul, 1986), 1.

12. Rupp, *Mobilizing Women for War.* See also Hartmann, *Homefront and Beyond.*

13. For analyses of the wartime effects on the status of women, see Anderson, *Wartime Women;* Campbell, *Women at War;* Chafe, *The American Woman;* Hartmann, *Homefront and Beyond;* Honey, *Creating Rosie the Riveter;* Meyer, *Creating GI Jane;* and Rupp, *Mobilizing Women for War.*

14. I do not mean to imply that race and class were absent as factors in the treatment of women during the war years; race in particular, resulted in a disproportionate number of arrests of African American women. Lower socioeconomic class made women vulnerable to charges of feeblemindedness and hereditary degeneracy. Rather, I wish to point out that during this period one can identify a broad use of a category—"woman"—to represent the danger/enemy on the homefront.

15. Joanne Meyerowitz, introduction to *Not June Cleaver: Women and Gender in Postwar America, 1945–1960,* ed. Joanne Meyerowitz (Philadelphia: Temple University Press, 1994), 5.

16. See, for example, Cynthia Harrison, *On Account of Sex: The Politics of Women's Issues, 1945–1968* (Berkeley: University of California Press, 1988); Meyerowitz, *Not June Cleaver;* and Paula Giddings, *When and Where I Enter: The Impact of Back Women on Race and Sex in America* (New York: Bantam Books, 1984), ch. 14.

17. Donna Penn, "The Sexualized Woman: The Lesbian, the Prostitute, and the Containment of Female Sexuality in Postwar America," in Meyerowitz, *Not June Cleaver,* 358–81. Also see Faderman, *Odd Girls.*

18. See Regina G. Kunzel, "White Neurosis, Black Pathology: Constructing Out-of-Wedlock Pregnancy in the Wartime and Postwar United States," in Meyerowitz, *Not June Cleaver,* 304–31. See also Rickie Solinger, *Wake Up Little Susie: Single Pregnancy and Race before Roe v. Wade* (New York: Routledge, 1992).

19. May, *Homeward Bound.*

20. Hartmann, "Prescriptions for Penelope."

21. Ferdinand Lundberg and Marynia F. Farnham, *Modern Woman: The Lost Sex* (New York: Grosset and Dunlap, 1947).

22. Joanne Meyerowitz, "Beyond the Feminine Mystique: A Reassessment of Postwar Mass Culture," in Meyerowitz, *Not June Cleaver,* 232.

NOTES TO APPENDIX I

1. Adopted by the Conference of State and Territorial Health Offices, May 7–12, 1940.

2. Familial contacts with naval patients will not be reported.

NOTE TO APPENDIX 3

1. Five-page document organizational information for the Social Protection Division. Copy provided by Tab Lewis, Archivist, National Archives, College Park, MD.

Bibliography

MANUSCRIPT SOURCES

National Archives, Washington, DC
    Record Group 215, Records of the Office of Community War Services, Social Protection Division
    Record Group 18, Records of the Army Air Force
    Record Group 52, Records of the Navy Bureau of Medicine and Surgery
    Record Group 287, Federal Bureau of Investigation, Uniform Crime Reports for the United States and Its Possessions, U.S. Department of Justice

COLLECTED PAPERS

American Social Hygiene Association Papers. Social Welfare History Archives Center, University of Minnesota, Minneapolis, Minnesota. (ASHA Papers).
Bureau of Social Hygiene Papers. Rockefeller Archives Center, Hillcrest, Pocantico Hills, North Tarrytown, New York (BSH Papers).
Columbus, Ohio, YWCA Papers. Ohio Historical Society, Columbus, Ohio.
Records of the Ohio War History Commission, Series 1142. Ohio Historical Society, Columbus, Ohio.

PRIMARY SOURCES

Books and Monographs

Annual Report of the Surgeon General of the Public Health Service of the United States for the Fiscal Year 1941. Washington, DC: U.S. Government Printing Office, 1941.
Annual Report of the Surgeon General of the Public Health Service of the United States for the Fiscal Years 1942–1943. Washington, DC: U.S. Government Printing Office, 1942–43.
Annual Report of the Surgeon General of the Public Health Service of the United States for the Fiscal Years 1944–1945. Washington, DC: U.S. Government Printing Office, 1944–45.

Broughton, Philip S. *Prostitution and the War: The Missing Man in the Front Line.* New York: Public Affairs Committee, 1942.

Carter, Dyson. *Sin and Science.* New York: Heck-Cattell, 1947.

Congressional Committee Hearings Index, part 4, 74th–78th Cong., 1935–44.

Congressional Record, 77th Cong. Washington, DC: U.S. Government Printing Office, 1942.

De Kruif, Paul. *Microbe Hunters.* New York: Pocket Books, 1940.

Federal Bureau of Investigation. *Uniform Crime Reports for the United States and Its Possessions.* Washington, DC: Department of Justice, 1941, 1942, 1943.

Flexner, Abraham. *Prostitution in Europe.* 1914. Reprint, Montclair, NJ: Patterson Smith, 1969.

Green, Howard Whipple. *Cases of Syphilis under Treatment in Cuyahoga County during March 1943.* Cleveland, OH: Cleveland Health Council, 1942.

Hazen, Henry. *Syphilis in the Negro: A Handbook for the General Practitioner.* Washington, DC: U.S. Government Printing Office, 1943.

Hearings of the House of Representatives Committee on Military Affairs, 1941. Columbus: State Library of Ohio. Microfiche.

Heller, Joseph. *Now and Then: A Memoir, from Coney Island to Here* (London: Simon and Schuster, 1998.

Johnson, Bascomb. "Vice Prevention and the Defense Program." In *Proceedings of the Seventy-First Annual Congress of the American Prison Association.* New York: American Prison Association, 1941.

Kneeland, George. *Commercialized Prostitution in New York City.* 1913. Reprint, Montclair, NJ: Patterson Smith, 1969.

Lombroso, Cesare, and William Ferrero. *The Female Offender.* London: Fisher Unwin, 1895.

Lundberg, Ferdinand, and Marynia F. Farnham. *Modern Woman: The Lost Sex.* New York: Grosset and Dunlap, 1947.

Munger, Elizabeth. "Indeterminate Sentences." In *Proceedings of the Seventy-Third Annual Congress of the American Prison Association.* New York: American Prison Association, 1943.

Myrdal, Gunnar. *An American Dilemma: The Negro Problem and Modern Democracy.* New York: Harper and Row, 1944.

The Operation of the Selective Service. Vol. 1. Special Monograph no. 17. Washington, DC: U.S. Government Printing Office, 1955.

Parran, Thomas, and Raymond A. Vonderlehr. *Plain Words about Venereal Disease.* New York: Reynal and Hitchcock, 1941.

Reckless, Walter C. *Vice in Chicago.* Montclair, NJ: Patterson Smith, 1933.

Safier, Benno, Hazel G. Corrigan, Eleanor J. Fein, and Katherine P. Bradway.

A Psychiatric Approach to the Treatment of Promiscuity. New York: American Social Hygiene Association, 1949.

State of Connecticut. *Public Health Report.* June 30, 1941.

Tappan, Paul W. *Delinquent Girls in Court: A Study of the Wayward Minor Court of New York.* New York: Columbia University Press, 1947.

Treadwell, Mattie E. *The Women's Army Corps.* United States Army in World War II. Special Studies. Washington, DC: Office of the Chief of Military History, Department of the Army, 1954.

Vonderlehr, Raymond. "The Venereal Disease Control Act." *Annual Reports of the Public Health Service*, 1942–43, 122–51.

Wilson, J. G. "The Female Psychopath." In *Proceedings of the Seventy-Second Annual Congress of the American Prison Association.* New York: American Prison Association, 1942.

Woolston, Howard B. *Prostitution in the United States.* Montclair, NJ: Patterson Smith, 1921.

Popular Magazines

"All Out War on Prostitution." *Newsweek*, September 29, 1941, 58.

"Along the NAACP Battlefront." *The Crisis*, July 1943, 211–16.

"Be The Thrill in His Furlough." *True Story*, June 1944, 2.

"Broad Street, Pa., USO." *The Crisis*, May 1943, 149.

"Camp Following Wives: Ask Your Soldier What He Thinks of Them." *Modern Romances*, December 1943, 32–33+.

"Canteen Hostess." *The Crisis*, June 1943, cover.

Carter, Michael. "She Makes the Wounded Wiggle." *Negro Digest*, April 1945, 67–69.

Chute, B. J. "Matchmaker." *Woman's Home Companion*, February 1943, 13+.

Close, K. "Sick Men Can't Fight." *Survey Graphic*, March 1943, 80–84.

Colcord, J. C. "Fighting Prostitution." *Survey*, August 1942, 214–15.

Cook, Zeke. "Battle Line Venereal Disease." *Newsweek*, November 20, 1944, 76–79.

Daniels, Jonathan. "Disease and Punishment." *Nation*, August 1941, 162.

Early, Eleanor. "A Soldier's Wife." *True Confessions*, December 1943, 26–27+.

Fleeson, Doris. "Within Sound of the Guns." *Woman's Home Companion*, January 1944, 4+.

Furnas, J. C. "Women Wanted." *Ladies' Home Journal*, November 1942, 20.

Gorham, E. "Lonely Wife." *Life*, December 21, 1942, 75–77.

Gorham, Thelma Thurston. "Negro Army Wives." *The Crisis*, January 1943, 21–22.

Greenbie, Marjorie Brastow. "Keep Up with Your Soldier." *Woman's Home Companion,* November 1943, 12–13+.

———. "Steps to Victory." *Woman's Home Companion,* May 1942, 22–23+.

Herbert, F. Hugh. "Tell Her the Score." *Woman's Home Companion,* July 1943, 20–21+.

Herbert, F. Hugh, and Hazel Rawson Cades. "OK with the Boys." *Woman's Home Companion,* July 1944, 32–33.

Hobby, Ovetta Culp. "Sweethearts at Ease: Army Chooses Woman Editor to Inform You about Soldiers' Behavior in Camps." *Cincinnati Enquirer,* August 2, 1941, 2.

"How to Treat a Soldier." Keeping Up With Hollywood. *Woman's Home Companion,* March 1942, 33–35.

Howitt, Florence. "How to Behave in Public without an Escort." *Good Housekeeping,* September 1943, 30.

"Just How Do You Land a Marine?" *Woman's Home Companion,* June 1944, 45.

"Keeping Up with Medicine." *Good Housekeeping,* April 1943, 119.

"La Guardia Backs Camp Zoning Bill." *New York Times,* March 12, 1941, 6.

Lochridge, Patricia. "V.D. Menace and Challenge." *Woman's Home Companion,* March 1944, 34, 129–31.

Moore, Virginia Bennett, and George de Zayas. "Begrimed, Bewitching or Both." *Woman's Home Companion,* October 1943, 80–81.

Newman, A. "V.D. in London: Battle of Piccadilly Circus among Our Army's Worst." *Newsweek,* June 14, 1943, 60.

Newton, Walter Lamb. "Bums, Burglars, and Blackouts." *Coronet,* March 1943, 5–7.

Parran, Thomas. "The New War against Venereal Disease." *Look,* May 16, 1944, 72–73.

"Parties Unlimited." Keeping Up with Hollywood. *Woman's Home Companion,* March 1942, 33–35.

"Plan to Land a Marine." *Modern Romances,* December 1943, 104.

"Prostitution Blamed; Suppression Near Army Camps Held Essential to the Control of Venereal Disease." *Science News Letter,* October 31, 1942, 278.

"Prostitution Major Wartime Threat." *American City,* February 1942, 71.

"Public's Health: Program to Prevent Young Girls and Women from Involvement in Prostitution and Promiscuity." *Survey,* May 1943, 152.

Ripperger, Harriet. "A Date with New York." *Woman's Home Companion,* February 1943, 17+.

Roemer, M. I. "Negro Migratory Workers in New Jersey." *The Crisis*, November 1942, 355, 364.

"Sell It to the Marines." *Woman's Home Companion*, October 1943, 131.

"Service Ribbon." *Newsweek*, November 13, 1944, 59.

Shallit, Rebecca. "Sleeping Beauty." *Woman's Home Companion*, October 1944, 26+.

"She Made Jive Respectable." *Negro Digest*, November 1942, 7–8.

Shields, Frances. "Love Is a Man Trap." *Woman's Home Companion*, March 1943, 13+.

"A Soldier on Sex." *American Mercury*, January 1943, 123.

Stevens, Alden. "Morale in the Camps." *Survey Graphic*, October 1941, 513–19.

Tooker, Helen V. "Venereal Disease Far from Beaten." *Harper's*, November 1944, 545–53.

"The Twain Do Meet: Oldest Profession Thrives in India." *Newsweek*, September 11, 1944, 63–64.

van Urk, J. Blan. "Norfolk—Our Worst War Town." *American Mercury*, February 1943, 144–51.

"When Love Catches Up with You." *True Story*, December 1943, 36–37.

Whitman, Howard. "Johnny Get Your Fun." *Coronet*, March 1943, 169–73.

Wickware, F. S. "The Army Fights VD." *Reader's Digest*, December 1941, 14–17.

———. "National Defense vs. Venereal Disease." *Life*, October 13, 1941, 128–30.

———. "War on Venereal Ills." *Science News Letter*, September 1942, 300.

Williams, Florence. "A New Kind of Army." *Woman's Press* (National Magazine of the YWCA), June 1943, 248–49.

Yerby, Frank. "Health Card." *Negro Digest*, July 1944, 69–76.

Professional Journals

Note: Issues of the *Journal of Social Hygiene* are all available online at http://hearth.library.cornell.edu/h/hearth/browse/title/4732756.html)? Issues of the *American Journal of Public Health* are all available online at www.pubmedcentral.nih.gov/tocrender.fcgi?action=archive&journal=259.

"Abstract of Proceedings: Conference with Negro Leaders on Wartime Problems in Venereal Disease Control." *Journal of Social Hygiene* 30 (November 1944): 76–83.

Anthony, Richard H. "The Girl and the Man in Uniform." *Probation* 21 (February 1943): 73–80.

Banay, Ralph S. "Emotional Factors in Wartime Delinquency." *Probation* 21 (April 1943): 103–8.

Bell, Marjorie. "In Times Like These." *Probation* 21 (June 1943): 140–42.

Boone, Joel T. "The Sexual Aspects of Military Personnel." *Journal of Social Hygiene* 27 (March 1941): 113–24.

Bost, Mrs. W. T. "The Welfare Worker's Recent Problem: The Camp Follower." *Jail Association Journal* 4 (November–December 1942): 20.

Bracy, Mildred B. "USO Travelers Aid Service to Women and Girls in Defense Areas." *Journal of Social Hygiene* 2 (January 1943): 8–11.

Brumfield, William A., Jr., James H. Lade, and Louis L. Feldman. "The Epidemiology of Syphilis Based upon Five Years Experience in an Intensive Program in New York State." *American Journal of Public Health* 32 (August 1942): 793–802.

Burke, M. A. "Improvement of Present Methods for Extrafamilial Contact Tracing." *American Journal of Public Health* 34 (May 1944): 548.

Burney, L. E., J. R. S. Mays, and Albert P. Iskrant. "Results of Serologic Tests for Syphilis in Non-syphilitic Persons Innoculated with the Malaria." *American Journal of Public Health* 32 (January 1942): 39–47.

Buwalda, Imra Wann. "The Policewoman—Yesterday, Today and Tomorrow." *Journal of Social Hygiene* 31 (May 1945): 290–93.

Charcot, J. M., and Valentine Magan. "Inversions du sens genital." *Archives de Neurologie* 3 and 4 (1882).

Chute, Charles L. "Juvenile Delinquency in Wartime." *Probation* 21 (June 1943): 129–34.

Cornley, Paul B. "Trends in Public Health Activities among Negroes in 96 Southern Counties during the Period 1930–1939." *American Journal of Public Health* 32 (October 1942): 1117–24.

Cory, Harriet S. "The Relation of National Defense to Social Hygiene." *Journal of Social Hygiene* 26 (November 1940): 358–61.

Curtis, Wilbur C. "The Prostitute before the Court." *Federal Probation* 7 (April–June 1943): 34–37.

Dumas, A. W. "National Negro Health Week Observance." *National Negro Health News* 4 (April–June 1936): 16.

Everett, Ray H. "Program Emphases for Preparedness Conditions." *Journal of Social Hygiene* 26 (November 1940): 364–66.

Hironimus, Helen. "Survey of 100 May Act Violators Committed to the Federal Reformatory for Women." *Federal Probation* 7 (April–June 1943): 31–34.

Hutzel, Eleanor L. "The Policewoman's Role in Social Protection." *Journal of Social Hygiene* 30 (December 1944): 538–44.

Jackson, Nelson C. "Community Organization Activities among Negroes for Venereal Disease Control." *Social Forces* 23 (October 1944–May 1945): 65–70.

Kolmer, John A. "The Problem of Falsely Doubtful and Positive Reactions in the Sereology of Syphilis." *American Journal of Public Health* 34 (May 1944): 510–14.

Lade, James H. Review of *Serology in Syphilis Control: Principles in Sensitivity and Specificity,* by Reuben L. Kahn. *American Journal of Public Health* 33 (September 1943): 1130.

Leider, M., S. Brookins, and V. McDaniel. "Biography of a Civilian Committee on Venereal Disease Control: The Negro War-Time Health Committee of Pensacola, Florida." *Journal of Social Hygiene* 30 (February 1944): 67–71.

"Lindbergh Home to Be V.D. Treatment Center." News from the Field. *American Journal of Public Health* 33 (February 1943): 195.

Lukas, Edwin J. "Digging at the Roots of Prostitution." *Probation* 22 (April 1944): 97–100.

Millikin, Rhoda J. "The Role of the Police Woman's Bureau in Combatting Prostitution." *Federal Probation* 7 (April–June 1943): 20–22.

Mountin, Joseph W. "Responsibility of Local Health Authorities in the War Emergency." *American Journal of Public Health* 33 (January 1943): 35–38.

Ness, Eliot. "The Federal Government's Program in Attacking the Problem of Prostitution." *Federal Probation* 7 (April–June 1943): 17–19.

"News from the 48 Fronts." *Journal of Social Hygiene* 27 (May 1941): 257–62.

"1943 Amendments to the Public Health Laws in Georgia." News from the Field. *American Journal of Public Health* 33 (June 1943): 769.

Norris, E. W. "Venereal Disease Epidemiology Third Service Command: An Analysis of 4,641 Contact Reports." *American Journal of Public Health* 33 (September 1943): 1065–72.

Oppenheim, A. "Health Education in Action." *American Journal of Public Health* 33 (November 1943): 1338–42.

Parran, Thomas. "The New Strategy Against V.D." *Journal of Social Hygiene* 32:3 (March 1946): 127–34.

Pennington, L. R. "The Challenge to Law Enforcement." *Journal of Social Hygiene* 30 (December 1944): 530–37.

Pinney, Jean B. "Social Hygiene a Generation Ago." *Journal of Social Hygiene* 29 (June 1943): 377–83.

"Prostitution Is an Axis Partner." *American Journal of Public Health* 38 (January 1942): 85.

"Psychiatric Service in Venereal Disease Clinic." News from the Field. *American Journal of Public Health* 33 (February 1943): 195–96.

Rayburn, Reba. "National Events." *Journal of Social Hygiene* 32 (April 1946): 202–3.

"Recent Developments in Washington." *Public Welfare News* 9 (October 1941): 4.

Reckless, Walter C. "A Sociologist Looks at Prostitution." *Federal Probation* 7 (April–June 1942): 12–16.

Reiger, Charles J. "Louisville's Welfare Director Sums Up His City's Approach to Its Defense Problems. " *Public Welfare News* 9 (April 1941): 7–10.

Reynolds, Charles R. "Prostitution as a Source of Infection with the Venereal Diseases in the Armed Forces." *American Journal of Public Health* 30 (November 1940): 1276–82.

———. "Statement." *Federal Probation* 7 (April–June 1943): 19.

"San Francisco Opens Social Hygiene Woman's Court." News from the Field. *American Journal of Public Health* 33 (July 1943): 921.

"San Francisco Opens Three Prophylactic Stations." News from the Field. *American Journal of Public Health* 33 (February 1943): 195.

"A 'Second Front' against Prostitution: Techniques for Repressing 'Unorganized' Prostitution, as Recommended by the Special Committee on Enforcement of the National Advisory Police Committee." *Journal of Social Hygiene* 29 (January 1943): 43–50.

Shenehon, Eleanor. "Fourth National Social Hygiene Day–February 1, 1940." *Journal of Social Hygiene* 26 (April 1940): 176–83.

Special Issue. *Federal Probation* 7 (April–June 1943).

Sullivan, Frances, and Milton Rose. "Public Health Planning for War Needs: Order or Chaos?" *American Journal of Public Health* 32 (August 1942): 831–36.

"Text of the Eight Point Agreement." *Federal Probation* 7 (April–June 1943): 7.

Turner, Thomas B. "Immediate Wartime Outlook and Indicated Post-war Conditions with Respect to the Control of the Venereal Diseases." *American Journal of Public Health* 33 (November 1943): 1309–13.

———. "The Suppression of Prostitution in Relation to Venereal Disease Control in the Army." *Journal of Federal Probation* 7 (April–June 1943): 8–11.

"U.S. Indian Medical Service Curtailed." News from the Field. *American Journal of Public Health* 32 (September 1942): 1078.

"War and the Health Department." *American Journal of Public Health* 33 (January 1943): 23–24.

Weitz, Robert D., and H. L. Rachlin. "The Mental Ability and Educational Attainment of 500 Venereally Infected Females." *Journal of Social Hygiene* 31 (May 1945): 300–303.

"What Army Blood Tests Reveal." *American Journal of Public Health* 33 (September 1943): 1137.

Whitehurst, Sara A. "Venereal Diseases and Prostitution Must Be Eradicated." *Journal of Social Hygiene* 29 (January 1943): 26–28.

Williams, W. C., and C. Y. McGinness. "Plans for Handling Special Health and Other Problems Incident to the Army Maneuvers in Tennessee." *Public Health Report,* October 24, 1941.

SECONDARY SOURCES

Adimara, Adora A., Holli Hamilton, King K. Holmes, and P. Frederick Sparling. *Sexually Transmitted Diseases: Companion Handbook.* 2nd ed. New York: McGraw-Hill, 1994.

Alexander, M. Jacqui. "Not Just (Any) Body Can Be a Citizen: The Politics of Law, Sexuality and Postcoloniality in Trinidad and Tobago and the Bahamas." *Feminist Review* 48 (Autumn 1994): 5–23.

Anderson, Karen. *Wartime Women: Sex Roles, Family Relations, and the Status of Women during World War II.* Westport, CT: Greenwood Press, 1981.

Appier, Janis. *Policing Women: The Sexual Politics of Law Enforcement and the LAPD.* Philadelphia: Temple University Press, 1998.

Bailey, Beth L. *From Front Porch to Back Seat: Courtship in Twentieth-Century America.* Baltimore: Johns Hopkins University Press, 1988.

Bailey, Beth L., and David Farber. *The First Strange Place: The Alchemy of Race and Sex in World War II Hawaii.* New York: Free Press, 1992.

Barry, Kathleen. *Female Sexual Slavery.* New York: New York University Press, 1979.

Bell, Shannon. *Reading, Writing and Rewriting the Prostitute Body.* Bloomington: Indiana University Press, 1994.

Berlant, Lauren. *The Queen of America Goes to Washington City: Essays on Sex and Citizenship.* Durham: Duke University Press, 1997.

Berube, Alan. *Coming Out under Fire: The History of Gay Men and Women in World War II.* New York: Free Press, 1990.

Braidotti, Rosi. "Mothers, Monsters, and Machines." In *Writing on the Body: Female Embodiment and Feminist Theory.* New York: Columbia University Press, 1997.

———. "Signs of Wonder and Traces of Doubt: On Teratology and Embodied Difference." In *Between Monsters, Goddesses and Cyborgs: Feminist Confrontations with Science, Medicine and Cyberspace,* ed. Nina Lykke and Rosi Braidotti, 135–52. London: Zed Books, 1996.

Brandt, Alan M. *No Magic Bullet: A Social History of Venereal Disease in the United States since 1880.* New York: Oxford University Press, 1987.

Brienes, Ingeborg, Robert Connell, and Ingrid Eid. *Male Roles, Masculinities and Violence: A Culture of Peace Perspective.* Paris: UNESCO Publishing, 2000.

Bristow, Nancy K. *Making Men Moral: Social Engineering during the Great War.* New York: New York University Press, 1996.

Brownmiller, Susan. *Against Our Will: Men, Women, and Rape.* New York: Penguin Books, 1975.

Brumberg, Joan Jacobs. *The Body Project: An Intimate History of American Girls.* New York: Random House, 1997.

Burchell, Graham, Colin Gordon, and Peter Miller, eds. *The Foucault Effect: Studies in Governmentality.* Chicago: University of Chicago Press, 1991.

Burnham, John C. *Bad Habits: Drinking, Smoking, Taking Drugs, Gambling, Sexual Misbehavior, and Swearing in American History.* New York: New York University Press, 1993.

Campbell, D'Ann. *Women at War with America: Private Lives in a Patriotic Era.* Cambridge, MA: Harvard University Press, 1984.

Chafe, William H. *The American Woman: Her Changing Social, Economic, and Political Roles, 1920–1970.* New York: Oxford University Press, 1972.

Chesney-Lind, Meda. "Equity with a Vengeance." *Women's Review of Books* 14 (July 1997): 5.

Chinn, Sarah E. "Liberty's Life Stream': Blood, Race, and Citizenship in World War II." In *Technology and the Logic of American Racism: A Cultural History of the Body as Evidence.* New York: Continuum, 2000.

Cohen, Patricia Cline. *A Calculating People: The Spread of Numeracy in Early America.* Chicago: University of Chicago Press, 1982.

Collins, Patricia Hill. *Black Feminist Thought: Knowledge, Consciousness, and the Politics of Empowerment.* Boston: Unwin Hyman, 1990.

Connell, R. W. "The Big Picture: Masculinities in Recent World History." *Theory and Society* 22 (October 1993): 597–623.

———. *Masculinities.* Berkeley: University of California Press, 1995.

Connelly, Mark Thomas. *The Response to Prostitution in the Progressive Era.* Chapel Hill: University of North Carolina Press, 1980.

Costello, John. *Love, Sex, and War: Changing Values, 1939–1945.* London: Collins, 1985.

D'Amico, Francine, and Laurie Weinstein, eds. *Gender Camouflage: Women and the U.S. Military.* New York: New York University Press, 1999.

Davis, Nanette J., ed. *Prostitution: An International Handbook on Trends, Problems, and Politics.* Westport, CT: Greenwood Press, 1993.

Degler, Carl N. *In Search of Human Nature: The Decline and Revival of*

Darwinism in American Social Thought. New York: Oxford University Press, 1991.

D'Emilio, John, and Estelle B. Freedman. *Intimate Matters: A History of Sexuality in America*. New York: Harper and Row, 1988.

Desowitz, Robert S. *Who Gave Pinta to the Santa Maria: Torrid Diseases in a Temperate World*. New York: W. W. Norton, 1997.

Dijkstra, Bram. *Evil Sisters: The Threat of Female Sexuality and the Cult of Manhood*. New York: Alfred A. Knopf, 1996.

Dubbert, Joe. *A Man's Place: Masculinity in Transition*. Englewood Cliffs, NJ: Prentice Hall, 1979.

Duffy, John. *The Sanitarians: A History of American Public Health*. Urbana: University of Chicago Press, 1992.

———. "Social Impact of Disease in the Late 19th Century." In *Sickness and Health in America: Readings in the History of Medicine and Public Health*, ed. Judith Walzer Leavitt and Ronald L. Numbers, 395–402. Madison: University of Wisconsin Press, 1978.

Elshtain, Jean Bethke. *Women and War*. New York: Basic Books, 1987.

Enloe, Cynthia. *Does Khaki Become You? The Militarization of Women's Lives*. London: Pandora Press, 1983.

———. *Maneuvers: The International Politics of Militarizing Women's Lives*. Berkeley: University of California Press, 2000.

Erikson, Kai T. *Wayward Puritans*. New York: Wiley, 1966.

Faderman, Lillian. *Odd Girls and Twilight Lovers: A History of Lesbian Life in Twentieth-Century America*. New York: Columbia University Press, 1991.

Fee, Elizabeth. "Sin vs. Sex: Venereal Disease in Baltimore in the Twentieth Century." *Journal of the History of Medicine and Allied Sciences* 43 (April 1988): 141–64.

———. "Venereal Disease: The Wages of Sin?" In *Passion and Power: Sexuality in History*, ed. Kathy Peiss and Christina Simmons, 178–98. Philadelphia: Temple University Press, 1989.

Feliciano, Antonio N., and Antonio E. Feliciano Jr. *Sexually Transmitted Diseases: You May Have One but Don't Know It*. New York: Vantage Press, 1992.

Fielding, Raymond. *The American Newsreel, 1911–1967*. Norman: University of Oklahoma Press, 1972.

Filene, Peter Gabriel. *Him/Her/Self: Sex Roles in Modern America*. New York: Harcourt Brace Jovanovich, 1974.

Fishman, Sarah. *The Battle for Children: World War II, Youth Crime, and Juvenile Justice in Twentieth-Century France*. Cambridge, MA: Harvard University Press, 2002.

Foucault, Michel. "The Dangerous Individual." In *Politics, Philosophy, Culture: Interviews and Other Writings,* ed. Lawrence D. Kritzman, trans. Alan Sheridan, 125–51. New York: Routledge, 1980.

———. *The History of Sexuality.* Vol. 1. *An Introduction.* Trans. Robert Hurley. New York: Vintage Books, 1980.

Freedman, Estelle B. *Their Sisters' Keepers: Women's Prison Reform in America, 1830–1930.* Ann Arbor: University of Michigan Press, 1981.

———. " 'Uncontrolled Desires': The Response to the Sexual Psychopath, 1930–1960." *Journal of American History* 74 (June 1987): 83–106.

Friedman, Lawrence M. *Crime and Punishment in American History.* New York: Basic Books, 1993.

Friedman, Lawrence M., and Stewart Macauley. *Law and the Behavioral Sciences.* Indianapolis: Bobbs-Merrill, 1969.

Fussell, Paul. *Wartime: Understanding and Behavior in the Second World War.* New York: Oxford University Press, 1989.

Gabor, Mark. *The Illustrated History of Girlie Magazines: From National Police Gazette to the Present.* New York: Harmony Books, 1984.

Gamman, Lorraine, and Margaret Marshment, eds. *The Female Gaze: Women as Viewers of Popular Culture.* Seattle: Real Comet Press, 1989.

Gerstle, Gary. *American Crucible: Race and Nation in the Twentieth Century.* Princeton: Princeton University Press, 2001.

Giddings, Paula. *When and Where I Enter: The Impact of Black Women on Race and Sex in America.* New York: Bantam Books, 1984.

Gluck, Sherna B. *Rosie the Riveter Revisited: Women, the War, and Social Change.* Boston: Twayne, 1987.

Goffman, Erving. *Gender Advertisements.* New York: Harper and Row, 1976.

Goldman, Marion S. *Gold Diggers and Silver Miners: Prostitution and Social Life on the Comstock Lode.* Ann Arbor: University of Michigan Press, 1981.

Goldstein, Joshua S. *War and Gender.* Cambridge: Cambridge University Press, 2001.

Goodwin, Doris Kearns. *No Ordinary Time: Franklin and Eleanor Roosevelt: The Homefront in World War II.* New York: Simon and Schuster, 1994.

Gordon, Linda. *Heroes of Their Own Lives: The Politics and History of Family Violence, Boston, 1880–1960.* New York: Viking, 1988.

———. *Woman's Body, Woman's Right: Birth Control in America.* New York: Penguin Books, 1977.

Gregory, Chester W. *Women in Defense Work during World War II: An Analysis of the Labor Problem and Women's Rights.* New York: Exposition Press, 1974.

Groneman, Carol. "Nymphomania: The Historical Construction of Female Sexuality." *Signs* 19 (Winter 1994): 337–67.

Gubar, Susan. " 'This Is My Rifle, This Is My Gun': World War II and the Blitz on Women." In *Behind the Lines: Gender and the Two World Wars,* ed. Margaret Randolph Higonnet, Jane Jenson, Sonya Michel, and Margaret Collins Weitz. New Haven: Yale University Press, 1987.

Haraway, Donna. *Modest_Witness@Second_Millenium. FemaleMan©_Meets _OncoMouse™: Feminism and Technoscience.* New York: Routledge, 1997.

Harris, Mark Jonathan, Franklin Mitchell, and Steven J. Schecter. *The Homefront: America during World War II.* New York: G. P. Putnam's Sons, 1984.

Harrison, Cynthia. *On Account of Sex: The Politics of Women's Issues, 1945–1968.* Berkeley: University of California Press, 1988.

Harrowitz, Nancy. *Antisemitism, Misogyny, and the Logic of Cultural Difference.* Lincoln: University of Nebraska Press, 1994.

Hartmann, Susan M. *The Homefront and Beyond: American Women in the 1940s.* Boston: Twayne, 1982.

———. "Prescriptions for Penelope: Literature on Women's Obligations to Returning World War II Veterans." *Women's Studies* 5, no. 3 (1978): 223–39.

Hegarty, Marilyn E. "Patriot or Prostitute? Sexual Discourses, Print Media, and American Women during World War II." *Journal of Women's History* 10 (Summer 1998): 112–36.

Heidensohn, Frances M. *Women and Crime: The Life of the Female Offender.* New York: New York University Press, 1985.

Heimel, Paul W. *Eliot Ness: The Real Story.* Coudersport, PA: Knox Books, 1997.

Henig, Robin Marantz. "The Lessons of Syphilis in the Age of AIDS." *Civilization* 2 (November–December 1995): 36–43.

Higonnet, Margaret Randolph, Jane Jenson, Sonya Michel, and Margaret Collins Weitz, eds. *Behind the Lines: Gender and the Two World Wars.* New Haven: Yale University Press, 1987.

Hine, Darlene Clark. *Black Women in White: Racial Conflict and Cooperation in the Nursing Profession, 1890–1950.* Bloomington: Indiana University Press, 1989.

Hobson, Barbara Meil. *Uneasy Virtue: The Politics of Prostitution and the American Reform Tradition.* New York: Basic Books, 1987.

Honey, Maureen. *Creating Rosie the Riveter: Class, Gender, and Propaganda during World War II.* Amherst: University of Massachusetts Press, 1984.

Horn, David G. "This Norm Which Is Not One: Reading the Female Body in Lombroso's Anthropology." In *Deviant Bodies: Critical Perspectives on Difference in Science and Popular Culture,* ed. Jennifer Terry and Jacqueline Urla, 109–28. Bloomington: Indiana University Press, 1995.

Jacobus, Mary, Evelyn Fox Keller, and Sally Shuttleworth, eds. *Body/Politics: Women and the Discourses of Science.* New York: Routledge, 1990.

Jones, James H. *Bad Blood: The Tuskegee Syphilis Experiment.* New and expanded ed. New York: Free Press, 1993.

Kamester, Margaret, and Jo Vellacott, eds. *Militarism versus Feminism: Writings on Women and War.* London: Virago Press, 1987.

Kennedy, Elizabeth Lapovsky, and Madeline D. Davis. *Boots of Leather, Slippers of Gold: The History of a Lesbian Community.* New York: Routledge, 1993.

Kerber, Linda K. *No Constitutional Right to Be Ladies: Women and the Obligations of Citizenship.* New York: Hill and Wang, 1998.

Kimmell, Michael. *Manhood in America: A Cultural History.* New York: Free Press, 1996.

Klassen, David, and Kay Flaminio. *Celebrating 80 Years.* Research Triangle Park, NC: American Social Hygiene Association, 1994.

Kunzel, Regina. "White Neurosis, Black Pathology: Constructing Out-of-Wedlock Pregnancy in the Wartime and Postwar United States." In *Not June Cleaver: Women and Gender in Postwar America, 1945–1960,* ed. Joanne Meyerowitz, 304–31. Philadelphia: Temple University Press, 1994.

Laska, Vera, ed. *Women in the Resistance and in the Holocaust.* Westport, CT: Greenwood Press, 1983.

Leavitt, Judith Walzer. "Gendered Expectations: Women and Early Twentieth-Century Public Health." In *U.S. History as Women's History: New Feminist Essays,* ed. Linda K. Kerber, Alice Kessler-Harris, and Kathryn Kish Sklar, 147–69. Chapel Hill: University of North Carolina Press, 1995.

Lerner, Gerda, ed. *Black Women in White America: A Documentary History.* New York: Vintage Books, 1973.

Levine, Philippa. *Prostitution, Race and Politics: Policing Venereal Disease in the British Empire.* New York: Routledge, 2003.

Lichtenstein, Nelson. *Labor's War at Home: The CIO in World War II.* Cambridge: Cambridge University Press, 1982.

May, Elaine Tyler. *Homeward Bound: American Families in the Cold War Era.* New York: Basic Books, 1988.

McWilliams, Peter M. *Ain't Nobody's Business If You Do.* Santa Monica, CA: Prelude Press, 1993.

Meyer, Leisa D. *Creating GI Jane: Sexuality and Power in the Women's Army Corps during World War II.* New York: Columbia University Press, 1996.

Meyerowitz, Joanne J. "Beyond the Feminine Mystique: A Reassessment of Postwar Mass Culture." In Joanne J. Meyerowitz, *Not June Cleaver: Women and Gender in Postwar America, 1945–1960,* 229–62. Philadelphia: Temple University Press, 1994.

———, ed. *Not June Cleaver: Women and Gender in Postwar America, 1945–1960.* Philadelphia: Temple University Press, 1994.

———. *Women Adrift: Independent Wage Earners in Chicago, 1880–1930.* Chicago: University of Chicago Press, 1988.

Michel, Sonya. "American Women and the Discourse of the Democratic Family in World War II." In *Behind the Lines: Gender and the Two World Wars,* ed. Margaret Randolph Higonnet, Jane Jenson, Sonya Michel, and Margaret Collins Weitz, 154–67. New Haven: Yale University Press, 1987.

Milkman, Ruth. *Gender at Work: The Dynamics of Job Segregation by Sex during World War II.* Urbana: University of Illinois Press, 1987.

Moss, Kary L., ed. *Man-Made Medicine: Women's Health, Public Policy, and Reform.* Durham: Duke University Press, 1996.

Nickel, Steven. *Torso: The Story of Eliot Ness and the Search for a Psychopathic Killer.* Winston-Salem, NC: John F. Blau, 1989.

Noble, David F. *America by Design: Science, Technology, and the Rise of Corporate Capitalism.* New York: Alfred A. Knopf, 1977.

Odem, Mary E. *Delinquent Daughters: Protecting and Policing Adolescent Female Sexuality in the United States, 1885–1920.* Chapel Hill: University of North Carolina Press, 1995.

Overall, Christine. "What's Wrong with Prostitution: Evaluating Sex Work." *Signs* 17 (Summer 1992): 705–24.

Palmer, Phyllis. *Domesticity and Dirt; Housewives and Domestic Servants in the United States, 1920–1945.* Philadelphia: Temple University Press, 1989.

Pateman, Carole. *The Disorder of Women: Democracy, Feminism and Political Theory.* Stanford: Stanford University Press, 1989.

Peiss, Kathy. "Charity Girls and City Pleasures: Historical Notes on Working Class Sexuality, 1880–1920." In *Powers of Desire: The Politics of Sexuality,* ed. Ann Snitow, Christine Stansell, and Sharon Thompson, 74–87. New York: Monthly Review Press, 1983.

———. *Cheap Amusements: Working Women and Leisure in Turn-of-the-Century New York.* Philadelphia: Temple University Press, 1986.

Penn, Donna. "The Sexualized Woman: The Lesbian, the Prostitute, and the

Containment of Female Sexuality in Postwar America." In *Not June Cleaver: Women and Gender in Postwar America, 1945–1960*, ed. Joanne Meyerowitz, 358–81. Philadelphia: Temple University Press, 1994.

Polenberg, Richard. *War and Society: The United States, 1941–1945*. New York: J. B. Lippincott, 1972.

Quetel, Claude. *History of Syphilis*. Trans. Judith Braddock and Brian Pike. Baltimore: Johns Hopkins University Press, 1990.

Rafler, Nicole Hahn. "The More Things Change . . . (Women's Prison System)." *Women's Review of Books* 14 (July 1997): 3–4.

Roberts, Dorothy. *Killing the Black Body: Race, Reproduction, and the Meaning of Liberty*. New York: Pantheon Books, 1997.

Roeder, George H., Jr. *The Censored War: American Visual Experience during World War II*. New Haven: Yale University Press, 1993.

Rosen, Ruth. *Prostitution and Victorian Society: Women, Class, and the State*. Baltimore: Johns Hopkins University Press, 1982.

Rosenberg, Charles E., and Janet Golden, eds. *Framing Disease: Studies in Cultural History*. New Brunswick: Rutgers University Press, 1992.

Rotundo, Anthony. *American Manhood: Transformations in Masculinity from the Revolution to the Modern Era*. New York: Basic Books, 1993.

Rupp, Leila J. *Mobilizing Women for War: German and American Propaganda, 1939–1945*. Princeton: Princeton University Press, 1978.

Saywell, Shelley. *Women in War*. New York: Viking Books, 1985.

Schur, Edwin M. *Labeling Women Deviant: Gender, Stigma, and Social Control*. Philadelphia: Temple University Press, 1983.

Sherman, Janna. " 'They either need these women or they do not': Margaret Chase Smith and the Fight for Regular Status for Women in the Military." *Journal of Military History* 54 (January 1990): 47–78.

Showalter, Elaine. *The Female Malady: Women, Madness, and English Culture, 1830–1980*. New York: Penguin Books, 1985.

Snitow, Ann, Christine Stansell, and Sharon Thompson, eds. *Powers of Desire: The Politics of Sexuality*. New York: Monthly Review Press, 1983.

Solinger, Rickie. *Wake Up Little Susie: Single Pregnancy and Race before Roe v. Wade*. New York: Routledge, 1992.

Spratley, Dolores R. *Women Go to War: Answering the First Call in World War II*. Columbus, OH: Hazelnut Publishing, 1992.

Styron, William. "A Case of the Great Pox." *New Yorker*, September 18, 1995, 62–75.

Suberman, Stella. *When It Was Our War: A Soldier's Wife on the Home Front*. Chapel Hill, NC: Algonquin Books, 2003.

Sumner, Colin. "Foucault, Gender and the Censure of Deviance." In *Feminist Perspectives in Criminology*, ed. Lorraine Gelsthorpe and Allison Morris, 26–40. Philadelphia: Open University Press, 1990.

Terkel, Studs. *The Good War: An Oral History of World War II*. New York: Ballantine Books, 1984.

Terry, Jennifer. "Anxious Slippages between 'Us' and 'Them': A Brief History of the Scientific Search for Homosexual Bodies." In *Deviant Bodies: Critical Perspectives on Difference in Science and Popular Culture*, ed. Jennifer Terry and Jacqueline Urla, 129–69.

———. "The Body Invaded." *Socialist Review* 19 (March 1989): 13–43.

Terry, Jennifer, and Jacqueline Urla. "Introduction: Mapping Embodied Deviance." In *Deviant Bodies: Critical Perspectives on Difference in Science and Popular Culture*, ed. Jennifer Terry and Jacqueline Urla, 1–18. Bloomington: Indiana University Press, 1995.

Tomblin, Barbara Brooks. *GI Nightingales: The Army Nurse Corps in World War II*. Lexington: University Press of Kentucky, 1996.

Tuchman, Gaye, Arlene Kaplan Daniels, and James Benet, eds. *Hearth and Home: Images of Women in the Mass Media*. New York: Oxford University Press, 1978.

Tucker, Sherrie. *Swing Shift: "All Girl" Bands of the 1940s*. Durham: Duke University Press, 2000.

Vance, Carol S. "Pleasure and Danger: Toward a Politics of Sexuality." In *Pleasure and Danger: Exploring Female Sexuality*, ed. Carole S. Vance. Boston: Routledge and Kegan Paul, 1986.

Walkowitz, Judith. *Prostitution and Victorian Society: Women, Class, and the State*. Cambridge: Cambridge University Press, 1980.

Washington, Mary Helen. *Invented Lives: Narratives of Black Women 1860–1960*. New York: Anchor Books/Doubleday, 1987.

Westbrook, Robert B. " 'I Want a Girl, Just Like the Girl That Married Harry James': American Women and the Problem of Political Obligation in World War II." *American Quarterly* 42 (December 1990): 587–614.

White, Kevin. *The First Sexual Revolution: The Emergence of Male Heterosexuality in Modern America*. New York: New York University Press, 1993.

Winchell, Meghan K. "Good Food, Good Fun, and Good Girls: USO Hostesses and World War II." PhD diss., University of Arizona, 2003.

Winick, Charles, and Paul M. Kinsie. *The Lively Commerce: Prostitution in the United States*. Chicago: Quadrangle Books, 1971.

Winkler, Alan M. "Politics and Propaganda: The Office of War Information, 1942–1945." PhD diss., Yale University, 1974.

Wood, James Playstead. *Magazines in the United States*. 3rd ed. New York: Ronald Press, 1971.

Yoshimi, Yoshiaki. *Comfort Women: Sexual Slavery in the Japanese Military during World War II*. Trans. Suzanne O'Brien. New York: Columbia University Press, 1995.

Index

African Americans, 66–69, 78–79; biological difference, 62; "cesspools of infection," 65, 156; health organizations, 82; "problem girl" arrests, 134, 135–142; race discrimination, 4, 5, 16, 35–36, 38, 43–44, 55–56; racial stereotyping, 80, 81–84, 123–125; sexual restrictions, Caribbean, 104; "syphilis soaked race," 103. *See also* Reckless, Walter, C.; Woolston, Howard B.

Alexander, M. Jacqui, 18

American Red Cross, and blood donations as "new kind of democratic citizenship," 4, 174n. 13

American Social Hygiene Association, 6, 13, 16, 22; and education, 56, 57–58, 66, 92, 101; and model for uniform prostitution law, 27; racial attitudes, 35–36, 43, 46, 48, 50; undercover studies, 52–53, 190n. 37

Anderson, Otis, coined term "patriotute," 1, 7

Arrests, 134–142; El Paso, 93; forced VD testing on incarcerated, 12, 27–28, 34; May Act, 37–40, 53, 67, 69; Oklahoma, 12; race, 142; "tens of thousands," 146–147; thousands during war years, 12

Asian American "conditional citizenship," 4

Bailey, Beth, 108, 160

Baker, Newton D., Secretary of War, WWI, 42

Baldinger, Colonel, and cleanup of Columbus, Ohio, 95–96; Stone Grill, 207n. 48

Bell, Marjorie, 146–147

Berlant, Lauren, 6

Braidotti, Rosi, 63, 195n. 14

Brandt, Alan, 5, 42, 62

British Contagious Diseases Act, 3

Brumberg, Joan Jacobs, on sexualization of young girls, 161

Buffer of whores, 85, 91, 99

Bureau of Medicine and Surgery (U.S. Navy), 13, 103

Bureau of Social Hygiene, 58, 66

Burgoon, Mrs., 29

Camp-followers, 17, 45, 46, 124, 125, 130, 146

Camp Forrest, May Act invoked at, 37, 40

Campaign against VD and prostitution, 2, 12, 13–14; arrests increase, 53; government, 16, 19; planning, 47; promiscuity and prostitution, 26, 44, 46, 52–53; protect national and male health, 7, 24, 177n. 15; surveillance of women's activities, 6, 13, 17, 18, 24–25, 35, 44, 52, 67, 93, 118, 119, 120, 132, 144–145, 152

Castendyck, Miss, 154

Cavour Act (Italy), 3

"Cesspools of infection," prostitutes as, 65, 156

Children's Bureau, 19–20; "observation visits" of Millikin and Hutzel, 22–23, 35, 48, 50, 134

Children's Division of the Domestic Relations Court (New York City), and female juvenile delinquency, 134

Citizenship: and military service, 3; giving and shedding blood, 3–4, 174n. 16

Civilian Conservation Corps (CCC) camps, 31–32, 77, 145

Clapp, Raymond F., 35

About the Author

Marilyn E. Hegarty is Senior Lecturer of History at The Ohio State University.